GLCSC
1625 N. Schrader Blvd.
Los Angeles, CA 9002

In a sea of reactionary propagandizing and mass media misinformation, Laura Flanders' voice is a desperately needed beacon of clarity and common sense. In column after column, her thorough reportage and smart analysis poke gaping holes in the culture's conventional wisdom. If only there were a hundred of her.

—*Susan Faludi*

Hey, George Orwell/Joan Didion: Roll over! On this otherwise dull and dismal landscape, Laura Flanders has arrived, scintillant with wit, intelligence, polemical grace, and contagious commitment to a righteous diminution of the problems of our time.

—*June Jordan*

An eloquent indictment of the mainstream media's dismissal of women's lives and perspectives. Flanders' compendium of columns and interviews confirms her stature as a leading media analyst in the progressive community The clear-headed writing and devastating truths gathered in this book sound an alarm, calling to activism all who care about women. Lively, topical and extremely informative.

—*Urvashi Vaid, author of* Virtual Equality: The Mainstreaming of Gay and Lesbian Liberation

Laura Flanders is a leading figure in contemporary media criticism. *Real Majority, Media Minority* makes a crucial contribution to our understanding of the news media and, in particular, the media's relationship with women and feminism. Flanders combines a rich and sophisticated understanding of politics and feminism with years of experience as a first-rate media critic. The book should be required reading for all who wish to understand media and for all who are dedicated to social justice. A very smart and important volume that is also is a pleasure to read. I couldn't put it down.

—*Robert W. McChesney*

GLCSC
1625 N. Schrader Blvd.
Los Angeles, CA 9

Y0-BXY-360

First-rate feminist *and* media analysis. Covering a vast array of issues—terrorism, women in prisons, the Promise Keepers, the biased pundit spectrum, the stolen feminism hoax, homophobia, the menopause industry, and many others—Laura Flanders handles them all with eloquence and skill.

—*Edward Herman*

With the clarity, vigor and panache that have made her a shining light of alternative journalism, Laura Flanders analyzes the ongoing sexism that pervades the public discourse on everything from welfare and rape to breast implants and lesbian mothers. An indispensable book—funny, angry, fact-filled and brilliant. I wish I had written it myself!

—*Katha Pollitt*

Laura Flanders has hundreds of thousands of fans around the country who have followed her marvelous radio broadcasts and critiques in *Extra!* over the years and who have come to rely on them to give the other sides of all the stories. Now this book confirms what a terrific heterodogmatiser she is. In the nature vs. nurture debate, some might say she inherited this talent from her grandmother Hope Hale Davis and her grandfather, Claud Cockburn. Maybe 20 per cent at most from that gene pool, 80 per cent comes from nurture in such crucibles as Belfast, the women's movement, Greenham Common, Beirut... Anyone who craves something different from the Authorised Version of life, politics and our history should have this book.

—*Alexander Cockburn*

Real Majority, Media Minority

The Costs of Sidelining Women in Reporting

Laura Flanders

COMMON COURAGE PRESS   MONROE, MAINE

First edition, first printing

Copyright ©1997 by Laura Flanders
Cover Design by Matt Wuerker and Doug Alexander

All rights reserved. No part of this publication may be reproduced or transmitted
in any form or by any means, electronic or mechanical, including photocopying,
recording, or any information storage or retrieval system, without permission in
writing from the publisher.

Library of Congress Cataloging In Publication Data
Flanders, Laura.
Real majority, media minority: the costs of sidelining women in reporting
Laura Flanders. —1st ed.
p.   cm.
Includes index
ISBN 1-56751-091-4 (cloth:alk. paper). — ISBN 1-56751-090-6 (pbk.: alk.
paper)
1. Women in the press. I. Title.
PN4784.@7F58 1997
070.4'493054—dc21   96-52246
CIP

Common Courage Press
Box 702
Monroe, Maine 04951
Phone: (207) 525-0900
Fax: (207) 525-3068

To Hope

for her attention
to detail
and to me.

Contents

Part III

Shifting the Blame

Part IV

Ripe for the Right

Part V

Confiding in Corporations

Part VI

Media Minority

Part VII

Real Majority

Acknowledgements

For reviewing parts of the manuscript and for lovingly pushing and pulling me through: Elizabeth Streb, June Jordan, Vivian Stromberg, Mab Segrest; also Hope Hale Davis, Claudia Flanders, (my grandmother and mother) and Robert Gorham Davis for years of teaching. For giving me a place to think: Helen Marden; to the staff and interns at FAIR, especially Jim Naureckas, Janine Jackson, Steve Rendall, Rachel Simpson and Tran Giang. THANK YOU.

Note

Except where otherwise indicated, these articles originally appeared in *EXTRA!* the bimonthly magazine from the mediawatch group FAIR. Some have been edited for republication. Interviews were broadcast on *CounterSpin*, FAIR's weekly radio program, recorded at Mercer Street Sound. They were conducted by Laura Flanders and Janine Jackson, research director at FAIR.

Information on *EXTRA!* can be obtained by calling 1-800-847-3993. *CounterSpin* is broadcast on around 100 radio stations in North America, and internationally on short-wave. Distribution information can be obtained by calling FAIR. Laura Flanders can be contacted c/o FAIR, 130 W. 25th St., New York, NY 10001; (212) 633-6700, fax (212) 727-7668. FAIR's web-page is located at http://www.fair.org/

Introduction

The Other Half of the Story

For as long as I can remember, it has been the conventional wisdom that females outnumber males on Earth, but before we went to press, I checked. Opening the United Nations 1995 Report on the World's Women, Trends and Statistics, I read the beginning: "There are fewer women in the world than men." I heard a statistical thunder-clap.

"Isn't that news?" I asked one of the UN researchers. "Well yes, actually," she replied excited, "but you're the first to call." A week later, the same researcher got back to me with answers to my other questions. She sounded chagrined. Women are a majority in the US she said (so, as this book is about US media, this title stands), but women haven't had the numerical upper hand worldwide since 1965.

My shocker story was thirty-one years old and yet to break. The only detailed discussion I could find of the documented decline of the world's women was a 1990 *New York Review of Books* article which estimated that although women naturally outlive men, the denial of food and healthcare to females had engineered a man-made shift in the planet's demography. The article was titled: "100 Million Missing Women."

One hundred million of us were estimated "missing" and for more than three decades it hadn't made the news? That's serious sidelining. Stumbling across the silence, I felt I'd downed a dose of the same contempt that determines who gets born and who survives. Simone de Beauvoir said that an understanding of the "genuine conditions of our lives" is what gives rise to the strength to change things. But for my entire life I'd been 100 percent wrong about the basic composition of the company I was in. The cost of sidelining women in this story was what it always is: the facts—but also, the possibilities for astute action. Neglect claims people's lives.

I grew up with halves of stories. In London in the seventies, for example, mainstream media taught us to fear the Irish and the Irish we saw were always men. When the Irish Republican Army (IRA) began hitting targets in England we lived with a constant slight anxiety. At any moment, we were led to believe, our surroundings might explode. Bomb-warnings appeared on London Underground trains: "Keep away from abandoned packages. Report all unattended suitcases to a guard." The phrase was repeated in German, Spanish, French and Italian and obediently as school-girls we memorized the subway grammar and worked the sentence somehow into foreign language essays.

One thing we were assured of: the terrorists were male. The identification was easy: the IRA wore trench coats topped by black berets and carried suspicious suitcases onto trains. The coverage gave us no explanation for why England was in danger. Reduced in the public mind to nothing but irrational, brute machismo, the hard guerrilla and all his kind were easy to despise. They were just violent; we were just scared.

Then one day I read about gray-haired women marching on the streets of Belfast (Northern Ireland), dressed in nothing but blankets, calling for justice for their imprisoned sons. I heard about thirty Republican women in jail in Armagh who were living in their own excrement to get word out to the world that they were in a war. Catholic, Irish, young, the women claimed they were political prisoners. The British called them criminals and to bully them into agreement the prison authorities withheld their "privileges"— like access to the toilets. For ten months the Armagh women smeared shit on their cell walls rather than trade their principles for chamber pots.

It was for me, as Muriel Rukeyser wrote, "a world split open." With women in the story, suddenly the picture became complex. I wanted to know who those women were and why they had joined in the IRA. What did they believe so strongly that they would risk their lives and why wasn't that in the news? I had a whole slew of questions that the BBC newsmen weren't asking. So you could say that sexism got me into journalism. Offered only half the picture, I was hungry for the rest.

In Belfast I learned that behind the headlines where bombings sometimes appeared, there were facts that fuelled the conflict and women in the fray. Though most news photographers focussed on boys in black masks hurling petrol bombs, those boys were outnumbered in every neighborhood by women and community activists whose struggle was not only with history but with housing conditions that poisoned their children, and employment so selective that workers were expected to be grateful for any job. Grandmothers endured the swagger by their door steps of teenaged British soldiers and arrogant policemen who had the legal authority to do almost anything, and regularly got away with killing kids. I watched the wife and small child of a man crouch by him as he died in the street from a plastic bullet wound and I interviewed British politicians who smiled as they told me that they'd prefer to fight to the death, and let their sons do likewise, rather than change a thing.

When riots broke out in London and Liverpool in 1980 and '81, the British police used the same tear gas that their colleagues had used in Belfast. They fired it at poor Black women and men who, like the Irish, were angry about discrimination in housing, police treatment, and jobs. "We should have seen it coming," Lady Margaret Simey, civilian chair of the Merseyside Police Authority told me. But she hadn't, and certainly not on TV.

In 1984, the National Union of Mineworkers called a strike to stop the wholesale closure of dozens of coal mines and the loss of thousands of jobs. Prime Minister Margaret Thatcher dispatched hordes of London cops to Yorkshire where they patrolled the strikers' picket-lines carrying shields and truncheons and plastic bullet guns. As foreign to the villagers as the troops were to the Belfast kids, the police presence got the miners thinking. One furious miner's wife, whose husband was a former soldier, muttered to me one morning: "I'm seeing another side of the story now." Her husband had served in Northern Ireland and ten years later, no thanks to the news media, the Yorkshire couple were wondering why.

Unisex Reporting

Filling the gaps in news reporting is not just about evening the score. Recording the stories of marginalized people, as Joan Nestle of the Lesbian Herstory Archives has said, isn't "revising history...but revealing it." Myths and stereotypes about who's to blame for an economy in decline, or whose behavior is a threat to your life aren't just classist, sexist, racist, rude—they're wrong.

As for sexism in reporting, it works in at least two ways. The first losers are women when the only people who walk, talk, think and count in mainstream media (not to mention politics and medicine) are men. But women aren't the only ones who pay for unisex reporting. Distilling an individual down to just his most macho profile is an effective way to make him look like a vicious brute. Stripped of a full quota of humanity (the female part), an entire group—Celt or Arab, poor or Black—can be made to seem not quite human and all the easier to imprison, starve and blame.

Not reporting on the fastest growing group of the world's workers, the people whose work styles and wages are likely soon to be the norm isn't only unfair and inaccurate but dangerous, not just for women and girls. And censorious coverage of peoples' movements robs the public of their news.

There was another bonus of travel beyond the realm of mainstream media: I found a women's movement that looked like mine. Different from the dry, derided thing that was sometimes glimpsed in the U.S. news, the women I met were part of something global and big-thinking. From Belfast to Beirut, from Appalachia to Port-au-Prince—I found women who refused to be shrunk into competing single-issues. Groups I came to know like the Women's Pentagon Action or New York Women Against Rape or MADRE were out for justice for women because women were society's root, but women's rights were wrapped up with the rights of others. Bigotry isn't boundaried they said: if it's ok to hate lesbians, it's ok to hate women. If scapegoating works anywhere, it works. If you can vilify women on welfare, the same technique can triumph against African Americans, immigrants, queers and Jews.

There is a history of women who always talked about power and justice that way. Anna Julia Cooper, a former slave turned teacher and writer, addressed the World Congress of Representative Women in Chicago in 1893, ninety-nine years before *Time* and *Newsweek* declared a "Year of the Woman" in politics. "If one link in the chain be broken, the chain is broken," said Cooper. "A bridge is no stronger than its weakest part, and a cause is not worthier than its weakest element. Least of all can woman's cause afford to decry the weak. We want, then, as toilers for the universal triumph of justice and human rights, to go to our homes from this Congress, demanding an entrance not through a gateway for ourselves, our race, our sex, or our sect, but a grand highway for humanity."

But the U.S. media's version of the women's movement hints at none of this diversity and expanse. Instead, having banished the movement to the media's margins and crammed its thoughts into bite-sized noises, the *New York Times* runs features on the "death of feminism" and television pundits declare feminists "marginal" and their analysis "simplistic." The coverage of the O.J. Simpson trial is just one 1990s example of reporters forcing women into deadly competing categories: white vs. African American, anti-sexist vs. anti-racist, soul vs. heart. Ignoring women's cross-race, cross-class, lesbian/straight organizing, the pundits love to cover conflict. They get to look like peacemakers as they anchor their own created-for-the-cameras "catfight."

In the 1980s, after years of reporting on mankind by reporters who meant just that (no females), activists called for equal time for women. Then the very people who had tried to talk about the implications for everyone of ignoring rights for women were called "separatist" or "divisive"—as if they were the ones separating the members of their sex from the State.

Feminist journalists were forced to squeeze their stories into niches. In mainstream media, a single sympathetic (usually embattled) editor could make the difference. In the alternative—usually, the women's—press the ones to thank were a small band of determined staffers and their loyal subscribers who were usually too few.

By the end of the 1980s, after years of outside pressure and insider effort, more stories with a women's angle were published, and more women in newsrooms won opportunities to tell them (and take pictures too). But instead of clarifying existing connections, most newspaper editors set reporting on women apart. Stories with a women's focus were "human interest" stories, I was told. At first I thought, so be it, what other kind are there? And then that line got old.

A newspaper would run a feature on the wages and working conditions of women in factories, but there was no word from those factory workers when the topic was NAFTA or GATT. A television team might investigate childhood sexual abuse or female self-esteem in school, but the same team would air only garbled words from teenage girls when the subject was poverty, welfare, or adolescents giving birth. No matter how clearly Palestinian, or Yugoslavian, or Israeli, or U.S. women documented the techniques of organized fundamentalists and described the political success and effect of religious nationalist groups, priority sources for national policy reporters remained the same oblivious inside-the-Beltway pundits. Journalists tended to mimic the politicians when they decided whose "expertise" was, as the *New York Times* says, "fit to print."

By the time FAIR founded the Women's Desk in 1992, a few more women were being seen and heard in mainstream media. But the vacuum between front-page news and "women's views" lived on, and it sucked away, black hole-style, the significance of what they said.

Free Speech Areas

Penned-in like the protesters outside the '96 Political Conventions to well-policed "free speech areas" several blocks away from the main event, it's tempting to shout a simple slogan just to get heard. Some thought that when we started the Women's Desk, our purpose was to shout a slogan: More Women. Getting more women power in mainstream media and more women quoted in news reporting is part of it. But only a part.

As French feminist Helene Cixous has written: "At this time

there are so many clandestine massacres of women that a woman has to say 'woman' a dozen times a day in order to protest." But, as she continues, "The more we say it in order not to be swept far away from our own banks by the current, and the more securely we moor ourselves to avoid being swept away from one another, the more we contribute to reinforcing limitations of strength, to restricting native territories and fortifying prejudices."

Some of the interviews and articles compiled here have to do with getting "woman" said more. A handful cover conspicuous sexism inside the media industry and the struggle of women to get good wages and jobs. A few of the interviews address the way that women or girls are represented, and some applaud the work of courageous women reporters working against the odds. But on *CounterSpin*, FAIR's radio program and in *EXTRA!*, FAIR's magazine, how a story is told is more important than who is doing the telling. The biggest problem isn't numbers, but an industry-created numbness to a whole range of ideas.

What infuriated conservatives at the Beijing Women's Conference, after all, wasn't "female," the biological adjective, but "gender," the political idea. Gender implies that vulnerability is not the characteristic of a class, but the consequence of certain conditions; power's not personal (or God-given), it's political, and it's maintained by human choice.

No wonder deep-pocket powermongers get nervous—from the Vatican to Wall Street to Pat Robertson's Virginia Beach. As the investigations included here document, in the last ten years as women reporters carved a tiny toehold in the media industry, simultaneously, right-wingers poured precious political power and dollars into hijacking the public debate. Ten years ago there were a handful of twenty or so major corporations controlling the jobs in the majority of media. Today, as the global economy concentrates all the world's resources into fewer hands, in the media arena, that handful is closing tightly into a fist. The purpose of the profit makers who determine the "news" in the 1990s is profit-making. And the places left—like community radio, public access television and independent publishing are shrinking in direct proportion to the big-boys' growth. In England, under Margaret Thatcher as in the U.S. under her buddies Presidents Reagan and Bush, and then Bill Clinton, the decline of independent feminist publishing happened concurrently with social policies that were devastating to women. News about women, still in the margins, is in slimmer margins than ever. And the openings for controversial reporters are rarer, making it ever scarier to dissent.

My purpose in pulling together this collection is to draw attention to an emergency. Counting beans, be they female or queer or multi-racial is not enough. When the Right got savvy to the media's "gender gap" they groomed well-connected women to fit the previously male-only pundit's chairs. Mainstream media obediently filled that gaping "women's" space with the anti-feminists who were driven to their doors. Now women's rights advocates are fuelling their own media machines to churn out daily press releases and editorials, or they're hiring good public relations firms to do it with them. And that's imperative. A serious effort to match the right's media assault with comparable vigor is crucial, if only to respond to those newspaper editors and TV anchors who claim they don't hear from feminists as they do from their opponents.

But as I write this, the producers of NBC *Dateline* are preparing to air—despite their subject's furious objections—a special report about a white woman's fight with the Santa Monica police. The producers were willing to tell her individual rape story and investigate her complaints about police sexism; what they stripped from the picture was her history as an activist, and her parallel efforts to document racism on the force. And in San Francisco, CNN is refusing to interview a white, male student poet who is hunger striking with several colleagues because he doesn't want to live in a world without affirmative action. Developing feminist media machines to duel with the right is one response to media intransigence. An equally reasonable alternative would be to say as Congresswoman Maxine Waters has said about progressives: "We haven't toned down: We've been tuned out."

There were always women in those jails, marching on those streets. Sometimes we see a smidgen of news about them on TV. Staying in rural Pennsylvania one night in August 1996, I watched a young reporter on the NBC affiliate cover a local event: a speech by Family Research Council leader, Robert Knight. Knight was shown speaking from a podium, lecturing the folks about the threats he thinks that gay marriage poses to heterosexual relationships. About a hundred men and women were there, nodding in agreement and quoting from the Bible in Knight's support. After what was apparently a good while of unadulterated fear-mongering, a light-haired woman in her 40s or 50s rose to her feet. Alone.

"This is a hate-rally. This is hate-speech and someone has to say something," she said.

Then she was gone. The camera moved. The reporter didn't interview her. He didn't even ask her name. Knight got the headline and the lead and the body of the story. She got so few seconds that if I'd blinked I would have missed her. But to me that was the news. News I had been waiting for. The glimpse of what communication through news media might be like. Used for community conversation, not corporate control—that sort of media might have given me some way to reach her, so that next time she'd not be standing there with me sitting somewhere else.

Women may not be the majority on the planet (for today) but there are still billions of us—millions engaged in work that improves our shared world. We have a right not to feel so alone, as I told the 30,000-strong non-governmental women's conference in China, because we're not. If profits can be global, why not conversation too?

But sidelines are no place to sit and wait. The media-moguls at huge corporations like Disney/ABC or Time Warner/Turner are not the ones we should expect to make the change. Horizontally, as well as vertically, the centuries-old movement for freedom of expression needs to be updated into a movement for the right to communicate. The ones who own the means right now aren't about to give them up. Why would they? As we say on radio: Over to you.

Part I

Cents and Sensibility

Media corporations are richer than ever, and the more that celebrity journalists, pundits and TV anchors are part of the economic elite, the less they are watchdogs of it. Turn the talk to blame and shame and those reporters rarely target their own employers and friends. Money may not buy happiness, but people with very little of it have few advocates in mainstream media.

Copyright © 1995 by Kirk Anderson

Compassion Rationed

For the past four years, the debate about welfare has targeted women. Politicians fingered poor women as the source of the nation's problems, and reporters followed, creating vivid, misleading images of lazy mothers-of-dozens draining to the dregs the nation's coffers. The pictures skewed the facts, inflating the proportion of AFDC receivers who are African-American, immigrant, urban and young.

But the scapegoating worked. By the time the Senate passed the1996 welfare bill, it was so acceptable to starve and impoverish women that even those editorial writers who opposed the president's signing of the bill generally did so on other grounds.

Editors across the country voiced concern about the effects that ending guaranteed federal income supports would have on some people. The *New York Times*' editors (7/18/96) worried that the House bill would "push a million children into poverty, victimize legal immigrants and leave no ironclad Federal safety net underneath families that search for but cannot find work." The *Boston Globe* mused that President Clinton "cannot in conscience send many thousands of Americans and legal immigrants–including large numbers of children–into poverty" (7/23/96). "Neither Governors nor Congress is likely to tolerate more malnourished or neglected children," wrote *Time* (7/29/96).

Neglecting and malnourishing *women* was apparently fine —for the nation, and for the press. If readers hadn't already jumped to that conclusion, the *Washington Post* (7/18/96) made it for them. "The central issue in reforming [welfare] has been the same for years. How do you increase the pressure on welfare mothers to go to work while continuing to support their children if they fail?" It's not quite acceptable to starve the little children. Yet.

Ninety percent of the adults the president and Congress cut off welfare are women: single female heads of households, women born outside the U.S., women whose partnerships aren't recognized as "marriage," poor women convicted of even a single drug crime. "Families" don't look for and fail to find work, single parents do, and in the case of AFDC receivers, the vast majority of those are women. Children surviving on an average AFDC grant plus food stamps ($7,968 a year for a family of three) aren't being pushed into poverty—they're there already (the poverty line is $12,320). And they're not suffering alone. Their moms typically feed them first and eat what's left.

Though feminists and others have fought for years for editors to use less sexist language, like parent instead of "mother," the welfare debate was no time to start. "Gender-neutral language is supposed to be a more accurate use of language, not used to obscure bias," columnist Rita Henley Jensen, a former welfare recipient, wrote in a letter to the *New York Times* (7/25/96).

Beneath the snow of talk about "families" and "children" and "immigrants" are as many as 75 percent of welfare mothers who have been victims of assault by a relative or so-called "friend." Fifty percent of homeless women are estimated to be fleeing men who've battered them (according to the NOW Legal Defense and Education Fund). If they leave violent homes without being able to support their children, then they're berated as "bad parents." If they turned to welfare (when there was welfare), they were portrayed as "welfare queens."

To many poor women in domestic danger, the shame of poverty looks more frightening than the terror of their next beating. The Congress and president just made the poverty a whole lot worse. Relentless media scapegoating made the shame worse, too. Domestic violence survivors and other experts know that what makes or breaks a woman's will to escape attack is her own sense of worth. But coverage of the welfare debate sent one message echoing loud. Like political undesirables after a coup d'etat, poor women can simply disappear. Coverage like that has consequences.

November/December 1996

Public Enemy Number One?

Media's Welfare Debate
Is a War on Poor Women

In a bizarre column blaming TV talk shows, in part, for the "sexually irresponsible culture of poverty," *Newsweek*'s Joe Klein (2/6/95) provided telling insight into how some in mainstream media see their relationship to poor people: "Television is the only sustained communication our society has with the underclass," Klein wrote. "It is the most powerful message we send." Recent mainstream news reporting on welfare and its "reform" has been full of messages about "us" and "them," with reporters leaving little doubt about who "we" and "they" are.

In a vivid example, ABC *PrimeTime Live*'s Diane Sawyer (annual salary: an estimated $7 million) devoted a segment to grilling a group of teenage mothers receiving Aid to Families with Dependent Children, or AFDC (2/16/95). Explaining that "to many people, these girls are public enemy No. 1," Sawyer harangued them on behalf of "taxpayers" who were "mad as hell." "Answer their question," she demanded: "Why should they pay for your mistake?"

One young woman commented that AFDC is "such a small percentage now, you know, of the amount of money of what taxpayers send in. Most of the money is going for defense." It's not a point that Sawyer followed up on.

ABC's star anchor was not alone in burying the economic lead on the welfare story in favor of a discourse on "shame" and "irresponsibility." Her moral inquisitor routine came in the midst of a media welfare debate that, for the most part, unimaginatively echoed the conservative Republicans' agenda—zeroing in on the relatively small AFDC program and the "pathology" of out-of-wedlock births, while reducing job loss, wage erosion and discrimination to background issues.

Whose Consensus?

FAIR surveyed the sources used in welfare coverage in half a dozen of the most influential news outlets (the *New York Times*, the *Washington Post*, ABC News, PBS's *McNeil/Lehrer NewsHour*, *Time* and *Newsweek*) for the period of Dec. 1, 1994 to Feb. 24, 1995. Revealed was a truncated spectrum of political opinion that favored conventional wisdom over dissent, a selection of policy experts that rarely stretched the debate, and a number of old myths persistently rehashed.

One of the most striking findings was how male-dominated the welfare debate was. Of sources whose gender could be identified, 71 percent (608 sources) were male—discussing policy proposals that will disproportionately affect women. Not counting welfare recipients, 77 percent of the sources were men.

Some of this gender imbalance resulted from reporters' reliance on government sources. In the period studied, reporters used current and former government officials as sources more than any other group, making up 59 percent of sources. Twenty-four percent of all sources were members of the U.S. Congress (72 percent Republican, 28 percent Democratic), 24 percent were state and local officials, while 9 percent represented the Clinton administration.

With specific proposals being debated in Congress, it's natural that Capitol Hill would provide the lead for many stories. But the D.C.-driven nature of coverage also limited the debate.

For example, since the Republican and Democratic leadership agreed that spending on the poor ought to be restricted, differing only on details, it was easy for reporters to emphasize consensus. The *New York Times*' David Rosenbaum (2/10/95) consigned any dissenters from the bipartisan view to invisibility, declaring "politicians and scholars from all points of the political compass agree...that, as Rep. E. Clay Shaw Jr. said today, [the welfare system has] 'destroyed responsibility, diminished personal dignity and created economic disincentives that bar people from success.'"

With 37 appearances, Rep. Shaw (R-Fla.), the chair of the House subcommittee that drafted the Personal Responsibility Act, was the single most quoted media source on welfare in the period examined. Shaw, who described the current welfare system as "pampering the poor" (*New York Times*, 2/16/95) was followed by Newt Gingrich with 34 appearances, and President Clinton with 26.

Cited as frequently as members of Congress were state and local officials—largely the Republican governors who run those "conservative state-of-the-art welfare reform programs," as the *Washington Post* called them (2/10/95). While a careful look at the track record of these state programs could be instructive, the largely uncritical attention given Gov. John Engler of Michigan (21 appearances) and Wisconsin's Tommy Thompson (17 appearances) only promoted the idea that "success" in dealing with welfare should be defined as cutting government assistance programs.

An *ABC World News Tonight* "American Agenda" feature on Gov. Thompson (1/13/95), for example, didn't include a single naysaying source—no one to contradict correspondent Rebecca Chase's claim that "Wisconsin has virtually turned its welfare offices into employment offices." Other reporters have found plenty of people critical of that state's new "Work Not Welfare" programs; see, for example, *Sacramento Bee* (2/17/95).

Good and Bad Victims

At the other end of the welfare issue from policy makers are the recipients of welfare and other social services, who made up 10 percent of media sources during the survey period. Stories on welfare were reminiscent of much reporting on the AIDS crisis, drawing a stark distinction between poverty's "innocent"and "guilty" victims. Although most of those quoted were young women receiving AFDC, mainstream reporters were emphatic in their rhetorical distinction between these "bad" aid recipients and "good" recipients, namely children.

A *New York Times* headline (12/18/94) said it boldly: "Despising Welfare, Pitying Its Young." The article, by Jason DeParle, suggested the central problem of welfare reform: "The more one seeks to punish the parent, the greater the risks to the child."

While poor children certainly need defenders, most welfare rights advocates note that poor children come from poor families. In the media, however, "innocent children" are often ominously separated from their guilty moms. Cutting off aid to young mothers, reports the *Washington Post* (2/14/95), "has drawn sharp criticism from advocates for the poor, who say innocent children would suffer."

And where are the women in *Newsweek*'s explanation (12/12/94) that "almost everyone agrees that millions of kids are in jeopardy"?

"Public Enemy Number One"

For centuries, U.S. culture has demonized "outsider" groups (African Americans, queers, feminists, immigrants, communists) by associating them with sex. In the media's welfare debate public enemy number one was sexualized too—and no group was presented as more "guilty" by virtue of their sexual activity than the teenage girl. Unmarried, but sexually active teenagers were linked to "every threat to the fabric of this country—from poverty to crime to homelessness" by Jonathan Alter (*Newsweek*, 12/12/94).

Alter and *Newsweek* frankly gloried in the theme of "shame" for poor young women, comparing them, in a Feb. 6 cover story, to "drunk drivers," and claiming that "the public is game for a little humiliation."

The relegitimization of such outmoded terms as "illegitimacy" reflected an eagerness to resurrect top-down blaming. But women were disproportionately targeted for shame. Sociologist Mike Males reports that 70 percent of so-called "teen" pregnancies are the result of sex with men over 20. Males's research (widely published in the alternative news media) suggests that 50,000 teen pregnancies a year are caused by rape and two-thirds of teen mothers have histories of sexual abuse by a perpetrator averaging 27 years of age. If, as syndicated columnist George Will wrote, the welfare crisis is a "crisis of character development" the statistics suggest that at least half the "blame" lies with impregnators who are not female or young. When men were mentioned in the welfare debate, it was usually only as a source of quick-fix dollars. On CBS, Clay Shaw told *Face the Nation* that "the irresponsibility of male partners is killing the American family" (1/29/94). Certainly, $34 million should *not* be owed in unpaid child support to women bringing up children, but evidence suggests that what's killing the family is poverty, not just bad dads. According to the Census Bureau, a two parent family living in poverty is *twice* as likely as its middle-class equivalent to break up during a period of two years. As for extracting the money owed to poor mothers, discussion of welfare in isolation from tax codes, the minimum wage, labor law enforcement and the bigger economic picture puts blame on poor parents, male and female—and keeps the focus off a system that benefits from keeping lots of people desperate for even low-paid jobs.

Direct interviews with welfare recipients could have added much to coverage of welfare, and might have helped to put a "human face" on the issue. But the poor women (and a few men) who appeared were constrained to a quite limited number of roles. At worst, as with Diane Sawyer, they were cast as the "embodiment" of a "problem" or a "pathology," forced to defend themselves in a way few public officials ever are.

The selection of certain women to represent "welfare mothers" did much to reinforce misleading stereotypes, especially with regard to teenagers and welfare. When the age of welfare recipients was given, they were generally 17, 18 or 19 years old—even though only 6 percent of mothers who receive AFDC are younger than 20. Only 1 percent are 17 or younger (*USA Today*, 1/20/95).

Some recipients were used to confirm "expert" opinion, as when, explaining that some legislators hope to reduce pregnancies by cutting off benefits, *Newsweek*'s reporters declare (12/12/94): "Sure enough, Julia Lestido, a 17-year-old welfare mother from Elizabeth, N.J. says that if the government abolished aid, 'I would prevent myself from having more children.'"

Other women got walk-on roles playing the temporarily misguided but ultimately "recovered"—like the women cited in the *New York Times* (2/17/95) who "hated [welfare] more than [they hated] the ex-husbands...who left them or beat them."

Even when these stories are sympathetic, as they sometimes are, they confirm the conventional wisdom that poverty is a personal problem, "dependency" a curable disease. A listener to FAIR's radio program *CounterSpin* decried this depiction: "My experience of welfare single moms is of heroines...women who are courageous, hardworking and creative," wrote Ann Mannering. "I would like to hear stories of these women in the media. Not just the ones who graduate from college and become a 'success,' but the ones who keep on doing their best for their kids under conditions that would daunt some of their better-off sisters."

Research? What Research?

In between the rhetoric of politicians and the anecdotal stories of welfare recipients should come analysis. And research and advocacy groups were 9 percent of media sources in the period studied. But even though reporters talked to people from a variety of think tanks and the like, a very limited range of policy proposals was permitted to direct the media debate.

One would have hoped that journalists covering the Republican plans would seek out proposals and ideas to contrast with those of the congressional leadership. Instead, the press constrained critics to responding to this or that aspect of conservative ideas, and no poverty-solving proposals other than cutting welfare were seriously explored. A job-creation program, or even a raise in the minimum wage, might do more for welfare recipients' economic futures than simply throwing them off the rolls—but progressive alternatives were virtually never given a space to be heard.

Critics of the Republican plan sometimes seemed to span a spectrum from A to B. Referring to a cut-off of benefits to unwed mothers under 18 and their children, the *New York Times* reported (2/10/95), "Liberals object to this idea because they think it punishes innocent children, and many conservatives are opposed because they fear it would encourage abortions." Critical voices—which neither defend the current welfare system nor embrace conservative alternatives—were not excluded from the discussion; their facts just weren't used to challenge political rhetoric. Articles might occasionally mention the fact that studies show no relationship between benefit levels and birth rates (e.g.,*Washington Post*, 2/14/95)—but reporters wouldn't be so rude as to confront a policymaker with that fact. And intermittent references to crucial issues like the health care needs of people on welfare—by people like Robert Greenstein from the Center on Budget and Policy Priorities (4 appearances)—just weren't enough to derail the Republican-led discussion about teenaged moms' morality.

The final paragraph of David Rosenbaum's 1100-word story on "The Welfare Enigma" (*New York Times*, 2/10/95) quoted the Urban Institute's Isabel V. Sawhill, who warned that welfare cuts wouldn't save money and would "leave people homeless." With Sawhill's perspective having been left for the wrap-up, no other source had to respond to her point—and no follow-up story appeared in which the Urban Institute's experts got to set the agenda.

Similarly, no one responded to the claim made by religious leaders in the *Washington Post* (2/22/95) that, despite politicians' claims, donations to churches and charities "would do precious little to offset the cuts to social programs." But that didn't stop mainstream outlets from heralding volunteers like Carol Doe Porter, of Kidcare, Inc. (named ABC's "Person of the Week" after the study period ended—3/24/95). Porter, according to the *New York Times* (2/6/95), was the "embodiment of the increasingly popular maxim that not all the country's problems need to be solved by throwing government money at them." Porter was singled out for media attention not because she feeds the hungry—thousands of people across the country do that—but because she personified a right-wing political argument. The implication of stories like the *New York Times*' profile—headlined "'Mother Teresa of Houston' Fights Hunger and Government Aid"—is that we can have *either* "communities that care" *or* government spending on programs for the poor.

It's a Myth, But It's Our Lead

After participating in two hours of "*Firing Line*" debate leavened with smug male jokes at the expense of poor women," professor-

Frances Fox Piven commented (*St. Petersburg Times*, 5/8/94), "I am struck by how little evidence matters in talk about welfare."

Myths prevailed in coverage of welfare reform, proving once again that it's easier to state the conventional wisdom than counter it.

ABC World News Tonight's Rebecca Chase (2/9/95) illustrated that phenomenon when she "examine[d] the premise" that welfare benefits are an incentive for poor women to have babies. Having opened with the analysis of Robert Rector of the Heritage Foundation (not identified as a right-wing think tank), she notes a statement from 79 social scientists whose combined research found little or no impact on birth rates from welfare benefits. "But numbers can be deceiving," she warns—and returns to Rector, who claims that "the best study on this" shows a 50 percent increase in benefits leads to a 42 percent increase in out-of-wedlock births.

Faced with conflicting claims from researchers, Chase does not examine their methodologies to see whose studies are more persuasive. Instead, she throws up her hands—"the correlation between benefits and babies is complex" is her conclusion—and returns to analysis by anecdote. (Chase to mother: "Do you think some women have babies just to get on welfare or get more money?" Mother: "Yeah, I know a couple that do.")

It's not that journalists don't know they're trading in stereotypes and impressions; sometimes they acknowledge as much. Here's *ABC World News Tonight's* Peter Jennings, introducing a lead segment on the crackdown on "fugitive felons" who've been "receiving welfare checks while hiding from the law": "This problem of welfare fraud does not eat up a particularly large portion of the money spent on welfare, but public anger at what fraud does occur has helped drive the movement for reform."

Missing: Anyone with a New Vision

One way to demonstrate the critical narrowness of the media discussion of welfare is to consider who is utterly absent. Of 890 people quoted, for example, not one was an out lesbian. Perhaps as a result, no one made the point that punishing people for not getting married discriminates against those whose partnerships are not recognized under U.S. law and whose children are "illegitimate" regardless of the stability of their unacknowledged family.

Whereas outspoken advocates from the conservative ranks were heard regularly, similarly "radical" advocates of women's rights were nowhere to be found. *The Bell Curve* author Charles Murray was cited five times during the period studied. He told *Newsweek* his opinion of teen mothers (12/12/94): "A great many of them have no business being mothers and their feelings don't count as much as the welfare of the child." But no feminist expert was heard from to offer the opinion that poor women have a right to live and to feed their children even when they are not married to the father of their children.

A handful of different groups dedicated to defending the rights of children were cited. But apart from a "women's rights advocate" who appeared on *20/20* (12/23/94), women's rights organizations were virtually absent from the source list. Groups like Planned Parenthood, for example, with its decades-long history of helping women to plan their pregnancies, seemed to be missing from reporters' rolodexes.

Union representatives were cited in only five stories in the periods studied (all but one in the *New York Times*). If reporters had sought out labor's voice more regularly, they might have resisted the invidious portrayal of welfare as a battle between workers and unemployed.

While acknowledging that the issue of poverty and public assistance is complex, deep-rooted and contentious, the mainstream media debate stuck so close to the well-trod path that it almost ensured no fresh ideas would squeeze through. By failing to incorporate perspectives that challenge the Republican/Democratic consensus, the media shut light out of a debate that sorely needs it.

Thanks to Janine Jackson and Dan Shadoan
for Research Assistance
May/June 1995

PATHOLOGICAL TARTS

"This is what we're learning about teen pregnancy: It is, too often, a form of child abuse," Joe Klein declared in *Newsweek*'s April 29 issue. Those who read EXTRA! learned this a while ago; we first discussed the fact that most "teen pregnancies" involve a father older than 20 in our July/August '94 cover story ("Bashing Youth: Media Myths About Teenagers," by Mike Males). But Klein put a somewhat different spin on the information: "Girls who become pregnant aren't just amoral, premature tarts—they are prey...The data are further proof that an intense social pathology—a culture of poverty—has overwhelmed the slums." Klein's solution: orphanages for wayward girls.

EXTRA!Update, 6/96

Five Media Myths
About Welfare

1. **Poor women have more children because of the "financial incentives" of welfare benefits.**

Repeated studies show no correlation between benefit levels and women's choice to have children. (See, for example, *Urban Institute Policy and Research Report*, Fall/93.) States providing relatively higher benefits do not show higher birth rates among recipients.

In any case, welfare allowances are far too low to serve as any kind of "incentive": A mother on welfare can expect about $90 a month in additional AFDC (Aid to Families with Dependent Children) benefits if she has another child.

Furthermore, the real value of AFDC benefits, which do not rise with inflation, has fallen 37 percent during last two decades (the *Nation*, 12/12/94). Birth rates among poor women have not dropped correspondingly.

The average AFDC recipient has 1.9 children—about the same as the national average.

2. **We don't subsidize middle-class families.**

Much of the welfare debate has centered on the idea of "family caps"—denying additional benefits to women who have children while receiving aid. This is often presented as simple justice: "A family that works does not get a raise for having a child. Why then should a family that doesn't work?" columnist Ellen Goodman wrote in the *Boston Globe* (4/16/92).

In fact, of course, families *do* receive a premium for additional children, in the form of a $2,450 tax deduction. There are also tax credits to partially cover child care expenses, up to a maximum of $2,400 per child. No pundit has suggested that middle-class families base their decision to have children on these "perks."

3. The public is fed up with spending money on the poor.

"The suspicion that poorer people are getting something for nothing is much harder to bear than the visible good fortune of the richer," wrote columnist Mary McGrory (*Washington Post*, 1/15/95). But contrary to such claims from media pundits, the general public is not so hard-hearted. In a December 1994 poll by the Center for the Study of Policy Attitudes (CSPA), 80 percent of respondents agreed that the government has "a responsibility to try to do away with poverty" (*Fighting Poverty in America: A Study of American Attitudes*, CSPA).

Support for "welfare" is lower than support for "assistance to the poor," but when CSPA asked people about their support for AFDC, described as "the federal welfare program which provides financial support for unemployed poor single mothers with children," only 21 percent said funding should be cut, while 29 percent said it should be increased.

4. We've spent over $5 trillion on welfare since the '60s and it hasn't worked.

Conservatives and liberals alike use this claim as proof that federal poverty programs don't work, since after all that "lavish" spending, people are still poor. But spending on AFDC, the program normally referred to as welfare, totaled less than $500 billion from 1964 to 1994—less than 1.5 percent of federal outlays for that period, and about what the Pentagon spends in two years.

To get the $5 trillion figure, "welfare spending" must be defined to include all means-tested programs, including Medicaid, food stamps, student lunches, scholarship aid and many other programs. Medicaid, which is by far the largest component of the $5 trillion, goes mostly to the elderly and disabled; only about 16 percent of Medicaid spending goes to health care for AFDC recipients.

Furthermore, the poverty rate did fall between 1964 and 1973, from 19 percent to 11 percent, with the advent of "Great Society" programs. Since the 1970s, economic forces like declining real wages as well as reduced benefit levels have contributed to the rising poverty rates of the last decade.

5. Anyone who wants to get off welfare can just get a job.

Many welfare recipients do work to supplement meager benefits (*Harper's*, 4/94). But workforce discrimination and the lack of affordable child care make working outside the home difficult for single mothers. And the low-wage, no-benefit jobs available to most AFDC recipients simply do not pay enough to lift a family out of poverty.

Although it is almost never mentioned in conjunction with the welfare debate, the U.S. Federal Reserve has an official policy of raising interest rates whenever unemployment falls below a certain point—now about 6.2 percent (*EXTRA!*, 9/10/94). In other words, if all the unemployed women on welfare were to find jobs, currently employed people would have to be thrown out of work to keep the economy from "overheating."

May/June 1995

WELFARE BY THE NUMBERS

AFDC accounts for 1 percent of the federal budget; food stamps are an additional 2 percent. Annual federal and state spending on AFDC totals $22 billion—less than one-tenth of what is annually spent on the military.

The average AFDC benefit is $415 a month, or $4980 a year, for a family of three. Many AFDC recipients also receive food stamps, bringing their average benefits to $7968 a year for a family of three—far below the poverty line of $12,320.

Of families receiving AFDC in 1992, 38.9 percent were white, and 37.2 percent Black (the *Nation*, 12/12/94).

Extra! May/June 1995

The Willie Horton of Welfare

Interview with Frances Fox Piven

We may take issue with the word "reform," but changes, anyway, in welfare policy are high on the agenda of the new Republican-controlled Congress. And although now and then someone mentions that Aid to Families with Dependent Children consumes only around one percent of the federal budget, the impression we get from both the quantity and the quality of the media coverage is that minority teenage mothers on public assistance are draining the public coffers dry. Depressing as it is, this is hardly the first time those at the bottom of the socio-economic ladder have been accused of ruining life for those above them and policy written up accordingly. Co-author of the groundbreaking book Regulating the Poor: The Functions of Public Welfare, *Frances Fox Piven has been observing U.S. welfare policy for years. What is it, Professor Piven, in the current social and economic climate that makes it okay to talk about putting children in orphanages?*

It probably isn't okay to talk about putting children in orphanages. It seems that that's a misstep that Gingrich quickly acknowledged. What has become okay is welfare bashing, the repeated, constant assertions by politicians, both Democrats and Republicans, that welfare is…a big problem, that the nature of the problem is minority women having out-of-wedlock babies…Having out-of-wedlock babies in turn has all sorts of repercussions. These women go on welfare, they become dependent, they bring up children who become delinquent. In other words, these women are "wanton." It's a kind of nineteenth-century mythology that we're constructing here. They have become, in this kind of political mythology that's being constructed, the explanation for everything that's wrong in the U.S.

So policy is being written up that's resting, essentially on false premises.

On entirely false premises. We can begin with the point that you already made, that welfare is a very small program. One percent of the federal budget. You're absolutely right. Sometimes the media in a sense rocket up the cost by adding in other things, like the costs of Medicaid. But obviously women and their children are not eating the Medicaid dollars. Those dollars go to the medical establishment, to clinics and doctors. We actually spend $23 billion on AFDC. That's what everybody is talking about, they don't mean other programs, in the U.S....We treat our people who are poor, we treat single parents much worse than other countries. Even a country like Canada, right across the border and in many ways very similar to the U.S., is much more generous in shoring up the income of poor people generally and single parents who are trying to raise children by themselves. Not only do we give them very little money; the average cash grant is $370 a month for a family.

Which doesn't even bring them up to poverty level.

It's much less than the poverty level. Some allowance should be made for the fact that most of these families also get food stamps, but even taking into account food stamps, no state brings a family on welfare up to the poverty level. One of the worst features of the experience is the insults. The insults partly have to do with deep traits in our culture. We don't like poor people. We have a kind of ferocious and unrealistic ethic of individual responsibility, and we're preoccupied with sex. Many of these women have had out-of-wedlock children, about half of them. That adds to the cultural symbolism, the denigrating symbolism of being on welfare. But then we have a whole generation of politicians who—being unwilling and unable to do anything about the real sources of anxiety in American politics: declining wages, an extremely uncertain economic future—use welfare as a kind of substitute for constructive and rational policy. You can always talk about welfare. You can always talk about those women and their out-of-wedlock babies; it's a kind of Willie Horton issue.

*So you think it's that search for scapegoats in times of perceived eco-
nomic scarcity or contraction that accounts for the intransigence of these
myths that we've been talking about? Because just as you've said, one
thing that we find particularly frustrating is that you will often see in the
final paragraph of a long story an admission that AFDC recipients don't
have any greater than the average number of children, or the TV segment
will announce that half or more of AFDC recipients are white, but all
the pictures that go with the story will be of Black women. What is it that
accounts for the inability to debunk these myths if the information and
the evidence is as you've just stated?*

I think that myths do have currency in American political culture, including our racism and our preoccupation with sexuality. I
don't think we like women very much or like the poor. All of those
things have deep roots. And the kind of welfare system that we have
in a sense keeps those cultural myths alive because it treats these
people so badly. It investigates them. When farmers or corporations
get money from the government, they don't have to appear for face-
to-face certification. They don't have to answer questions like, Don't
you have anything at all in the pantry? Where did you get that
watch? Nothing like that. It's all matter-of-fact and straightforward.
Those procedures color in the eyes of many people, influence in the
eyes of many people, the meaning of welfare.

*I would think that as someone who has done years of work in this area
your phone would be ringing off the hook with TV and newspapers wanting to get your ideas and your expertise on this issue. Have you in fact
been called on by the media?*

Not very much. Occasionally PBS or Pacifica News. But by and
large I and other people like me, people who have spent years study-
ing welfare, scholars who know about the history of welfare, who
know about comparative welfare state policies, have not been turned
to by the media. The people who have been turned to are the pub-
licist think-tank characters like Charles Murray [author of *The Bell*

Curve] or to some extent the administration's own policy experts. But a very narrow kind of perspective has been put before the American people, and very limited kinds of information about welfare.

You're involved currently with other women academics who are working in this area in a campaign to bring these concerns to the public's attention. What are your plans? What are you trying to achieve with that?

Last summer, Linda Gordon, a historian at the University of Wisconsin, and I developed a statement criticizing the Clinton administration's welfare proposal. We thought we would circulate it among a few other women academics who do research in this field to see if they were interesting in signing it. To our surprise, instead of getting 50 women we ultimately got 500 women academics who signed our statement and who contributed money. We're going to publish that statement in *The New Republic*, *Roll Call*, *The New York Review of Books* and in *The Nation* over the next two weeks or so. So that's one kind of effort. But while I don't get a lot of calls from the Donahue show or Oprah Winfrey, I do get a lot of calls from local grassroots groups, from Women's Studies programs that are planning teach-ins and speak-outs. I think that there is growing recognition that the Personal Responsibility Act in particular goes too far, that it is in a sense overreached. I think women in particular are beginning to see this attack on women and children born out of wedlock as of a piece with a larger attack on the rights that women have won.

Frances Fox Piven is Distinguished Professor of Political Science at City University of New York. Her book, Regulating the Poor, *co-authored with Richard Cloward, was recently re-issued and is as relevant as ever.*

January 7, 1995

Family Values

Single Motherhood and Welfare

Interview with Theresa Funicello

On November 29th, NBC Nightly News featured a segment on the scourge of single motherhood now spreading, according to the report, from the Black community to whites. Here's a segment from that program:

(children): Hickory-dickory-dock, the mouse ran up the clock ... (commentator) At age 18, Christine is one of the oldest in this group of single mothers. She has two children. "How old were you when you had your first?" "Fifteen." "Fifteen. Do you think it's a good idea for you to have two children at your age?" "Yeah." Robin's second baby is on the way. "Why did you want to have a baby?" "Just so I could love somebody and they could love me back." Erin also wanted to be a mother, but not a wife. "Who pays for this baby? [pause] You or welfare?" "Welfare." Melanie's not interested in getting married either. "How come?" "I don't know. I'm just not good with commitments."...Society is a lot easier on mothers like this than it used to be. Welfare will support them, and the stigma of being an unwed mother is history. "Do you feel any shame about this?" "No." Why would they be ashamed when both their friends and so many famous women they see as role models do the same thing?

This kind of framing of the issue is par for the course in mainstream media. Women are presented describing their experience, but rarely if ever are they sought for their expertise, their ideas about policy. That's left to the experts back in Washington, or to the network analysts. Veena Cabreros Sud prepared this report for Counterspin.

Theresa Funicello is a welfare mother. In 1973 she gave birth to a baby girl. Three months later, the child's father left. For years she held on to survival and sanity on what poor people call "the welfare." She also became one of the most vocal activists in the welfare rights movement. Funicello recently authored Tyranny of Kindness: Dismantling the Welfare System to End Poverty in America. *Today in the U.S., women represent two-thirds of those in poverty. Almost all are mothers. Social Security survivors are also almost all mothers. Yet women whose husbands die get society's support to raise their children. They are not called "pathological," "lazy" or "irresponsible." Women whose husbands leave them are.*

One of the things that amuses me is to read the social policy experts who over and over and over again say, "They don't work," referring to welfare mothers. And "what we've got to do is make them work". Then they start talking about this "social contract." They love this thing. This is great stuff. The state has these obligations and the individual has those obligations. It's all one big happy family. The thing that they keep forgetting when they say, "You have responsibilities and then you get certain things," is that the women didn't walk away from their responsibilities. They're holding onto their kids by a thread under the most intensely complicated and difficult and dark and even horrifying circumstances, really hard work, even though they have the option of getting rid of them just like the guy who walked away. They could. Why are the adults on welfare in families and AFDC where they have children, why are they almost all women? How dare any man question, even think about the mother as being irresponsible under the circumstances? She's the one person who has been responsible.

In 1990 the average welfare grant for a family of three was $377. All that to cover rent, food, utilities, some medical expenses, laundry, diapers, clothes, furniture, transportation. Survival on that kind of money is indeed work. According to Funicello, the term "working poor" is a misnomer.

Mothers are working poor. People on welfare are not the *lumpen*. They are the working class. They may have periods of time in which they are on welfare, but they also have periods of time in which they are not on welfare, at which point they're in the wage market. No matter how you look at it, work gets done. The only people I know who have the luxury of doing nothing are very wealthy people. And they have a choice. But even people who are on the streets, homeless single people, theirs is not an easy task, to stay alive. It isn't simple to survive on the streets, even for a single adult. Try being a mother with some children without anyplace to live, or living in a slum that's so bad it's literally life-threatening.

Throughout the 1980s, the health of pregnant women and infants in the U.S. plummeted. In 1991, American ran twenty-first worldwide in infant mortality rates. In her book, Funicello documents children who died from preventable diseases, lack of food, lead poisoning, babies dying of heart failure, not to mention stray bullets. Many mothers now take out funeral insurance for their children.

Poverty is the number one killer of children. Period. No question about it. There have been several studies that proved it, and it's true whether you're white or Black or Hispanic. It just is true. And when you think about that, not only for the children, but for the mothers, that is considered to be the worst thing that can happen to a human being, which is to have your child die. Not to have you die, but to have your child die.

This is how it works if it happens and you're on welfare: You don't have the money to bury the kid. The welfare department has a limit on how much it will give you to bury your baby. That limit will not get your baby buried anywhere, because it's just not enough. No undertaker will do the job. So you have two choices. One is to go out and get the money any way under the sun, whether you collect it from neighbors, friends, relatives, whatever, and then you maybe get an undertaker and maybe then you can bury your child and you will know where your child's buried. Maybe you have to prostitute yourself. You might do anything. Say you succeed in collecting a certain amount of money and then you assume that you can get the rest of it from the welfare because they said you could get whatever that figure is. It's different in different states. You go back to the welfare department and say, Okay, now I've got the rest. I want to bury my child. They will not give you the original amount that they would have given you, because they then say that if you have been able to get the rest of that money to bury your child, then you had hidden resources that you could have tapped. So now not only will we not give you the additional money, we're cutting you off welfare. So every mother in that situation is in a terrible bind. The other option she has is to let the baby be buried by the city of New York or whatever public institution it is. When that happens, the child is buried in a pauper's grave, an unmarked grave. The mother will never know where the child is. She can never know where the grave site is because they're all just dumped someplace. I watch the news all the time, and I see this New York story about the dog cemetery and everybody went nuts because the dogs were not buried properly. It has been a news story over and over again. Why isn't it a news story that poor women do not know where their children are buried if they can't get the money to bury them?

Theresa Funicello documents that in New York City alone the waiting list for public housing exceeds 250,000 families. Instead of helping poor women and children in need, Funicello says the state comes down with an iron fist.

How we can say that they're not working is beyond me. How we can not look at them almost as heroic is beyond me. Instead all we hear about in the major media, just every politician, is how screwed up they are, or they take drugs, or they drink. If we went into the households of middle and upper-class people and requested their urine to find out what they did, you know damn well that we'd find a lot of people who drink and/or take cocaine and/or smoke this, that or the other, and we wouldn't be talking about how bad parents they are. The minute they find a poor women with some kind of substance in her body, it translates immediately into this totally debauched human being. It's pretty outrageous. A couple of days ago a woman was arrested for prostitution. She's got two kids. What's the story? The real story is, she has two kids and she's been cut off welfare. A million people a year who are eligible for welfare at that point in time are cut off. When you're cut off, you don't have too many choices. And yet, she's now a criminal and God knows what they're going to do with her.

This woman's story, and many like hers, are rarely covered in the media. Their words are even less believed. Reagan's mythic "welfare queens" has seen to that. Another media myth has captured the headlines today: welfare fraud. National hysteria has resulted in proposals from fingerprinting welfare mothers to cutting off all benefits completely. According to Funicello—once a welfare mother herself—this is one of the crueler headlines.

Even when I was on welfare in the mid-1970s, the welfare grant was slightly lower than it is now, but you couldn't live on that money, no kind of way, and everybody, including the workers, knew it. So if you were living on welfare, you had to figure out all kinds of ways to manipulate, maneuver, whatever to get by. If somebody wants to call that welfare fraud, they're sick, is all I can say, just plain sick. We read Les Misérables and feel bad about the guy who went to prison for stealing a loaf of bread, and we're going to stick this woman in jail for prostituting because she couldn't buy a loaf of bread, is what the bottom line is. The real welfare fraud, to the extent that it's ever been found in any significant way, isn't committed by women. It's committed by thieves, serious, well-organized thieves. You have to be well organized to get a system working for you where you pile up checks or pile up food stamps. We're mixing all of this stuff up and blaming it over and over again on the poor women and then saying, If they just get a job. What job? Somebody tell me what job they're talking about?

Theresa Funicello is the author of Tyranny of Kindness: Dismantling the Welfare System to End Poverty in America.

December 4, 1993

Budgets Made Boring

Covering Economics
Without Women

Close to a million French women and men screamed a furious, collective "Non!" when they heard President Chirac's scheme to slash public spending on pensions, health services, and income supports for the unemployed. "We must fight—our backs are to the wall! It's now or never!" a striking railwayman declared on French TV as thousands of angry workers took over dozens of French towns in the fall of 1995.

The French workers were shocked into action just as the U.S. Congress spat out an even more inhumane budget. But most U.S. media managed to avoid the comparison. In fact, the dominant media response here to the French strikes was a giant, distracted snore. The *New York Times's* European correspondent fixed his trained reporter's eyes firmly on the banal: baguette delays and snarled-up boulevards. *Time* magazine dismissed the protesting public workers as "coddled." The *Wall Street Journal* explained the root of the problem: The French people just don't understand.

But perhaps they understand more than American women, lulled to inaction by media assurances that the budget negotiations are the dullest subject on earth. Marion Wright Edelman, president of the Children's Defense Fund, was one of the few who seemed to notice. "It is immoral what is going on in Washington today. The country is sleeping through this revolution," she seethed to *New York Times* columnist Bob Herbert, calling the U.S. Congressional plan "an unbelievable budget massacre of the weakest."

As no class is more perilously poised than women—who, with children, make up the majority of the poor—it might have unglazed some eyes if reporters had covered the fiscal future from a working woman's point of view. Instead, we heard about "budget gridlock"— a traffic metaphor that implies that no one's really at fault, there are just too many interest groups on the road.

The same TV networks that sent crews to the Grand Tetons to bemoan vacation-time closure of the federal wilderness ignored the provisions in the budget that would cut by a quarter the staff of the already-stripped Environmental Protection Agency. *Newsweek* called the pre-Thanksgiving government shutdown "a stubborn name-calling standoff." The *New York Times* referred to the "blame game" when 280,000 federal workers were furloughed for Christmas and 460,000 emergency employees toiled through the New Year without pay. Then came the professional wrestling reports: the endless accounts of men in D.C. "bickering," "groping," "blood-letting," and "inching towards a budget deal." In fact, although President Clinton got to play the people's protector in many news accounts, he strongly supported a Senate bill that would flatten the working poor and shove 1.1 million more children into poverty.

Consider the impact of just one budget provision on the welfare of American women: the cuts aimed at the Occupational Safety and Health Administration (OSHA). Who are the more than 200,000 workers who have been killed and the two million who have been permanently disabled from job injuries since the Administration's founding in 1970?

Even though writers like syndicated columnist Ellen Goodman or the *New York Times*'s Maureen Dowd haven't taken up the threat to OSHA as a "women's issue," heavy industry is no longer a male preserve. There are almost as many poultry workers as steelworkers in U.S. today, and poultry workers are almost entirely poor, African American, and female. The average poultry processor makes 78 hand motions every minute, enabling companies to process 90 birds in that time, with an injury rate worse than that of coal mining, construction, or auto work.

In an unusual piece of reporting last January, Tony Hurwitz of the *Wall Street Journal* wrote about life at a contemporary poultry plant where women workers peed on themselves because they were forbidden to leave the production line without permission. And if this didn't clue reporters that OSHA was a women's concern, memories of the 25 locked-in women workers who lost their lives in the

1991 chicken-factory fire in Hamlet, North Carolina, should have set them straight. Clinton mourned for Hamlet in his pitch for the presidency at the '92 Democratic National Convention, but Vice President Al Gore is all for the relaxing of government regulations—he calls it "Common-Sense Government."

Common sense for whom? Who benefits when OSHA's feeble staff financing, which covered only 2,000 inspectors to monitor six million businesses nationwide, is reduced by a quarter? One rider to the '96 appropriations bill bars any regulation of, or even research into, the hazards of repetitive stress injuries such as carpal tunnel syndrome, and bars workers from filing any complaint on the subject with OSHA—until they've checked with their bosses.

Public protest might have occurred if the impact of budget-slashing on women were visible in the news. While the *New York Times* and the *Washington Post* dedicated over 100 editorials each to the budget between November 1 and December 15, only two women were among the writers of signed opinion pieces, and no writer addressed the threat to women, except to those who receive welfare. Women are assigned the role of social scapegoat (the welfare "queen")—or they get no role at all.

It's not asking for special favors for economic writers to stop editing women out. Women dominate the two fields (public service and health care) that are showing the strongest union growth. Women make up two-thirds of the most quickly expanding job sector, the "contingent" or "part-time" workforce which receives the poorest benefits and the skimpiest job security. Excluding women from financial reporting is like covering the SuperBowl without mentioning the players. It's not just sexist, it's getting the story wrong. And it's no small reason why economic reporting is such a bore.

It wouldn't be difficult to make pocketbook issues exciting. Far more tedious topics are pumped up to titillate the public. Night after night, the dips and leaps of the Dow Jones average are vigorously reported, though only a smidgen of the U.S. population actually trades stocks.

If journalists adopted a women's perspective as often as they viewed the world from Wall Street, the public might not sleep through the budget battle, but join the French at the barricades. But don't worry, that story would be considered much too dull to make it onto national TV.

Reprinted with permission of ON THE ISSUES:
The Progressive Woman's Quarterly, *Spring 1996,*
copyright ©1996 by Choices Women's Medical Center, Inc.
To subscribe to ON THE ISSUES, *call 1-800-783-4903, M-F 9am-8pm*

EUROPE

Days of Rage in Paris

Europeans won't give up the 'good life' without a fight

Paris is burning: *Students striking in 1968 helped topple Charles de Gaulle. Last week they targeted France's austerity-minded regime*

POWELL   the Hudson Institute, an India   think. "the

With Jobs At Stake, Women are Ignored

The North American Free Trade Agreement (NAFTA) will disproportionately affect women, yet the voices of women workers were barely heard in the mainstream media's discussion of the pact.

NAFTA's most likely impact, according to the World Bank, will be on multinational corporations operating south of the U.S.-Mexico border and on those who work for them—predominantly women and girls. Multinationals already employ almost half a million people in Mexico, 70 percent to 80 percent of whom are women between the ages of 16 and 25. NAFTA may open up new job opportunities for these women, albeit in industries that pay as little as 40 cents an hour for 14- to 16-hour days, but the freer rein their employers will enjoy is widely expected to decrease what slim protection the women have against workplace violence and abuse.

Similarly, in the United States, the smaller textile and assembly plants which are particularly likely to close if the U.S.-Mexican border is opened, employ a high concentration of women workers. Women in these U.S. factories tend to be the last hired, most weakly protected workers on the job, as they are in Mexico.

Given the above, it would have made interesting copy to consider the attitudes of women workers toward the pact. But a study of coverage in the *New York Times*, the *L.A. Times* and ABC news broadcasts during the week the pact was signed(10/4/92-10/11/92) found only 10 quotes from women in 42 stories.

Four of those quotes were from Carla Hills, the U.S. Special Trade Representative who represented the Bush administration in negotiations. One quote came from Lynn Martin, Bush's secretary of labor; two more from Bush campaign staffers Mary Matalin and Torie Clarke. The remaining women quoted were businesswomen: the president of a Newport Beach marketing firm that helped Bush on the agreement, and two securities and bonds saleswomen, inter-viewed by Lydia Chavez in a story in the *L.A. Times* (10/4/92).

Women workers (and their advocates) were overlooked by all of the outlets studied. They did, however, remain the favorite subject of advertisements aimed at industry, tempting them to relocate south of Texas with promises of cheap, vulnerable, female labor

January/February 1993

The Celebrity
and the Sweatshops

Kathie Lee's "Star Power"
Outshines Child Workers

Kathie Lee Gifford was caught off guard when labor rights activist Charlie Kernaghan and his team at the National Labor Committee revealed the unperky truth: The Wal-Mart clothing line that bears her name (and picture) was partly made in sweatshops by Central American kids.

But before the month was out, Gifford's "Scramble to Save Face" (*New York Times*, 5/24/96) had been transformed into a crusade: with help from damage-control king Howard Rubenstein (PR consultant to Leona Helmsley and Donald Trump) Kathie Lee became a "committed labor activist" (*New York Times*, 6/13/96). Suddenly it was Gifford, not Kernaghan, who had "called for a crackdown on sweatshops" (*New York Times*, 7/3/96). And all without giving up the profits from her lucrative "Kathie Lee" line of clothes.

To get the story of sweatshop exploitation into the U.S. limelight, Kernaghan and the NLC went where the media torch shines most sharply: on the rich and famous. Journalists joked about their industry's pro-celebrity proclivities: "Star Power. There's nothing like it to get people's attention," admitted *USA Today* (6/12/96).

Ted Koppel (*Nightline*, 6/19/96) adopted the defensive tone that he perfected during the excesses of the O.J. Simpson era, absolving himself for routinely ignoring labor rights stories that came fame-free: "We would not be paying as much attention to the issue of child labor…were it not for the fact that celebrities rent out their fame to help sell the items that are produced under those conditions. That's a given."

L.A. Times reporter Barry Bearak blamed the audience (6/14/96), quoting a historian who said the fascination with fame was cultural:

"To get Americans to engage in a difficult subject there has to be some entertainment value.... That's the nature of social issues and politics these days." No word from Bearak about the nature of commercial media and what it takes to get most journalists to engage in critical coverage of issues touchy to their sponsors.

Disney to the Rescue

Conveniently equipped with a live, national, daily TV show—syndicated by Disney which also reaps profits from child labor—Gifford launched her defense in person (*Live with Regis & Kathie Lee*, 5/1/96). "I started my clothing line to benefit children...Up to 50 percent of the profits go to the little children. Now, if anybody is calling that into question, this is all verifiable."

With no TV program of their own, labor rights activists couldn't immediately contradict the uncontrite Kathie Lee. In fact, only $1 million of the reported $9 million-$10 million profits from the Kathie Lee line go to children's charities; the rest Gifford keeps. "One for the kids, nine for Kathie Lee," Kernaghan told FAIR's radio show *CounterSpin* (5/31/96).

When the accusations against Gifford continued to catch attention, Disney's ABC News came to her aid, airing a *PrimeTime Live* segment (5/22/96) that gave Gifford plenty of time for anguish: "I felt like I was being...kicked in the teeth for trying to help kids," she complained through tears.

Only when she was connected to a scam at home—a sweatshop subcontracted to make Kathie Lee clothes just a few blocks from the ABC studio where she tapes her show—did Gifford start her conversion. Her husband, ABC Sports personality Frank Gifford, burst into the factory with $100 bills for unpaid workers, and an eager press corps. "I have the money to pay them," he said (*New York Observer*, 6/3/96), "I just need to know who the hell they are."

Public: Enemy

With the spotlight off Gifford's profits, a safer scapegoat emerged: the public. According to the *L.A. Times* (6/14/96), "the great beneficiary" of "filthy fly-by-night rag shops" that pay sub-minimum wages is "the consumer, grown used to bargain shopping at national chains."

ABC's *Nightline* (6/19/96) devoted a whole show to the issue of exploitation of Third World workers, including children, but their starvation wages were blamed on consumers: "Those of us who buy the products...pay very little attention to where and how those products are manufactured, as long as we feel that we're getting a bargain, which is, of course, what encourages the manufactuers to search out the lowest-paid hourly workers."

Nightline mentioned that its corporate parent, the Disney Corporation, uses subcontractors in Haiti that pay workers the unlivable—but legal—wage of 28 cents an hour. The producers shied away from any mention of the corporation's profits. In the first quarter of 1995, Disney's soared to half a billion dollars. Big profits can be reaped from Disney's clothes and dolls when the purchase price is roughly 100 times what the workers are paid.

Koppel noted the absence of representatives from Nike, Reebok and other manufacturers on his program: "We invited [them] but they won't be joining us." He didn't apologize for the fact that his in-studio discussion failed to include a representative of a labor group. Had such a person been included in the debate, she or he might have pointed out that it is corporate profits, not consumer pockets, that are swollen by sweatshop work. Wages could be quadrupled without raising prices and profits would still be huge.

Feeling Her Pain

Instead, Kathie Lee's "pain" made bigger headlines than that of the workers assembling clothes for Wal-Mart: "Mrs. Gifford...has become Exhibit A in proving that what you don't know can hurt you after all," the *New York Times* reported (6/27/96). Close on Gifford's heels in the victim parade came bewildered investors and the companies themselves. In "Investing Abroad with a Conscience: It's Not Easy" (*New York Times*, 6/2/96), reporter Ken Brown referred to companies—not workers—with "problems." "No matter how careful an investor tries to be," he concluded, "the potential for an error is great."

One could say that such obfuscation was an improvement. The last time the *New York Times* did a front-page story on sweatshops, "65 Cents an Hour: A Special Report" (3/12/95), writer Jane Li went under cover in a Brooklyn sweatshop and found that the blame for poverty lay with the poor: "Week in Sweatshop Reveals Grim Conspiracy of the Poor."

But, like that story, which mentioned the effects of NAFTA only in its penultimate paragraph ("Federal labor inspectors say they have eased enforcement since the passing of the North American Free Trade Agreement because they do not want to drive jobs out of the United States"), most Gifford-related reports focused tightly on women—the celebrity, the buyers of dressers, the workers—and kept off the big picture: international trade policy, or the (male) CEOs.

Women's Empowerment?

There were some exceptions, like syndicated columnist Bob Herbert, who hammered corporate heads (*New York Times*, 6/24/96). Reporting on the tremendous wealth of Philip Knight, Nike's founder and chief executive, Herbert condemned Nike's move from repressive Indonesia to even lower-paid Vietnam: "What's next? Employees who'll work for a bowl of gruel?" And he used similar straight talk to describe Nike's advertising strategy: riding a "so-called women's empowerment campaign to new heights of wealth while at the same time insisting that most of its products be made by grossly underpaid women stuck in utterly powerless and often abusive circumstances."

The *LA Weekly* (5/10/96) illustrated the wealth of Disney CEO Michael Eisner with the help of a diagram of an 18th Century slave ship. In 1993-95, the *Weekly* reported, Eisner made an average of $292,871 per day, or just about 100,000 times the daily wage of the Pocohantas pajamas tailors and seamstresses in Haiti. At a density of 291 people per slaveship, the paper noted, "it would take 344 deckfuls of Haitians to approximate Eisner's earning power."

But if readers are looking for the lasting impact of the Kathie Lee saga, there's not much to celebrate. Though the Giffords have made much of the fact that Wal-Mart moved its operations out of Honduras, the move was to Nicaragua, where workers are paid less, not more.

As for celebrities who cash in on product endorsements, *Entertainment Weekly* (6/14/96) wrote: "Fearful of tarnishing their images, will luminaries stop vending their names? Three words: Are you kidding?" Sacrificing none of her profits as she metamorphosized, with the media's help, from "ignorant" exploiter to hero of the working poor, Kathie Lee showed that media chivalry can be a wonderful thing—for wealthy celebrities, that is.

September/October 1996

The Exploitation of Workers in Chinese Restaurants

Interview with Joanne Lum

Joanne Lum is one of the coordinators of the Chinese Staff and Workers Association in New York. Joanne recently got into an interesting dialogue with the New York Times. *How did you get into this wrangle?*

The Chinese Staff and Workers Association is a workers organization based in Manhattan's Chinatown. We organize Chinese workers of all trades: construction, restaurant, garment, building maintenance. We had a campaign that we supported that started last August, supporting the Silver Palace Restaurant workers. The Silver Palace Restaurant in Chinatown is the only unionized restaurant among the 300 or so restaurants in Manhattan's Chinatown. It was unionized about 13 years ago. In March of 1993, the management started union-busting efforts because the contract was up for renewal. It was putting forth all these proposals, some of which were illegal, to the workers, such as having the waiters share some of the tips with management, arbitrarily trying to force the *dim sum* workers into a tips-recipient category and slashing their wages to $2.90 an hour, trying to take away all kinds of benefits like medical benefits, sick leave, etc. Basically they were saying to the workers, Sign or forget it. We're going to lock you out. The workers didn't want to sign this illegal contract, so they were locked out on August 20th of last year and began what ended up being a 7-month campaign that actually involved other workers from the community, but also other workers from other trades, races, activists from a lot of different organizations. It was a campaign that was really powerful because it brought together so many different workers and activists and it put a message out there to a lot of workers in Chinatown that you can really fight and win. That was the big point about this campaign—that the workers won. Last month, the workers managed to force management to sign a fair contract to rehire all the picketing workers.

The New York Times *gave the lockout very little attention, but once the victory happened there was a story.*

Actually, during the campaign there were three short stories in the *New York Times*. What they tried to do each time was to appear as if they were giving the full story by going back and forth, like the workers say this, the management says this. But the tone was always that the business had good reason for doing what it was doing. You know, times are rough, competition's hard, so you can understand why management is trying to do what it's doing. It always gave management the last word.

After the victory rally that was in part a victory for the Silver Palace workers, but also drawing attention to what else was going on in Chinatown—lack of government attention—the *Times* ran a story trying to assess the impact of this victory. What it did was, it ran one story suggesting that this victory didn't have much impact in Chinatown, that the workers in Chinatown were powerless victims, that they probably didn't want to fight, and it quoted one person in particular who heads this huge, multi-million dollar social service agency as saying, This victory has no ripple effect. It's not going to do anything to the other workers in Chinatown. It doesn't represent anything significant. Yet it doesn't tell you anything about the source, the fact that this source, David Chang, who is the head of the Chinese-American Planning Council, heads an agency that's been found guilty by the National Labor Relations Board and by different level courts of firing workers who are trying to organize and of failing to pay prevailing federal wages for certain programs and of discriminating against senior workers.

Along with this story about the impact of the victory they ran a story, a profile of a Chinese waiter. This profile was full of the stereotypes that people love to hear about Chinese workers—that we love to be slaves, that it's in our blood, that we don't like to make trouble, that we don't like unions because it's just not in our culture. Basically that we don't really care about labor law violations because it's our work ethic.

Is that the essence of the letter that you wrote to the Times?

I was pointing out, first of all, that the assessment of the victory was really off base. There were all these factual errors. There was omission of key information. The reporter used sources whose labor records were totally questionable. I pointed out what some of her errors were. I was saying, too, that the *New York Times* obviously doesn't really care about labor issues or immigrant issues, because you assign someone who doesn't know much about the Chinese community…The editor, actually to his credit, called me and said, We want to run the letter, but it's got to be totally edited. First of all, we can't run attacks on our writers—which I felt okay about it. The *New York Times* as an institution, it should assume responsibility for the coverage. But what they did in cutting out the attacks was took all the bite out of the letter. When he called me back after he had cut out about half of the letter, he told me that he had to pass the letter by the reporter to see what she thought. He said that she had three problems with it. I said, This is supposed to be a letter to the editor from readers. Why does it have to be approved by the reporter?

Joanne Lum is one of the coordinators of the Chinese Staff and Workers Association in New York City.

April 23, 1994

Part II

Silence and Scapegoats

"Familiarity breeds contempt" or so the saying goes. But students of homophobia, for example, have found that in fact the reverse is true. The likelihood of someone supporting equal rights for homosexuals increases massively if that person knows someone who is lesbian or gay. Reporters could familiarize their public with people who are marginalized. Instead, powerful media tend to accept rather than challenge prejudices—and the vilified rarely get to speak for themselves.

Copyright © 1989 Kirk Anderson

Women ARE the News

In 1990, the executive editor of the *New York Times* responded to a critical study of his paper by saying, in effect, that when women were making the news, they would be in it. But women are making news daily. Usually, they *are* the news, yet Frankel and his colleagues, as Jane O'Reilly would say, still "don't get it."

When young women organize against rape and claim their right to sex on their own terms, *Newsweek* calls it "Sexual Correctness," and asks, "Have We Gone Too Far?" When Antioch College supported a student initiative to promote consent-seeking rather than blame-assigning in sex, it becomes a media laughing-stock.

On the medical front: According to the *New York Times*, some 194,000 people in the U.S. have died of AIDS since 1980; 450,000 have died of breast cancer. Yet when ABC in September produced a special on breast cancer, it was called "The Other Epidemic." When women organized for increased federal funding for research into breast cancer, the *New York Times*' Gina Kolata reported (10/20/93), "The question is not whether breast cancer is worthy of research. Instead, it is whether the nation benefits when vocal advocacy groups get their way."

As for lesbians, the media's favorite minority of 1993: Where were *Vanity Fair* and *Newsweek* in 1992, when an African-American woman was burnt alive in her home by skinheads? Hattie Mae Cohen's death received barely a murmur. In September, Sharon Bottoms had her two-year-old taken away from her by the Virginia supreme court because she made her family with another woman. "The mother's conduct is illegal and immoral and renders her an unfit parent," said Judge Duford M. Parsons. Is this what the media call "Lesbian Chic"?

And as '93 came to a close, the biggest headlines had to do with genital mutilation. Not the kind that affects more than 100 million women in parts of Africa, the Middle East and Asia who are ritually mutilated before adolescence. The mutilation that became a media magnet this autumn was the castrating act of Lenora Bobbitt. She hacked off her husband's privates and newspapers from coast to coast picked up the sordid story. In New York's *Daily News*, a full-page headline screamed the brilliantly incisive, "It Really Hurt." Cutting off a penis is a crime—but so is this coverage.

The same outlets that present feminists as hysterical whiners and lesbians as having all the fun routinely shut women's perspectives out of most of their reporting. Women are made invisible, along with all our differences, our difficulties and our points of view.

Consider almost any major issue up for debate today—you'll find that women are at the heart. Take NAFTA: Women are the workers already employed in huge majorities by the transnational corporations most likely to expand in Mexico. They're also the ones last-hired, first-fired in the textile and electronic factories most likely to be displaced here in the U.S.

When you talk about welfare and the poor, you're talking predominantly about women; 90 percent of the adults on welfare are female. Those who most use the health system and are most devastated by it—women, the elderly; the education system—the same. They are precisely the voices that, according to FAIR's studies, are often excluded—even from discussions addressing issues, like abortion or family leave, that have been deemed legitimate "women's" affairs.

On Oct. 18, the *New York Times* ran a story on a massive demonstration protesting U.S. and UN actions in Somalia. The accompanying picture featured a woman at the head of the demonstration. Writer Douglas Jehl explained that the thousands-strong demonstration was made up "mostly of women and children." Did Jehl think to speak to a woman? All the named sources were male; all but one, a U.S. or UN official. The women were seen, but never heard.

When FAIR complains about the coverage of women, we're not looking for special coverage or special supplements—where advertisers can sell us things to keep us young, content and in the home.

We're calling for accurate coverage of what's actually going on, and that includes women. Not just as the acted-upon, but as actors and as analysts: not just as those who have experiences but among those who have expertise.

To *Newsweek*'s question, Have We Gone Too Far? Yes. Way too far to go back.

January/February 1994

Whose Story Is It Anyway?

A Forum on Coverage of Women's Stories

From Heidi of Hollywood to Lenora Bobbitt, from the raped daughters of Bosnia to the starving mothers of Somalia—the most frequent roles for women in the mainstream news are sadly familiar.

"Women are more likely to get into the mainstream media as the victim of crime than in any other role," Helen Benedict, author of *Virgin or Vamp: How the Press Covers Sex Crimes*, told the audience at a Nov. 10, 1994 panel discussion organized by the Women's Desk at FAIR.

The panel posed the question: "Whose Story Is It Anyway? How the Media Tell Women's Stories." In a commercial media fixated on sales, the three big sellers are sex, power and death. Women find themselves squeezed into stories that the press associate with these categories; the alternative, often, is to be written out of the story altogether. Given that scenario, FAIR's panelists discussed: Is any coverage at all necessarily better than no coverage?

"You couldn't get a story on prostitutes or sex workers on the Lower East Side, or anywhere, until the Joel Rifkin murders," said panelist Lisa Napoli, coordinator of the Lower East Side Women's Center in New York. Napoli's center was besieged by the press after it was discovered that 18 women, whose murders had virtually been ignored, had apparently been killed by a single serial killer, who found some of his victims in the center's neighborhood.

"Violence devastates our lives, but it only gets attention when we're dead," she said.

The problem of lack of access coupled with blatant bias is particularly pronounced in international coverage. "Muslim women don't have enough identity to have countries," said Nahib Toubia, the author of *Female Genital Mutilation: A Global Call to Action*.

"They're just referred to in the media as 'Muslim.'"

That sort of coverage, said Toubia, has a lot to do with what she called the selling of the American Dream. "People in the U.S. have to have someone to look down on," said Toubia, and for the under-privileged in the U.S., who better than people in the Third World?

"For all these years, no one has wanted to talk about African cultures, the positives, the negatives, the history. Then the first time you get mass attention particularly to women, it's to something like female genital mutilation," said Toubia. A Sudanese surgeon and a long-time anti-mutilation organizer, Toubia published her book specifically to give the Western press factual information on female mutilation and to profile African women "not as victims but as activists," she said.

When they arrive in the U.S., Third World women also get inadequate press attention, unless they arrive in a dramatic way or come from a country with a high political profile. Earlier this summer, the *Golden Venture*, a ship carrying 300 immigrants from China, ran aground off the coast of New York City. "Suddenly the media discovered Chinese immigrants," said Joanne Lum of the Chinese Staff and Workers Association, another panelist.

In the wake of the *Golden Venture*, Lum's desk was piled high with messages from the media. "Mostly they said: wants illegal alien. If you could find a woman, they particularly liked that," Lum remarked.

What the press didn't want was serious discussion of the living and working conditions of immigrant laborers. At a time when the press is blaming women for talking too much about what Katie Roiphe calls "victimhood," these stories of women who work in sweatshops have received close to no attention. Involving not physical but economic violence, the experience of striking Chinese workers doesn't make it onto the front page.

The victims that do get attention are the ones the press associate with sex. A lusty model promoting a story on "Sexual Correctness" sells more copies of *Newsweek* than would a similar shot of a striking garment worker accompanying a report on sweatshop labor.

But more doesn't equal better, especially when it comes to sex-crime coverage.

As Helen Benedict, professor at Columbia's Graduate School of Journalism, concluded, "Given that a woman in this country is being raped every five minutes, according to the FBI, or every 3.5 minutes, according to another national survey, covering rape is an essential duty for the press."

"Women are too often reported as victims, not because there's too much coverage of sex-crime, but because it's covered in the wrong way," said Benedict.

"Instead of looking at victims, the press should be looking at perpetrators; it should be looking at rape—and sexism. And that's what the press is utterly failing to do."

January/February 1994

Far-Right Militias
and Anti-Abortion Violence

Media Disconnect

When the Oklahoma City bombing captured the attention of the mainstream media, some women's rights activists expected that the attack would end mainstream media's reluctance to report on violence against abortion-providers and other domestic terror threats. That reasonable hope was dashed.

With its first reporting of the Oklahoma story, the *New York Times* (4/20/95) ran a list headlined "Other Bombings in America," which spanned four decades and included some attacks that claimed no injuries or lives. But none of the 40 officially documented bombings that have targeted women's clinics in that period was mentioned.

Media investigations of where right-wing militants get their violent ideas generally ignored the Army of God manual, which recommends 65 ways to destroy abortion clinics and includes an illustrated recipe for making a "fertilizer bomb" from ammonium nitrate and fuel oil. The manual turned up in 1993, buried in the backyard of an anti-abortionist indicted for arson and acid attacks on nine clinics. But headline-writers avoided describing it as a "Manual for Terrorists," as the *New York Times* identified a militia document in 1995 (4/29/95).

The first person convicted of violence against a women's health center ignited a gas can in a crowded New York City clinic in 1979. Since 1982, according to the Bureau of Alcohol, Tobacco and Firearms, there have been 169 arson and bomb attacks on women's health centers in 33 states. In the '90s, when five workers in such clinics have been murdered, people calling themselves "pro-life" publicly advocate violence as a way to make legally sanctioned abortion impossibly unsafe.

In January 1994, the Supreme Court agreed with pro-choice groups that anti-abortionists could legitimately be investigated for conspiracy, but influential media have been harder to convince. In fact, the national media's gentle handling of the anti-abortion story has amounted to a quasi-conspiracy itself.

See No Terrorists

Four days before the first abortion provider was killed in Florida in 1993, directors of women's health centers in that state and Texas held a news conference to call attention to an organized campaign of terror that was striking clinics across the U.S. The *New York Times* (3/6/93) portrayed that event as a pro-choice publicity stunt: "Like a conclave of unreconstructed Cold Warriors, [pro-choicers] appeared intent on fighting new battles, to avoid becoming victims of their own success," the *Times*' Felicity Barringer wrote.

When Dr. David Gunn was shot three days later outside his clinic in Pensacola, rather than investigate the feminists' claims that Gunn's killing was part of an organized strategy, the newspapers of record reported the death as if it had been fated: "A Collision of Causes," the *Washington Post* labeled it (3/13/93); "Separate Visions on Bettering Lives Collide" was the *New York Times*' headline (3/14/93). Dr. Gunn and his killer were presented as somehow equivalent: both men were "consumed by abortion," according to another *Post* story (3/12/93) that was headlined "Doctor, Accused Killer both Impassioned."

The World Trade Center bombing, a month earlier, had been reported without the talk of "impassioned" victims and terrorists "colliding." Nor were advocates of anti-Western terrorism turned into credible media commentators.

But after Pensacola, anti-abortion zealots, even criminals, were regularly sought out by media for their views. Many news organizations quoted John Burt, the regional director of Rescue America, the group whose anti-choice demonstration Michael Griffin attended on the day he shot Gunn. The *Washington Post* (3/13/93) cited Michael Bray, "another Project Rescue leader," without mentioning that Bray was a convicted clinic-bomber. (He'd targeted several abortion clinics and the offices of the National Abortion Federation and the ACLU.)

In late 1993 (12/8/93), *Nightline's* Ted Koppel hosted an in-studio discussion of doctor-killing. His only guests were Helen Alvare, a representative of the National Conference of Catholic Bishops (which issued a statement post-Pensacola comparing the violence of murder with the "violence of abortion"), and Paul Hill, director of the anti-abortion group "Defensive Action," which advocates killing doctors on the grounds that abortion is violence.

Ted Koppel echoed this definition of violence when he opened the show by comparing the number of legal abortions with the number of murdered doctors—what he called "the latest casualty count from the battlefield between the pro-life and the pro-choice movements." Although terrorism is one of Koppel's favorite subjects— FAIR's study of *Nightline* counted 52 programs on the topic in 40 months (*EXTRA!*, 1-2/89)—the word "terrorism" was never used by him to describe anti-abortion violence. Instead, a sympathetic Koppel said that Hill's advocacy of murdering doctors raised a "very, very difficult moral question." (See *EXTRA! Update*, 2/94.) Hill, like Griffin, was a protege of Burt, whose group issued a wanted poster for Dr. John Bayard Britton, Gunn's replacement. The poster "exposed" Britton "for the butcher that he is." Seven months after his appearance on *Nightline*, Hill gunned down Britton and James Barrett, his escort, at the same Pensacola clinic.

See No Agenda

With all the media's familiarity with these "pro-lifers," it's surprising that Koppel, the *Washington Post*, the *New York Times*, et al. have had such a hard time cottoning on to the fact that militia men and anti-abortion zealots can sometimes be one and the same.

Not all anti-abortionists are advocates of violence, nor do all militias put stopping abortion on the top of their list of goals. But while it would be wrong to lump both groups entirely together, it's equally indefensible for mainstream media to have kept militia who target federal agents, and the anti-abortion militants who target feminists (and women, especially poor women), so far apart.

John Burt, a former Klansman, borrows tactics like his "wanted" posters from the KKK, and says that "fundamentalist Christians and those people [the KKK] are pretty close" (The *Progressive*, 10/94). Paul Hill told *USA Today* (3/7/94), "I could envision a covert organization developing—something like a pro-life IRA."

Anti-abortion activists like these share agendas, rhetoric and tactics with the militia. Others, like Matthew Trewhella, director of Missionaries to the Preborn, have formed militia groups of their own. Trewhella pastors a church-based militia whose priority is defeating abortion. He's also a member of the National Committee of the U.S. Taxpayers Party (USTP), what *Covert Action* (Spring/95) calls "one of the largest political manifestations of the theocratic wing of the Christian right."

In 1994, Planned Parenthood released a video showing Trewhella speaking at a Wisconsin state USTP convention. "What should we do?" Trewhella asked. "We should do what thousands of people across the nation are doing. We should be forming militias." According to Planned Parenthood, the USTP sold a "Free Militia" manual on how to form an underground army. Defending the "right to life" against "legalized abortion" is the first of the manual's stated reasons why one should take up arms.

Following the December 1994 shootings of two health clinic workers in Brookline, Mass., *Reuters* ran an investigative story, "Chilling New Link Suspected Among Anti-Abortion Activists" (1/13/95), that connected Brookline murder suspect John Salvi with militia activism, but the *Reuters* piece was overwhelmingly ignored.

See No Link

In December 1994, NBC refused to air a segment of the program *TV Nation* in which Roy McMillan of the Mississippi-based Christian Action Group said that assassinating Supreme Court justices would be justifiable homicide, and that the president was in "probable harms way." *TV Nation* producer Michael Moore believes that the airing of the segment could have led to arrests that might have prevented the Brookline clinic killings. "It's a federal offense to say the president should be killed," Moore told *USA Today* (1/16/95). Eventually the interview aired on the BBC in Britain, but not in the U.S.

Long before the Oklahoma bombing sent reporters scrambling for militia information, mainstream media had Planned Parenthood's research. "All the national networks and the major dailies have had our material for over a year," Planned Parenthood's Fred Clarkson said in May 1995. But most national news outlets skipped the story. Last fall, in the wake of Paul Hill's arrest, *Newsweek* went so far as to commission a special investigation of rising right-wing violence, including anti-abortion militants and extremist militias.

After the Oklahoma City suspects turned out not to be Arabs, the networks' favorite terrorist experts were flummoxed, so producers had to find other people who knew something about militias. And national news outlets did turn to researchers like Clarkson and others who could draw the lines between various violent far-right movements. A news producer at one major cable network, however, rescinded an invitation for Clarkson to appear just hours before the scheduled broadcast. "He said they couldn't have someone from Planned Parenthood on about militias," Clarkson told *EXTRA!*, "because they'd have angry pro-life viewers calling in and they didn't want to take that heat."

That kind of intimidation does influence how these issues are covered. *New York Times* columnist Frank Rich has been one of the few journalists to pick up on Planned Parenthood's information about Trewhella's involvement with militias— his column "Connect the Dots" ran April 30—but it's a connection that his own paper has been loath to make. After a May 15 press conference, Clarkson heard from reporters that the "evidence of a link" between anti- abortion and militia activity was inadequate. "For some reason, the same blind eye that's been turned to the domestic terrorism we call clinic violence remains turned that way even when we have militia groups among whose major issues is being opposed to abortion," Clarkson told FAIR's radio show *CounterSpin* (5/19/95).

"When people say can you prove a link between militias and anti-abortion groups, I have to say no," said Clarkson. "There's no link. They're the same people in very many cases.... Abortion is part of the agenda. It's not a separate issue, it's the same."

July/August 1995

Homophobia, Racism and Sexism?

The Connections are Clear to Far Right

After the Oklahoma City bombing, the *New York Times* (4/13/95) reported surprise at the existence of right-wing terror-gangs: "New Images of Terror...A suspect, a white drifter, evokes new fear." But right-wing terror is hardly surprising to those who've been on the receiving end of it over the years; nor would the pale image of the suspect have been "new" to mainstream readers if media had been doing their job covering hate crimes.

There were 2,064 homophobia-motivated acts of violence in nine U.S. cities last year. According to New York's Gay and Lesbian Anti-Violence Project, anti-gay hate crimes are the fastest-growing kind (*New York Times*, 3/7/91). But when a disabled man and an out lesbian were murdered in a firebomb attack on their home during Oregon's Ballot Measure 9 campaign, mainstream reporters hardly covered the event at all.

In 1994, when the U.S. attorney general had to send federal agents to Mississippi to protect the women of Camp Sister Spirit from armed mobs, media outlets from AP to *Oprah* churned out stories about small town bigotry; few researched the mainstream context out of which the mobsters sprang.

Even when reporters finally scrambled to report on right-wing militias, the homophobia that is a central part of the radical right's agenda has escaped serious scrutiny. This isn't just an expression of bias; it's bad reporting.

Unlike mainstream media professionals, former KKK leader Tom Metzger, leader of the White Aryan Resistance, is clear about the interconnection of racism, anti-Semitism, misogyny and homophobia: "Almost all abortion doctors are Jews," he ranted (*Covert Action Quarterly*, Spring/95). "Abortion makes money for Jews. Almost all abortion nurses are lesbians. Abortion gives thrills to lesbians. Abortion in Orange County is promoted by the corrupt Jewish organization called Planned Parenthood."

And Metzger is clear about the "need" for violence: "Jews must be punished for this holocaust and murder of white children along with their perverted lesbian nurses."

Samuel Sherwood of the United States Militia Association warns that Bill Clinton "is determined to seize your guns, steal your food, take your children away. In his term, he will have killed more babies than Hitler, put more homosexuals in government than Sodom and Gomorrah" (Scott Nakagawa op-ed, 5/9/95).

Violence-friendly homophobia isn't restricted to militiamen; the rhetoric of gay-hate has been central to mainstream efforts to legislate discrimination. George Matousek, the leader of Michigan's anti-gay ballot measure, plays to fears of the New World Order in an effort to stir support: "Where sodomy is acceptable, the nation declines...The homosexual movement will destroy the military." Says Matousek: "Clinton, or whoever's in office, will turn all our troops over to the United Nations." Matousek's plan? "Step one, stop the homos" (Nakagawa op-ed, 5/9/95).

July/August, 1995

Haitian Women
Are Out of Frame

And Their Abusers Are Out of Sight

When President Clinton sat down in front of U.S. television cameras to explain "why the U.S. is leading the international effort to restore democratic government in Haiti" (10/16/94), he emphasized the violation of Haitian women's human rights. "International observers uncovered a terrifying pattern of soldiers and policemen raping the wives and daughters of suspected political dissidents," Clinton said, "young girls, 13, 16 years old...children forced to watch as their mothers' faces are slashed with machetes."

In Haiti and in the United States, there was hope that these words would translate into action. But a month after the landing of approximately 20,000 U.S. troops, there's no indication that the women's assailants are being brought to trial. And there's just as little evidence that the U.S. press corps cares.

Landing in Haiti a week to the day after the return of Aristide, this writer found herself traveling against the tide of U.S. mainstream media reporters. Having "done" the Haiti story, journalists were leaving the hotels en masse. "We're among the last to leave," Charlayne Hunter-Gault, of the *MacNeil/Lehrer News Hour* and *Rights and Wrongs*, said on October 22, 1994.

There's nothing the U.S. press corp likes better than a videotapeable "moment" and a "great man" making history. Aristide's return to Haiti offered both. No matter how many times President Aristide and his staff said things like "the house of democracy does not stand on a single pillar alone," U.S. cameras focused exclusively on the individual.

Ellen Braune, who runs a non-profit public relations firm, invited journalists to interview leaders of the large popular organizations that constitute Lavalas, the movement that brought Aristide to power. "News producers would say: Well, that's nice, but can't you get us Aristide?" Braune told *CounterSpin* (10/8/94).

The media's failure to see the movement behind the man left most of the Haitian people, and all the women, outside the frame. Remaining in camera-center were "Americans." When *ABC World News Tonight* discussed the damaging effect of poverty in Haiti (10/22/94), who were the victims? U.S. GIs. "Among the stresses that every soldier feels is the shock of seeing Haiti's poverty," explained John McWethy in a segment about why three U.S. soldiers had committed suicide since the Haitian mission began in September. U.S. soldiers appeared on the screen in close-up, with impoverished Haitians in the background. The *Miami Herald* ran headlines like "To Black GIs, Haiti Misery Especially Touching," and "Bad Conditions Cause Morale Problems for U.S. Troops in Haiti" (10/22/94).

For the most part, large, impersonal forces like "poverty" and "power" received scant coverage. It's hard to capture "structural readjustment"—the austerity program imposed on Haiti by foreign lenders—in a graphic photograph; it's far easier to catch a snapshot of the smiling infant or the raising of a U.S. flag.

The question asked by the women of SOFA, a broad-based Haitian women's organization, is what happens when the U.S. troops go home. "The U.S. troops have opened up a space, but what will fill it?" said Marie France, one of the leaders of the group, speaking to a delegation from MADRE, a U.S. women's organization that is supporting a women's health project in Haiti. As fast as reporters were leaving Haiti in the week after the restoration, businessmen were arriving. As the *Miami Herald* reported (11/7/94), "Haiti is open for business."

To Marie France and the women of SOFA, the revival of business as usual in Haiti means a return for women workers to the sub-poverty (14¢/hour) Haitian wage. In addition to purely commercial investment, some $800 million in multilateral aid (most of it from the U.S.) is expected to be invested in Haiti over the next 15 months for "elections assistance" and "stability" development (*Miami Herald*, 11/7/94).

"The intent of many of these programs," Jane Regan writes in the Port-au-Prince-based newsletter *Haiti Info* (10/22/94), "is to counter the democratic and popular movement's demands for radical economic change and social justice." But the *Christian Science Monitor* reported investment solely as a boon (10/24/94): "Aid Windfall Propels Sweeping Change in Haiti."

"The U.S. media provide a very limited picture of just what constitutes a human right," said Vivian Stromberg of MADRE. "Freedom from torture is more or less understood; freedom to develop your own institutions to serve your own needs is not."

As for the torturers? "When the people turn criminals over to the [U.S.] troops," said Anne Marie Coriolon of SOFA in the fifth week of the U.S. occupation, "they see them on the streets again in three days or less." "Our mission," one young U.S. MP on the ground explained, "is to professionalize the army and the police here, not to judge them."

So far, none of the close to 100 rape survivors whom SOFA works with on a regular basis has felt secure enough to try identifying her abuser to the U.S. GIs. One boy did point out the man who forced him to rape his mother, and got U.S. forces to take the accused man away, said Coriolon. "But no one's watching to see if that man is kept in jail," she said. "If he's let out, that boy's life's in danger."

No one's watching because the abusers of women never did get put into the spotlight, and in any case, the media moment has passed.

January/February 1995

Locked-Up Women
Locked Out of Coverage

There is no shortage of reasons why women end up in jail. Women earn less, are responsible for more and are among the least well-protected people in the country. A recent article in *Harper's* magazine (4/94) pointed out that a single mother is almost required to resort to illegal activity if she is to feed and clothe two children on the roughly $300 to $400 cash grant she gets per month from AFDC.

Yet some reporters still drag out the old tired feminist villain to explain the rise in female offenders. "Female Crime Rate Alarming, Law Officials Say; Drugs, Women's Movement Called Factors in Arrests, Prosecutions," an *Arizona Republic* headline announced (10/26/93). A *Houston Chronicle* report took a similar approach (5/10/92): "Some argue that the participation of women in crime parallels women's entrance into previously male-dominated roles." The desperate stab at women's rights activists would be funny if it didn't mask a dangerous failure to investigate the reasons for women's imprisonment. "Stereotypically, victims are female and criminals are male," says Meda Chesney-Lind, director of Women's Studies at the University of Hawaii at Manoa. There's little comprehension of why women end up in jail, says Chesney-Lind, because "women offenders are basically media roadkill."

It's not that there aren't newspaper stories on women in prison— well-informed reports crop up regularly. But when the discussion is national crime policy, women—consistent with the media's notion that they are separate from the category of regular humans—fade away.

A cover story in *U.S. News & World Report* (1/17/94) painted a picture of U.S. crime in which perpetrators were basically men. Apart from an unidentified African-American "gangster girl" in a photo collage, the only female profiled in the piece was one of four women who abducted a 12-year-old and tortured her to death. The "ringleader" of the group was reported to be Melinda Loveless, who "allegedly wished to kill the child because of her closeness to Loveless' lesbian lover." Hardly a representative offense, the sensationalistic Loveless story did satisfy the media's taste for the vicious killer dyke.

"The [crime] story in the press is as if women don't exist," said Brenda Smith of the National Women's Law Center in Washington, D.C. And that's not just a problem for women, who still make up only 5.7 percent of the prison population—it's a problem for the policy debate.

In 1980, the Bureau of Justice counted 13,420 women in federal and state prisons. At the end of 1992 that number stood at 50,409—a roughly 275 percent increase, compared to 160 percent for men. According to the FBI's statistics, women weren't landing in jail for their participation in violent crime: Women's share of arrests for murder, aggravated assault, robbery, etc. had barely moved, from 10.0 to 11.3 percent, in the same period. What did increase was women's incarceration for non-violent crime: shoplifting, check forgery, welfare fraud, substance abuse crimes and "possession for sale" of illegal drugs.

A large part of this increase has been triggered by mandatory sentencing guidelines, under which judges are required to impose minimum sentences for certain federal crimes (including both welfare fraud and drug offenses) without discretion.

"Women offenders are being incarcerated where, previously, they would have been given different types of community-based sentences such as half-way houses or supervised probation," Judge Gladys Kessler of the National Association of Women Judges told the Senate Judiciary Committee last June. Thrown into jail for their work at the lowest, most easily arrested rung of the drug crime business, the majority of these women, said Kessler, are "precisely the kind of offender who is usually an ideal candidate for community placement."

A 1990 study by the American Correctional Association indicates that these women are overwhelmingly young, poor, women of color (57 percent) and mothers of children (75 percent). Female offenders are largely women who ran away from home; about a quarter have attempted suicide; more than half have been abused physically—and 36 percent sexually. Twenty-two percent had been unemployed in the three years before they went to prison. They're in the same world as their brothers, only more so; unlike their brothers, the mainstream media don't consider them part of the picture.

"What happens to the children of the incarcerated mothers?" Judge Kessler asked the Senate. What happens to the *women*? Dubbed "getting tough" in the press and by the politicians, mandatory sentencing remains a common plank in both the Senate and House Crime Bills, perhaps aided by scant coverage of the very people the policy has been proportionately toughest on.

May/June 1994

STUDENT BODIES

Number of newspaper stories in the Nexis computer database about Gina Grant, high school student, being denied admission to Harvard when it was revealed that at age 14 she had killed her abusive mother: 107.

Number of stories about Gen. Hector Gramajo, former military chief of Guatemala and Harvard Kennedy School class of '91, being found responsible by a U.S. federal judge for "thousands of civilian deaths" (*New York Times*, 4/13/95): 21.

EXTRA!Update June 1995

Women In Prison

Interview with Bobbie Stein

Diane Sawyer was at it again not long ago. This January the $7-million earner went behind bars for ABC's Prime Time Live. Sawyer produced a special report about what she called "women's flooding this country's jails." But in the segment she failed to ask why the population of incarcerated women has been rising, who or what is to blame. The New York Times skimmed over that part of the story, too, when they dedicated the cover of the Sunday magazine to the subject of women in jail on June 2. Their focus was on female bonding, sexuality, and how women inmates are different from men. If you turned to the Progressive magazine this month, you'll find quite a different approach: a stinging story about serial rape and the diminished rights of women prisoners, nothing to do with floods or acts of God, but the direct result of specific acts of legislation. With us to try to get the facts on women in jail is Bobbie Stein, the author of one of the articles in the current issue of the Progressive. She is a law professor at New College School of Law and the director of the school's in-house criminal defense clinic.

What do you think were the major differences between the way that your story approached this topic and the Times piece by Adrienne Leblanc?

The Adrienne Leblanc piece talked about the softer side of what's going on with women in prisons. There was basically accurate reporting with regard to the rise of women in custody. She really didn't talk anything about what's really going on with women, what kind of services are provided for the women in prison. It was focused on personal relationships that women were having with other women on a friendly basis and sometimes the sadness that comes along with women in prison not being able to see their children. My piece focused on very specific incidents that happened at the prison in Pleasanton, California, the federal prison, they call it Dublin now, where three women inmates were being housed in a men's facility. They were in single cells and one specific prison guard was opening the prison cell door to other men to come in and basically rape these women. This is a cold reality that's happening not just in California prisons, but in prisons all around the country.

As I alluded to in the introduction, the cold reality didn't just materialize out of the air. There have been legislative and policy changes in recent years that have led to the current situation. Could you clarify for our listeners what some of those changes have been?

There's been an incredible rise in women in prison, about 500% since 1980. There are about 69,000 sentenced women prisoners now in the country, largely because of new laws around drugs and the harsher sentencing laws. There is less violent crime among women, but there are more and more women caught in other kinds of activities that are landing them behind bars. The mandatory sentencing laws have increased the number of years that people in general spend behind bars.

One trend that we've followed is that when the major topic for discussion is prison policy or penal reform, women seem to drop out of the picture. The explanation is, women are such a small minority of inmates. Yet you do see an interest in women prisoners in human interest stories. Clearly there's something to be said for taking a specific, special look at women in jail, but how do you think the coverage suffers from this kind of gender apartheid?

I think it suffers because people aren't actually discussing the issues. What I see happening now with this influx of articles in various media publications around women in prisons is that they are focusing on the human interest aspect. It's like a novelty: "Look, we've got a lot of women behind bars now." It's being sensationalized: Women Behind Bars. The *New York Times* piece: A woman behind bars is not a dangerous man. The little blurb in the *New York Times* piece was that they're beginning to create a world all their own, one without weight-lifting gangs and violence. That doesn't really talk about what's going on with women in prisons. There are lots of the same kinds of things that go on with women in prisons that go on with men in prisons, but there's a whole host of other problems.

On July 21, another article appeared in the New York Times *Sunday magazine, this time by Betsy Israel, on the subject of Amy Fisher and the time that she's spending in jail. The subhead is, "She went to jail at 18 for shooting her boyfriend's wife, but not before becoming a tabloid Lolita. Four years into her five-to-fifteen-year sentence, her life is still the stuff of made-for-TV movies." The writer implies that she looks down on that spin, but the article takes something of a similar approach and a mention even of quite a serious charge that Fisher seems to be making about rape in jail is skimmed over. What did you make of that?*

The focus of the article was the sort of Lolita kind of gal in prison, and isn't this something we should all be interested in and want to see it portrayed in a miniseries. The allegations of rape seem to be glossed over as, "Oh, this is just Amy Fisher. This is another ploy that she has to get attention for herself." I read today in the paper that she's actually filed a lawsuit alleging rape and some other abuses. I think that I know from my research that this is a reality that's happening across the country, that women are being raped in prison. They're being raped by correctional officers. If they're not being raped by correctional officers, in many cases correctional officers are allowing it to happen by either looking the other way or actually, as I reported in my story, opening the cell door and letting other people in. I think this article about Amy Fisher certainly didn't want to focus on that.

Finally, before we close, we have seen this week the possible passage of a welfare bill that eliminates women and men who have ever received any kind of sentence for a drug-related activity from having access to any welfare programs. This is just one piece of legislation that will affect the population that you work with. Another is the legislation that President Clinton signed in April called the Prison Litigation Reform Act. How would you characterize the way that that piece of legislation was covered, and what do we need in the way of better reporting on this issue if we're to understand some of the legislation that's going down and its long-term repercussions?

The Prison Litigation Reform Act pretty much wasn't covered at all. It was something that was just sort of tacked on the budget bill and went through, and nobody seemed to care much about it. But it has really serious ramifications with regard to prison litigation. The reason, ostensibly, behind this legislation was to stop what's called "frivolous" lawsuits from being filed by prisoners. But in reality it's going to curtail any prisoner filing any kind of lawsuit at all. Most of these lawsuits are not frivolous. Just a couple of examples of lawsuits that have been filed: prison staff engaging in sexual relations with women prisoners and allowing male inmates to enter into their cells for forced intercourse, like what happened in Dublin. There's already a suit that has been filed in Louisiana. Suicidal children being transferred to state mental hospitals where they were placed naked and put in restraints so that they can inject them with psychotropic drugs, and they call this "aversion therapy." That's another lawsuit that's pending somewhere. These are very serious lawsuits.

Is there simply no interest among reporters in this kind of story?

I don't know if there's a lack of interest among reporters. I think that the way certain things are presented to the public, it may not seem like a hot issue, and it may seem like something nobody's interested in. I think one of the ways I heard this prison litigation reform bill being talked about was in the context of attorneys' fees being limited, which has a very serious effect. That's what it does. It limits how much money attorneys could get. But frankly, who cares? Nobody likes lawyers. This is not the age of attorneys, particularly around criminal issues, particularly in the wake of the O.J. Simpson case. So anybody who is a lawyer assisting a criminal, somebody on trial for a criminal case is bad enough, but we're talking about people who are already convicted. We're talking about somebody trying to help a prisoner. I think that's the kind of thing that the public doesn't care about.

Bobbie Stein is a professor at New College School of Law and is the director of the school's in-house criminal defense clinic.

July 26, 1996

Prisoners Are People

Interview with Laura Whitehorn

In October 1995, in the same month that the desision to acquit was announced in the O.J. Simpson murder trial, Congress rejected a proposal to change federal drug sentencing guidelines. Under current law, the recommended penalty for crimes related to crack cocaine are 100 times stiffer, ounce for ounce, that the penalties related to cocaine powder. As black people are more often convicted for crack and whites more often for powder, the result is a starkly different rate of incarceration for the two races. Shortly after Congress decided not to change those guidelines, the Bureau of Prisons declared a nationwide lockdown of federal prisoners, claiming that there had been riots inside several jails. The BOP announced a ban on journalists entering those jails and some state Bureaus, like California's, have kept those restrictions in place.

Shortly after the lockdown, CounterSpin spoke to a prisoner in a federal correctional institution (FCI) for women in Pleasanton, California. Laura Whitehorn was convicted on politically-related conspiracy charges in the 1980s. She was interviewed from her cell block for CounterSpin by freelance reporter Suzie Day.

Let me begin by describing the prison I'm at. It used to be called FCI Pleasanton. Now it's called FCI Dublin at California. It's one of the only two FCI's for women in the federal system, although there is still a control unit in Florida. It houses about 1,100 women. It was built originally to house approximately 325 prisoners. So you can see that it's completely overcrowded. We live three to a cell, and the cells were built for one person. There's no living room at all. All the programs are either intensely overcrowded and overenrolled, so that there are waiting lists to get on typing classes that go for a long time. If you have a long sentence, you're not permitted to sign up for a computer class, because they figure by the time you get out there will be such new developments it won't do you any good anyway. There are very few programs because the Pell grants that enabled prisoners to get higher education have been cut out. That's just one example. All recreation programs are being cut back. There's a new law that just came out in Congress that cuts back use of monies from Bureau of Prisons funds for things that are called "amenities" for prisoners, which include things like television and any electrical appliances. We don't have kitchens, so obviously we need electricity. The racism at the women's institutions is exactly the same as at the men's. For anybody who is familiar with the penal system and the history of the U.S. government, this should not be at all surprising. It goes from who gets written up for petty infractions to who gets the choice jobs and who is trusted to have the jobs that pay better and have less physical labor. For example, the work jobs in the kitchen are almost always held by women of color, by Black and Latino women, in this prison and in every other federal prison I've ever been in. It's palpable. It's every day. It's very wearing.

When the O.J. Simpson verdict came down, we celebrated. This whole institution, people who didn't celebrate kept their mouths shut because everyone was so happy no one could disagree loudly. The upper echelons of the administration were furious. The warden was absolutely livid that O.J. had been acquitted, for the same reasons that a lot of white people were, because they don't mind seeing Teddy Kennedy and other white figures who maintain respect getting off for the killings of white women, but if they suspect that a Black man had gotten away with it, that's a whole different thing. On the day that O.J. was acquitted, one Black women who serves on the cafeteria line said to a friend, quietly, joking along on the line, "Power to the people." The warden saw it and threw her in the "hole" immediately. A number of Black women walked up to the building that has the "hole" in it and demanded to see the lieutenant, and within half an hour she was released. But that was the atmosphere. Everyone knew that Congress was considering changing the penalties for crack and powder cocaine. Everybody knew that it was a racial issue. It's been absolutely clear. Even the least liberal white commentators in the media have been saying it's a racial issue.

Did most people in prison, to your knowledge, know that the Congressional debate was going on about the sentencing?

Absolutely. There are very few of us who receive newspapers, who subscribe to newspapers because it's so expensive to do so. We generally try to inform people of important news that affects prisoners and affects criminal laws. We post things, we xerox articles. I would have to say, I heard about the pending debate in Congress from a wide variety of people in here. People sent in letters to their Congressmen taking positions, saying that the penalties for crack should be lessened, since they were a hundred times greater than for powder cocaine. When the Congress refused to change that sentencing disparity, it was such a blatant act of racism, it felt very much like the Rodney King verdict in Simi Valley, when the cops got off the first time. It was like being told, "So what? We don't care." Racism is the order of the day, and like it or lump it. People felt completely abandoned. Who cared? No one cared. But nobody was running around saying, Let's do something. There was nothing happening. Two or three days later, on October 20, we were just arbitrarily locked down. Everyone was returned to their living units and forced to go into their cells. We were made to stay in our cells, locked into our cells, all that evening. They turned the TVs off. They unplugged all the phones. We had no contact with the outside world, even for those few minutes that we were allowed out of our cells to get dinner. But we listened to our radios.

Have you had any word from other prisons as to how many people from other prisons got transferred or what happened in the prisons since the lockdown was taken off?

No, I don't know what's happened since the lockdown's been taken off. I read in the newspaper that Lewisburg (PA) was particularly hard hit, but they didn't have a rebellion when the crack law was not changed. Instead what happened was that about ten guys got drunk and started some stuff. The reaction of the prison was to crack down so hard that there were twenty or so prisoners who were hurt so badly that they had to go to the hospital. They forced the men in the units, stripped them and had them lying naked for eighteen hours. If they tried to move or talk they were kicked in the head. So that they were pissing and shitting right there. I assume they weren't fed. It sounds like the aftermath of Attica without the Attica rebellion. So I think that the government has become increasingly repressive, and they bank on the fact that no one on the outside is going to care.

What do you think the press missed about this whole experience?

The fact that prisoners are human beings. I think that if the press as a whole and society as a whole could remember that when we talk about this percentage of people are locked up out of each community, that those are human beings that they know, that they grew up with, and that we shouldn't be demonized, that there would be a whole different relationship to prisons. How many different great philosophers and writers have said things like, If you want to judge the nature and the quality of a society, look at its prisons, look at those who are the most powerless? Look at the treatment that the powerless people get in a society and you will see, you'll have a window to the soul of the society.

Federal prisoner Laura Whitehorn, spoke to freelance reporter Susie Day for CounterSpin. *Under current conditions in California, no journalists have access to Laura Whitehorn.*

February 3, 1996

The Media
and Mississippi's
Mothers of the Disappeared

Interview with Andrea Gibbs and Louise Bernikow

Andrea Gibbs is a former police officer in Gulfport, Mississippi, who made history when she and three of her colleagues blew the whistle on violence in custody. This March, civil rights leaders convened hearings in Mississippi to bring attention to deaths in police cells. Andrea, what was the testimony heard at those hearings?

I was the witness coordinator. We brought forward seven [relatives of people who had died in custody]. Out of seven [dead], five were alleged suicides by hanging. One was an alleged overdose of crack cocaine. The other one was an alleged heart attack. With all of the cases, the similarities primarily—because there were just as many white families as there were Black families—was the fact that all of these people were poor and simply did not have the resources, lawyers, independent pathologists to come in behind the Mississippi authorities to see if indeed there was discrepancy. The other interesting part about the majority of these cases was that the family members had difficulty receiving the autopsy reports and clear defining documents to explain to them exactly what happened to their family members.

What has been the outcome of the hearings? What kind of change has happened?

The panelists presented the information to the Justice Department and the Senate Judiciary Committee. Primarily because of all the national publicity and people being up in arms about it, Janet Reno yesterday, which was the 14th of April, ordered an investigation into what is happening here in the state of Mississippi. I know deep down in my heart because I have been fighting this battle, it feels like all by myself, for three years here within the state of Mississippi and have gotten absolutely nowhere, but now there's this national publicity that's coming in, and that's exactly what has made this happen.

Your demands made it to Reno, but they also made it to the president. At a press conference on March 23, President Clinton was asked a question about whether he was going to convene an investigation. Somehow that question was edited out of the transcripts of the press conference as they appeared in the Washington Post. *What else do you think has been edited out of the press coverage of the story?*

There's no telling. We were making this wonderful national publicity, front page of *U.S.A. Today* and a lot of really big-name papers. Here in the state of Mississippi we were in the back of papers. Information was left out. They were interviewing tourism officials rather than panelists or witnesses that came forward at the hearings. So they basically, as far as the state of Mississippi goes, they do anything they want and they slant the stories to portray the image that they want the public to know. When I got home— I live on the Gulf Coast of Mississippi, which is three hours away from the capital city where I was—there was a two-minute segment played on WLOX-TV, which is where I live, about how this was ruining the state image and was costing us tourism dollars. They interviewed people off the street: "What do you think about what's going on?" "Well, it looks bad for the state. People think we're still backwards." Rather than interviewing the panelists, talking about what the hearings were about and what the goals were going to be— it was all about how awful this is and about how this is all making us good Mississippians look bad.

Louise Bernikow is a writer and the author of five books. She traveled to Jackson, Mississippi to cover the hearings for the Women's Action Coalition. Louise, what did you make of press behavior there?

It was interesting to see when the TV cameras went on and when they didn't. That's the way a courtroom is different from a movie set. You know when they think they've got a "moment." The moment usually was when a Black person was talking about atrocities. One of the things that you saw on the TV screen was that it looked as though this problem was only about Black people when in fact there were quite a lot of white families and white people in other capacities testifying when the lights weren't on. There was a press conference at which there was a piece of behavior I want the world to know about. It was when *New York Times* reporter Peter Appelbaum asked the commission how they felt about not having a representative of the government there. He meant the governor himself or someone like that. The answer to him was that there were two people who were members of the Mississippi State Legislature on that commission. He didn't consider them members of the government. I think that affects the kind of coverage that he writes, too.

You would think that in March of this year, when the whole topic of police violence was in the air a propos of the trial of the LA police who beat motorist Rodney King, that you would have seen quite a lot of coverage of a hearing in Mississippi convened by civil rights leaders, including Ben Chaney. The hearings addressed 47 hangings in custody since 1987?

Every one of them ruled a suicide. Every one. I think there was a lot of coverage, actually. Every major network covered it. I was surprised about that. It was on the ABC evening news. CNN gave it very prominent play. I want to applaud them for their coverage too, because I think the problem is not that this is being denied in the press. I think it's being reported in a way that makes people dismiss it easily, that sort of ghettoizes it entirely in every sense. This is only about Black people. It's only about Mississippi. The CNN reporter actually had in his piece the most bizarre testimony. That was that a white coroner came forward, he wasn't asked to testify, to give us his version of how a young man could hang himself in his jail cell with one sleeve of his shirt over a doorknob and the other sleeve of his shirt over the bedpost, the bunkbed post, and then bend his knees. This coroner, who by the way weighed more than 300 pounds, stood up in the courtroom and showed us how it was done. I felt that if you wanted to give a picture to the world of how bizarre it is there in Mississippi, all you had to do was put this on the air. Bernard Haraldsen of CNN led his report about Jackson with that image. I think it told people how crazy and weird the police system is in Mississippi.

You went there to cover this event for the Women's Action Coalition in New York. What did you make of the sexism in both the events and the coverage?

All the newspapers said that "family members" testified. In fact, for each of the cases of hangings, a mother testified. I think of these as the American mothers of the disappeared. Nobody noticed them. Nobody reported their extraordinary courage. These are people who are poor and powerless, who are willing to defy the local authorities in their communities and say that they think they're being lied to, say that they think that their sons and one daughter—not all the people hanged in jail were men—say that they were lied about. That's one thing that they never mentioned. I think their pictures should be in the newspaper. What we get are pictures of men with titles, powerful men. Maybe that's what it takes to bring this to the government's attention, but I think in terms of letting the public know, the courage of these women was amazing.

Andrea Gibbs was the connection between WAC and these hearings. We have been supporting her work with her organization, the Victim's Voice. She's a deputy who blew the whistle on brutality in her own district. She testified brilliantly and didn't get very much coverage. The only thing that the newspapers liked was the fact that she cried, but there was very little about what she actually had to say.

You mentioned the mothers of the disappeared. Perhaps what the women

*involved in this hearing needed to do precisely is move south of the border
to Mexico, or at least move outside of the U.S. How do you think this
story would be covered if it were occurring outside of U.S. borders?*

It's interesting you say that, because the very night that I was in
Jackson watching television, on *Unsolved Mysteries* there was a piece
about an American who was arrested in a Mexican jail and hanged
there. When the family was told he had committed suicide they
didn't believe it. They acted immediately. They got their Congressman. They sent a delegation down. And they actually got the
police who had hanged this man. He was murdered. The piece was
so full of rage that this could happen. I thought, I get it. If it happens to an American in *another* country, we'll get up in arms. But
when it happens in the South, then we're just going to be very cool
and say, "Well, maybe it's true and maybe it's not."

*That was Louise Bernikow, a writer who traveled to Jackson, Mis-
sissippi to cover civil rights hearings on deaths in police custody.*

April 15, 1993

Media
Turned Population Debate
Into Pope vs. Veep

"The Cairo Conference will probably be remembered as the Great Abortion Showdown," exclaimed a *Wall Street Journal* report (9/13/94) as the International Conference on Population and Development drew to a close this September. But whose fault is that? For all the "isn't it a shame" tone of journalistic commentary, most of the mainstream media allowed that debate to dominate coverage of Cairo.

United Nations conferences are bureaucratic affairs; the anti-contraception dogma of the Pope against a most-of-the-world, pro-choice chorus provided a dramatic angle on the story. "Clash of Wills in Cairo," headlined *Time* magazine (9/12/94); "Population Wars," *U.S. News & World Report* called it (9/12/94). Illustrated in *Time* by head shots of Al Gore and John Paul II, the Veep vs. the Pope condensed complicated issues revolving around women into a show starring—surprise, surprise—men.

Having found their lead, the press presented a two-character scenario. The U.S. delegation and its allies were portrayed as fighting for women's rights, reproductive choice and economic development to slow global population growth. The Vatican, along with some Islamic allies, articulated the woman-as-instrument-of-God opposition.

The bipolar framework missed most of what was interesting about Cairo. It was also misleading. The Clinton administration's program at Cairo was more feminist-friendly than the anti-abortion platform of the Reganites at the 1984 conference in Mexico City. But the official U.S. point of view which dominated news reports had its roots as much in security concerns as concern for women's rights.

Speaking to *ABC World News Tonight* (9/6/94), Timothy Wirth, undersecretary of state for global affairs, told reporter Ned Potter that

"you have too many people chasing too little land, too little food...
You're inevitably going to have conflicts." Potter went on to use
Wirth's examples of crises in Haiti and Rwanda as evidence of the
link between population density and conflict.

This link went unchallenged in most media—despite the facts:
The Netherlands has twice the population density of Haiti; Taiwan
twice that of Rwanda. Of all the continents, Europe is the most
densely populated, with almost twice the crowding of Africa and
nowhere near the poverty and strife.

"The major problems facing the planet have less to do with
human numbers than with human systems of resource and labor
exploitation," Betsy Hartman, director of the Hampshire College
Population and Development Program, told FAIR's radio show
CounterSpin (9/16/94). In an article in Dollars & Sense (9-10/94),
Hartman suggests that Ted Turner's CNN was instrumental in forg-
ing what she calls a "population control consensus." (Turner's wife,
Jane Fonda, is the UN Family Planning Association's "goodwill
ambassador.") Refocusing public attention on population as a security problem, Hartman told FAIR's radio program CounterSpin,
"helps create, intentionally or not, a kind of fear of numbers that
gets translated into fear of poor people and immigrants."

The projection of the U.S. program as "pro-development" is also
disingenuous. Although U.S. officials promised generous new funding for international family planning programs after Cairo, the total
grant for foreign aid in 1995 is down $400 million from '94 (Wash-
ington Post, 6/19/94).

As for the U.S. commitment to women's choices, few reporters
scrutinized the position of the Clinton White House in light of the
administration's record at home, where federal funding for abortion
had been bargained away in the healthcare debate. CNN's cele-
bratory news footage of free, local health clinics in remote rural
regions of the globe must have looked odd to viewers in the U.S.,
where comparable health services do not exist. As for abortion,
access to affordable abortions has been denied to poor women in
most states since 1977.

Some reporters did paint a broader picture. Sonia Correa and Rosalind Petchesky pointed out in *Ms.* magazine (9-10/94) that "Southern advocates of women's reproductive and sexual rights have increasingly brought home to feminists in the North [that] securing such rights for women is inseparable from transforming the economic and gender inequities of societies."

And Kim Murphy in the *Los Angeles Times* (9/8/94) gave her readers an unusual opportunity to hear from women medical experts and development activists outside of the U.S. whose perspective was distinct from both the "population control establishment" *and* the Vatican.

What actually happened in Cairo, according to participants who were there, was that an approach that integrated women's empowerment, development, and consumption issues got a high-level airing. Sadly, observers who were dependent on the U.S. mainstream media were offered little chance to listen in. As in the welfare debates, so in the discussion of population growth: Poor women are the ones society—and the media—hold accountable for the planet's fate.

November/December 1994

WHICH SIDE ARE YOU ON?

CNN had an "exclusive" during the World Population Conference in Cairo: The network aired footage (9/7/94) of the genital mutilation of a 10-year-old girl. After it aired, three men were arrested by the Egyptian government for their role in the event that CNN taped. The D.C.-based *Feminist Faxnet* (9/15/94) denounced the coverage as "exploitation"; a CNN spokesperson told *EXTRA!* that the segment increased awareness of genital mutilation, and that the girl's maiming "definitely would have happened whether we were there or not." Meanwhile, the *Washington Post*'s story on the incident (9/12/94) explained that the procedure is "called genital mutilation by opponents and female circumcision by its advocates." So what was the *Post*'s headline? "4 Men Arrested in Circumcision of 10-year-old girl."

EXTRA!Update 11-12/94

Population Fictions

Interview with Betsy Hartman

The coverage of the Third International Conference on Population and Development, which took place in Cairo is beginning to fade. In an article that appears in the September 1994 issue of Dollars & Sense, *Betsy Hartman, who is the Director of the Hampshire College Population and Development Program, started as follows: "In the corridors of power, the tailors are back at work, stitching yet another invisible robe to fool the Emperor and the people. Cloaked in the rhetoric of environmentalism and—ironically—women's rights, population control is back in vogue." Betsy Hartman, it's a very hard charge you're making there. Explain for our listeners what exactly is the essence of your thesis in "Population Fictions," the story that's in* Dollars & Sense.

I think we're seeing a resurgence of population control right now in the 1990s as an international development strategy. Not that it's ever gone away, but certainly with the Clinton administration, we're experiencing it yet again, and internationally, too, more and more funds are going to be earmarked for family planning programs in the Third World. I'm not opposed to family planning, but I think we have to ask, "What kind of family planning programs, and are they really in women's interest?" Also, the mainstream environmental movement, particularly in the U.S., is increasingly saying that population growth is one of the main causes of the environmental crisis. I think this is very dangerous. It diverts attention from the real problems facing the planet. There's an alliance now between the mainstream environmental movement and the international population agencies. It's a very powerful alliance, and I think it needs to be challenged.

Your article suggests that alliance also extends to the mainstream news media. What do you think are the problems and what do you think the media have been doing right?

I think they were right to talk about the issue of the Vatican trying to fight any progressive feminist language on abortion rights. But at the same time I think claiming the conference as a victory for the world's women is a mistake, and it obscures some of the underlying issues. For example, is women's empowerment really possible in a population stabilization context in which targets are acceptable? How can we have real women's empowerment also in the situation where living standards for the poor majority in the world are deteriorating, where wealth is concentrated in fewer and fewer hands, where military violence is increasing? These kinds of broad questions were not asked at the Cairo conference and were not presented in the press.

One of the specific examples that you mention in your article where the press sometimes has only taken one angle on the story is the situation of Bangladesh, which was brought up even this week in an article in the New York Times. *Can you give us a specific example of the problems with that piece of reporting?*

I find it incredible that Bangladesh is being heralded as a great family planning success story in the *New York Times* and elsewhere. Bangladesh, they say, has managed to drive down its birth rate in the absence of social and economic development due to what they call a vigorous or aggressive family planning program. When you look at the experience of Bangladesh, you note two things. First of all, to claim that the fertility decline is due mainly to the family planning program alone ignores the complex demographic changes that have occurred in the country. True social and economic standards have not improved for the poor majority, which I think is really not a cause for celebration. It's a cause for saying, "What's going on here?" But I think population growth rates have come down because there is increased women's employment, because people themselves realized smaller family sizes made sense, at least that was my experience when I lived in Bangladesh in the seventies. People then wanted smaller families, for a variety of reasons. Secondly, the kind of family planning that's been promoted in Bangladesh is mainly sterilization of poor women through the use of incentives. Also, the family planning program has received much more money and attention than basic health care. In fact, population control absorbs one-third of the government's total health care budget. As a result you have a situation in Bangladesh where people may have access to contraceptives, but not basic health care. In fact, even though birth rates are coming down, maternal mortality rates remain at tragically high levels because the government has not invested in safe pregnancy, in the kinds of care that would really ensure that women and children survive.

Betsy Hartman is director of the Hampshire College Population and Development Program.

September 17, 1994

The China Syndrome

When Women Talk,
Media Listen...to Politicians

The topic was women. The place was China. And mainstream media in the United States still managed to focus on men and politicians in D.C.

Consider any topic, from the global economy to health care, to education and technology—the women in China were discussing it. Looking for a variety of perspectives on those issues? The diversity was there. The Beijing conference was not just the largest gathering of women in history, it was probably the largest gathering of marginalized experts the world has ever seen. But did the press focus on justice, equality and the way that women have moved an international agenda from the bottom up? Not quite.

When the global conference began, the same U.S. media that remained tight-lipped when Ronald Reagan approved sales of police equipment to China's internal security force, and praised Vice President Bush's visit to Beijing in 1985, were suddenly concerned about Chinese security operations and the claims of Capitol Hill conservatives that Hillary Rodham Clinton was disrespecting human rights by attending a rights conference.

The London *Guardian* got it right in an editorial (9/11/95) "Points of conflict with China and the starring role of Hillary Clinton were legitimate news stories, yet the complex issues raised by the conference should not have been reduced to a struggle between our 'free speech' and their 'secret police.'"

Non-governmental organizations (NGOs), whose meeting in nearby Huairou began before the main event in Beijing, got trace-coverage in U.S. newspapers, but Chinese officials often got the lead. "Challenging the Censors in Beijing" was the headline of a *New York Times* editorial (9/1/95) that declared: "There is no place for censorship at an international conference like this."

But the focus on the difficulties of grassroots in getting heard in China struck many participants as ironic. As one delegation of women from Delhi explained, the obstacles faced in Huairou were minimal in comparison to what they face every day getting taken seriously by the media in their hometown. (Many U.S. women felt the same way.)

Some women were seen, but silenced. The front page of the weekend *International Herald Tribune* (9/2-3/95) featured a large photograph of two Tibetan women from the NGO Forum who were taking part in a protest. They were gagged—in the picture and in the paper. Looking inside for the follow-up story, readers found no word from either of the two.

When the government delegates discussed homophobia, Long Island *Newsday* ran a story "Delegates Mull Ban on Bias Against Lesbians" (9/14/95). But the story quoted none of the activists involved, including South African Palesa Beverley Ditsie, a lesbian who made history when she addressed the plenary on behalf of more than 50 non-governmental organizations. *Newsday's* caption-writers described her as "representing a lesbian group" and quoted nothing of what she said.

Given the opportunity to air new viewpoints from women from around the world, the *New York Times* op-ed page (9/1/95) preferred to publish a familiar tract from professional anti-feminist Camille Paglia. Her column referred to women's organizations as representatives of "special interests" (a neat way to make half the population sound "elite") and attacked them for being "strident"—as if she herself hadn't made a career of sounding just that way.

Although Paglia dismisses such figures, UN statistics show that women are 75 percent of refugees, two-thirds of the world's illiterate and 70 percent of the 1.2 billion people who are poor. Given those sorts of figures, it shouldn't require the United Nations in order for mainstream media to pay attention to women's rights advocates.

The women gathered in China have expertise in dealing with the concerns of the majority of people on the planet (the poor, the female, the displaced, the young). They are full of ideas, experience and strategies; what they don't have (unlike Paglia) is access to mainstream media—or the resources to buy their own.

The gathering in China did provide an occasion for some unusual coverage. CNN's special series on the Fourth World Conference gave a taste of what it might be like to have women taken seriously. The network's daily half-hour report by Judy Woodruff (9/4/95-9/15/95)—when not pre-empted by breaking Bob Packwood or Randy Weaver news—showcased a cast of female experts whom CNN viewers had probably never seen before. The World Conference on Women is a once-in-a-decade occurrence; let's hope this sort of reporting is not.

November/December 1995

© Donna Binder/Impact Visuals

Part III

Shifting the Blame

Journalists used to believe that, as H.L. Mencken said, their job was "to comfort the afflicted and afflict the comfortable." Many still believe that. They are just confused about who's afflicting—and who's comforting—whom.

Covering Rape

"To Friends, a Fab 4"

Rape, and in particular acquaintance rape, has become something of a human interest story-of-choice for mainstream newspaper editors. But more coverage has usually not meant better.

When five St. John's University students were charged in the rape of a fellow student, the New York *Daily News* went out of its way to present the assailants as more than just nice guys. "To Friends, a Fab 4" was the headline on one story (5/11/90) that quoted the men's lacrosse coach as saying, "They are the types to give something back to the community."

Not only tabloids promote this theme. "After Rape Charge, 2 Lives Hurt and 1 Destroyed," was the *New York Times* headline (11/12/90) above a story about a University of Rhode Island student who committed suicide before giving testimony to police about a rape he had witnessed. The story, by William Celes 3rd, presented the rape survivor and her attacker as equally "hurt," the real victim being the 20-year-old young man with "personal problems" who couldn't bear the memory of the assault he'd witnessed without trying to prevent. (Celes points out, however, that "some said the real victim was Mr. Lallymand," the man charged with the rape.)

Reporters gave few facts about the survivors of the assaults in these stories, except the victim-blaming detail that the women were reportedly drunk at the time of their assaults. (The *Times* mentioned this twice in their story.) While there are conventions protecting the identity of rape victims, there is nothing to prevent them being "humanized" at least as fully as their assailants. In each of these stories the reporter made no attempt to do that.

In a special report on rape on campus (*New York Times*, 1/2/91), Celes suggests why the *Times* might show equal or greater sympathy for rapists than for the women they assault. "Sexual activity that goes too far and becomes abhorrent to the woman is not new among college students," writes Celes. "But calling it date rape is...defining sex between dates or acquaintances without the woman's consent as a form of male assault rather than a form of female error."

The report describes as "agony" not the women's ordeal, but the confusion on campus stimulated by discussion of the subject. Celes revives the old argument that men cannot help raping women—he repeatedly blames co-ed dormitories for the rise in rape on campus, although more rapes occur in single-sex fraternities. The underlying premise is that changing social relations have caused the problem: "Assumptions about the roles of men and women seem to be shifting, with a resulting confusion on both sides about what is and is not acceptable behavior." A new brand of "blame the victim," this thesis blames rape on the movement that fights for women's survival.

In his section on "Women," Celes quotes university administrators saying the problem is "partly the result of mixed signals sent by women." Even feminist author Susan Brownmiller is taken out of context to defend this blaming of the female, saying, "Women need to react more quickly."

Meanwhile, under the topic of "Men," the emphasis is not on individual responsibility. Interviewed sympathetically is a troubled young man who, after attending several workshops on the subject, had to admit that probably he had raped "some" of the women he had dated.

Syndicated columnist Mona Charen (*Newsday*, 1/9/91) blamed the feminist movement for eroding the "old sexual mores" that she seems to think once kept rape at bay. "While it seems plausible that reporting of date rape is up, it is obvious that there is simply much more of it than there used to be. And for this the feminist movement must take its share of the blame."

There is a lot of blame, and (to judge by the mainstream press) far too few feminists to take it. The Senate Judiciary Committee in June 1990 reported that rape is increasing four times as fast as the overall crime rate (*Time*, 10/1/90).

It is possible to treat violence against women in a way that helps to fight the crime. A three-part ABC News series on rape (1/7/91 through 1/11/91) included more insightful comments than a culling of print articles produced in a year. "Violence against women is done by men, and it's time that men took the responsibility to stop the violence," one male anti-rape activist was quoted. "What we want is the recognition that any sort of forced sexual contact is unacceptable, plain and simple," said Mary Ellen Shone of the King's County Sexual Assault Center.

But helpful reporting on rape is the exception, not the norm. Instead of hearing the cries of survivors, the press is hearing the complaints of apologists; instead of condemning cruelty, the press promotes excuses.

March/April 1991

Campus Feminists

The Media's New Bogeywomen

In her new book, *Where the Girls Are*, Hampshire College media studies professor Susan J. Douglas argues that to grow up female with the mass media in the United States is to grow up confused, or, as she puts it, "with the bends."

When it comes to the women's movement, or the dreaded F-word, "No wonder young women, who were infants and toddlers at the height of the women's movement, say, 'I'm not a feminist, but...'" says Douglas.

Time magazine's Dec. 4, 1989 cover asked the question, "Is there a future for feminism?" Inside, the story revived old ghosts: "Hairy legs haunt the feminist movement, as do images of being strident and a lesbian." "Hmm, wonder where those specters came from?" Susan Douglas asks.

Almost five years after *Time*'s cover, media myths about feminists are in season once again—with some revisions. For the last two decades, body hair and loving women were the most horrifying things about the women's rights movement. Today, feminist opponents of violence are the ones spoiling life for females—especially young female students on campuses nationwide. In 1993, *New York* magazine chose March 8, International Women's Day, to run their special report, "Crying Rape: The Politics of Date Rape on Campus." Author Peter Hellman wandered uptown to Columbia University to interview women he depicted as engaged in internecine squabbling over campus sexual assault.

"There are growing questions about how real the campus rape threat is and how much of the controversy is fueled not so much by psychosexual concerns as by political ones," wrote Hellman. He brought on literary critic, not rape expert, Camille Paglia to discuss the options. Having defined rape as *at most* a "psychosexual concern," Hellman tracked down a campus psycho: an activist at

Princeton's 1991 Take Back the Night rally who declared in public that she had been "date raped" and then recanted, admitting that her story had been a hoax.

Conveniently, Katie Roiphe studies at Princeton. The same story of the hateful hoax turns up in her book, *The Morning After: Sex, Fear and Feminism on Campus*. Her thesis on "rape-crisis feminists" draws a tight link between anti-violence workers on campus and anti-porn theorists like Andrea Dworkin and Catharine MacKinnon. Feminism, according to Roiphe, isn't about changing power relations for the future, it's about "nostalgia for the days of greater social control."

The "hoax" theme also haunted Sarah Crichton's "Sexual Correctness" *Newsweek* cover (10/25/93). "In the rape-crisis mentality," she wrote, "the numbers keep being bloated." Crichton, too, sees anti-violence activism as anti-sex. It's a revealing connection for the mainstream press. Try to think of one major feminist theme that has received mass coverage that couldn't in some way be turned into a debate about sex.

Mother Jones, whose namesake knew that violence against women was political, not psychosexual, weighed in with its own assault on campus feminism in 1993. *Mother Jones'* article "Off Course" (9-10/93) looked at women's studies as part of an issue devoted to problems in U.S. education.

Having surveyed four college programs, writer Karen Lehrman condemned feminist academics for having "infected" women's studies with ideology. To back up her claim that "over the past 25 years, feminists have been among those who have devalued womens traditional roles most vigorously," Lehrman provides no statistics, no cites, no explanation.

"I never took a porn class when I went to college 10 years ago," writer Karen Lehrman told her readers. "In fact, I never took a women's studies class." Being feminist, for Lehrman, "didn't depend on external affirmation."

Campus feminists better not count on external affirmation in 1994—in fact, with media models like these, it's a wonder that there are feminists on campus at all. Perhaps they survive because they've never held their breath to be the cover story. The women's move-ment that's got the headlines has usually been one that had little or nothing to do with what was going on on the ground.

Where once there were hairy lesbians, a sort of stand-in for Com-munists in the anti-feminist war, now there are "New Victorians," "politicized" women's studies professors, and "rape hype" in an era when young women are encouraged to be sexually hot, politically cool and into conspicuous consumption. (How else to sell those magazines?) A few foul-ups in the feminist ranks get top-billing; the mass movement that spans the globe gets zip. Shocking-sounding talk about sex gets sound bites; reasoned debate about wages and childcare is dead air.

If after all of this, you still somehow hanker after justice for women, mainstream media even have an acceptable brand of fem-inism ready, the "Do Me" feminists who have it all: good looks, good connections, no hang ups about sex (or capitalism)—and the cover of *Esquire* (2/94).

The future for feminism? It's as bright as the perfume ad is pun-gent. A perennial target, as long as there is advertising space to sell.

March/April 1994

Paula Jones
and Sex Harassment

The World Stayed Right-Side Up

It seemed like May madness had hit—at least as far as sexual harassment was concerned.

Hoards of previously unreconstructed misogynists supported a working-class female who charged a powerful man with grimy sexual misconduct. *New Republic* editor and PBS pundit Fred Barnes, who once derided Anita Hill as "delusional," claimed that Arkansas state employee Paula Jones' accusations against Bill Clinton were "credible" (*McLaughlin Group*, 5/8/94). Rush Limbaugh, who'd previously boasted of a sign on his office door that read, "Sexual harassment at this work station will not be reported…. It will be graded," evinced sympathy for a woman who said she'd been harassed.

At the same time, liberal pundits often trivialized the accusation against the president. In an offhand comment that conflated consensual sex and sex harassment, columnist Mary McGrory remarked (NBC's *Meet the Press*, 5/8/94), "This debate was held two years ago in New Hampshire, where people knew this president was not a model husband." Clarence Page of the *Chicago Tribune* (5/8/84) called sexual harassment "a vehicle for witch hunts"—apparently forgetting who killed whom in Salem.

Newsweek's Joe Klein lamented on CBS's *Face the Nation* (5/8/94) that "we're going to end up with government by goody-goodies." He went on to claim that historically, presidents with "interesting sexual histories" have made better leaders. Klein also seems to have a problem distinguishing sex from assault—isn't that what feminists are accused of?

One might have thought spring lunacy had taken over—especially when Rush Limbaugh started criticizing feminists for being *too quiet* about sexual harassment. But in fact, plenty of conservatives stuck to their traditional, dismissive line. William Safire (5/9/94) called sex harassment statutes "loosey goosey"; the *New York Post*'s Ray Kerrison(5/11/94) wrote a column headed "Anita and Paula: Sisters in Sleaze."

Talk show host John McLaughlin (5/8/94) moaned about a "rush to judgement...against the male" in sex harassment cases, then rushed in with his own verdict: Paula Jones' suit was "largely bogus." "You can sue anybody for anything," whined McLaughlin. He should know: He's been accused of sexual harassment by several female employees, settling a suit out of court with one in 1989.

And feminists, contrary to media assumption, were not so silent. On his TV show, Limbaugh (5/4/94) lined up Jones and Hill in mirror image, and claimed that NOW, which "organized marches for Anita Hill," was "just yawning" about Paula Jones. Neither claim was true. NOW, which never held a demonstration for Hill, issued a statement on the day Jones' suit was filed, stating, "Every Paula Jones deserves to be heard, no matter how old she is and how long ago the incident occurred.

Feminists, wrote *USA Today* columnist Joe Urschel (5/10/94), "have not rushed to [Jones] defense in ideological lockstep as they did with Hill." At least Urschel interviewed leaders of women's organizations for his story. (One corrected the record in a letter the next day.) The *New York Times*' Maureen Dowd (5/8/94) cited no leaders of women's groups as she asserted vaguely that "some women" who supported Hill "are wishing they could cut the ground from underneath Paula Jones."

U.S. News & World Report provided phony fodder for the pundits when they printed a claim by Jones lawyer David Traylor that his client had been refused help by the NOW Legal Defense and Education Fund. In fact, NLDEF hadn't been approached on the case, and did send technical help once Jones' team got around to asking—which is more assistance than NLDEF ever gave to Anita Hill. Traylor admits now he was referring to a call made to an Arkansas chapter of NOW, a separate organization, but no one at *U.S. News* had checked the facts.

In the absence of a hearing—or many facts at all—the Paula Jones debate took place almost entirely in the realm of politics and personalities. Participants were brought into TV studios to take sides on the basis of political loyalties.

The silenced reality is that sex harassment comes all too often as a surprise. Most perpetrators aren't recognizable creeps, but men who women dared to think might interact with them as equals. According to the National Council for Research on Women, at least half of all women will experience sexual harassment at some point in their lives.

But prime time left it to the afternoon talk shows to ponder the real toll harassment takes in U.S. life. Partisan debates fit better into snappy sound bites. Maybe they sell more papers, too.

July/August 1994

Super Bowl Success Sparks Good Ol' Boys' Backlash

Shortly before the start of the Super Bowl on NBC this January, viewers saw a public service announcement that warned: "Domestic violence is a crime." For some, the PSA came as a surprise, but not for those involved in the campaign to get 30 seconds of airtime donated to the ad. The moment (worth roughly $500,000 to advertisers) was the result of many weeks of work by FAIR and a coalition of anti-violence groups in negotiation with executives at NBC and NBC Sports.

Workers at women's shelters, and some journalists, have long reported that Super Bowl Sunday is one of the year's worst days for violence against women in the home. FAIR hoped that the broadcast of an anti-violence PSA on Super Sunday, in front of the biggest TV audience of the year, would sound a wake-up call for the media, and it did.

"Since the Super Bowl it seems as though public awareness has increased dramatically on this topic," the executive director of a women's shelter in McKeesport, Pa. wrote to FAIR. "We believe you've played a major role in bringing domestic violence out in the open."

But a handful of reporters and editors decided to "debunk" the story. These journalists, mostly men, apparently felt affronted by FAIR's success in getting NBC to dedicate 30 seconds, in between the beer ads and the car commercials, to a crisis that, according to the National Coalition Against Domestic Violence, claims thousands of women's lives per year.

The "debunkers", led by Ken Ringle of the *Washington Post* (1/31/93), claimed that FAIR, in coalition with women's groups, slanted the facts in their effort to get NBC to run the PSA. Ringle (and journalists at AP, the *Boston Globe* and the *Wall Street Journal*) asserted that the coalition had claimed "national studies" linked Super Bowl Sunday to increased assaults. No such claims were made. In fact, FAIR made the point repeatedly that domestic violence is understudied and prevention work is gravely underfunded.

Critics charged that the coalition was forced to "acknowledge" that its evidence was largely "anecdotal." "Anecdotal" was the word used in countless interviews by FAIR; stories from women on the front lines were something that made the campaign stronger, not something anyone was forced to "acknowledge."

In the *Washington Post*, Ringle attacked those who fought for the NBC public service spot as "causists" who "show up wherever the most TV lenses are focused." The article painted a picture of a feminist mob strong-arming the networks with myth and false statistics.

But it was Ringle who distorted the facts. *Post* readers would not know that of the four experts cited by Ringle, only one agreed with the article's thesis that there is no "evidence that a link actually exists between football and wife-beating."

Ringle quoted psychotherapist Michael Lindsey to defend his point that the Super Bowl PSA campaign was misguided: "You know I hate this," Ringle quotes Lindsay saying. But Lindsey told FAIR that he was referring to Ringle's line of questioning, not the anti-battering campaign. "He was really hostile," Lindsey added. On the same day as Ringle's "debunking" story, Lindsey was quoted in the *New York Times*, saying, "That PSA will save lives."

Ringle claimed triumphantly that a speaker at a press conference co-hosted by FAIR had "misrepresented" a study by Old Dominion College on violence and sports. FAIR interviewed the authors. While due to the small sample involved, they chose not to express the study results in percentage terms as the activist had, they did not see this as misrepresentation. "We have not accused anyone of distorting the results of our study," the authors stated.

Following the lead of the *Washington Post* and editorialists at the

Wall Street Journal, Rush Limbaugh jumped into the act on his TV show (2/16/93). He berated the PSA as "just a bunch of feminist bilge" because the man it featured is not a credible batterer: "Like people who beat their wives wear ties," Limbaugh scoffed.

The backlash articles bore all the traits of typical coverage of domestic violence: They belittled the victims, minimized the crisis and missed the point—which is that, according to FBI averages, a woman is battered every 18 seconds. That is enough to deserve attention all year long.

FAIR's goal was to open up debate. We did. The PSA was seen by more people than any anti-battering message in history. Weeks later, TV news and talk shows were still covering the issue intensely and constructively.

The fact that some good ol' boys managed to miscast the campaign came as no surprise. Some journalists' determination to undermine the Super Bowl effort was just a reminder of how many in mainstream media typically disbelieve women when they talk about the violence in their lives.

April/May 1993

Some Families' Values

Rocking the Cradle of Sexual Politics

Interview with Louise Armstrong

Rocking the Cradle of Sexual Politics: What Happened When Women Said "Incest" *is a new book by Louise Armstrong about incest and about the abuse of power. Louise Armstrong, author of what was considered a wake-up call to the American public about incest, the book* Kiss Daddy Goodnight, *refers to herself as "television's first walking, talking incest victim." We spoke with Louise Armstrong about her new book. But first we asked her about the media response to that earlier wake-up call.*

Back then we truly were breaking the silence. A kind of a gasp went up. "The world's first walking, talking incest victim" is, of course, ironic. It was like, "Are you scarred forever?" "Tell me, Louise, does this really happen?" A breathless quality. For the first few minutes I really thought that the interviewers were listening. I thought that the world was listening. I thought, "Oh, good." We went out there with a tremendous amount of passion and, I guess in retrospect, naïveté...It was the seventies, and the women's movement was fairly strong. We thought, "Good. The world has never said, 'Stop.' We'll say, 'Please stop. Please.'" And we will begin to reduce the incidence.

You also say in the introduction to your new book that you had a goal in mind beyond just starting a conversation. What did you mean by that?

The goal was social change. In the seventies, what was the goal of speaking out on battering? Social change. Rape, same thing.

The conversation, however, did get started. How do you think it's gone?

Straight downhill. We were not out there for five seconds in all of our glorious optimism before over the horizon rode hordes of new-found experts, professionals. They were selling "intra-familial child sexual abuse"—gender-neutral. They were selling "decriminalization," which was an interesting thing, because this had never effectively been treated as criminal. Somehow the media managed to print "decriminalization" with a straight face and absolutely no further reflection on the fact that they were decriminalizing something that had effectively been legal. The mental-health professionals were selling this as a family illness. They came up with profiles of everybody, and it was all not to worry. You had Daddy, and Daddy might be a little weak or a kind of a nebbish or a little aggressive or what have you. He was pretty normal, though. Mom, however. Mom. When we got to the profile of the "non-offending parent," as they kept saying, she sounded offensive indeed. She was passive-aggressive, manipulative, domineering, cowardly, sexually rapacious or frigid. Most damning, she always knew, on some level. She was said to be "collusive." And that led to statutes in virtually every state, very quickly, like by 1980, that faulted the woman who knew or should have known or the woman who failed to protect. So moms were at risk of losing their kids to the state simply because they didn't know.

You see this as a connection between the media depiction of the issue of incest, which has a direct connection to the legal and policy responses to that problem.

Absolutely. If the media had heard the feminist message, or at least given voice to the feminist message, if we'd had even a minute more of air time, of any kind of time, I think that nobody could have swallowed that "decriminalization," nobody could have said it with a straight face.

Where do we stand now? Who do you think are the chosen protagonists in the media, the different positions? What do you think has hap-

pened to your initial agenda, your initial goal of change?

We got lost. I am hoping that *Rocking the Cradle of Sexual Politics* catches some attention, enough at least to get our voices back out there. I think what's happened to women and children since is urgently, desperately awful. Things have gone downhill. And it's hard to say that we should have kept our mouths shut. That's not what I mean. But we've got to recapture some control of this. We get "false accusation syndrome." We had "parental alienation syndrome." Now we've got "false memory syndrome." We are being thrown into a panic about "ritual abuse." We're having all sorts of conversations on what incest "causes." Incest has been turned into a disease of women. Women have been infantilized. We are no longer talking about what causes incest, the power abuse that causes incest. It's very difficult, unless we can get the media's attention on this. This illness thing has been so wildly oversold that women are really in jeopardy of being made sicker than they need to be.

Louise Armstrong's new book is Rocking the Cradle of Sexual Politics: What Happened When Women Said "Incest."

November 26, 1994

Virgin or Vamp

How the Press Covers Sex Crimes

Discussion with Helen Benedict

At a panel discussion hosted by FAIR's Women's Desk in November, 1993, Columbia journalism professor Helen Benedict, the author of Virgin or Vamp? How the Press Covers Sex Crimes, *addressed the coverage of rape.*

I spent five years looking at how the mainstream and the alternative press in this country cover sex crimes, particularly rape. I read all the local and national stories about several notorious sex crimes from the past decade, and I interviewed the reporters and editors who worked on those original stories. What I found is that the way the press covers rape today is dominated by three factors: the age-old sexist bias inherent in the English language, the fact that the American press only really began covering rape a hundred years ago in the context of lynchings, and the rape myths dating back to the Bible and beyond. These three factors dominate both which women make it into the news and how they are covered. For the purpose of this discussion today—which women make it into the news and why and how they're treated—I'm going to talk about the second two factors: the history of rape coverage in lynching and the rape myths.

The lynching of Black men and women reached its peak between 1890 and 1910, although it went on for longer. Often the excuse for lynching was an accusation of rape. Historians have shown that rape was only the third most common excuse given for a lynching and was most often a false accusation. Nevertheless, that was the narrative that usually captured the press's and the public's imagination. Up until this time, the mainstream American press had stayed away from rape, considering it too indelicate to include in their pages. But once it began covering lynching it couldn't avoid the subject, or didn't want to. Unfortunately, and obviously for racist reasons, this habit stuck, leading to an unchangingly and steadily racist bias in rape coverage. The rape of a white woman by a Black man is the most commonly covered kind of rape, still, while the rape of a Black woman by a Black man is the least commonly covered, still. This habit is not only inaccurate statistically—most rapes are carried out by men of the same race and class of the victim as well as by someone she knows—but it reflects and perpetuates the attitude that white women are more valuable than Black women. It also raises the specter of blaming white women for the conviction of Black men, dividing white feminists from civil rights activists and leaving African-American women out of the debate altogether.

To illustrate: the only big rape stories I could find involving African-American women over the past six decades—and by big I mean national stories—were one story from 1959 about a "Negro coed" raped by four lower-class white boys, called the "Tobacco Roaders' Case," the Tawana Brawley case of 1988, and the recent rape of Desirée Washington by Mike Tyson. The fact that the victim of the Jones University gang assault was Jamaican, while her assailants were white Americans, was covered up for some time by the white press. In the *New York Times*, for example, it wasn't mentioned until the very bottom paragraph on the jump page, and most people I asked casually didn't even get that far in the story. To give a smaller local example, the director of the rape crisis center in Buffalo, New York told me that 80% of the women in the African-American community there had been raped. Yet to read the paper you wouldn't know about one.

Meanwhile, the bigger stories about white women attacked by Black men have dominated rape coverage since the 1890s, the Scottsboro boys, Willie McGee, Emmett Till—which wasn't a rape but an alleged wolf whistle—Kitty Genovese, the Central Park jogger case, and so on. I got these numbers, by the way, by looking at *Time* and *Newsweek* for the past six decades and the major newspapers. So it's pretty amazing when you can only come up with three cases of when the victim was African-American, over six decades, that made big stories.

My second point, the rape myths: the rape myths, I'm sure, are familiar to most of this audience. In the press they boil down to two narratives, or story lines which I found reporters tend to impose on sex crime stories like a cookie cutter on dough, stamping them out unwittingly. The most common rape narrative is that the woman by her looks, her behavior or her generally loose morality drove the man to such extremes of lust that he was compelled to commit the crime—a myth because it assumes that rapists attack out of desire and not out of the urge to dominate, punish, torture, and because it ignores the fact that a woman would no more ask to be raped than she would ask to be murdered. I call that version the "vamp image," which is half the title of my book.

When circumstances make it impossible to paint the woman as the alluring vamp, then the alternative myth is called to work, which is the virgin image of the victim. This narrative holds that a pure and innocent woman was attacked by a perverted monster, usually of a lower class and, yes, a darker skin than she. The virgin narrative is also a myth because it assumes that a woman must be pure to be raped—whatever that is—and ignores the fact that most rapists, as I said before, are of the same race and class as their victims and are usually known to the victim. It also ignores the fact that rapists tend to have more normal psychological profiles than any other kind of criminal, rather than being monsters and weirdos and wackos.

Almost all the women who make it into the mainstream press as sex crime victims do so because the press can make them fit neatly into one of these two images. The woman must either be the virgin, and thus illustrate the age-old racist myth of the pure white woman raped by the savage Black man—such as the Central Park jogger; or the woman must be a vamp, usually somebody who has had the audacity to incriminate a man who doesn't fit the criminal stereotype of the dark-skinned, sinister or crazy assailant. Examples of famous vamp stories, of women who had such audacity, were Jennifer Levin, killed by preppie Robert Chambers, Patricia Bowman, who accused William Smith, a Kennedy no less, of raping her, and the Glen Ridge, New Jersey woman assaulted by the gang of upright high school jocks. Each one of these women was subject to an appalling amount of trashing and insults by the press, as I've documented in my book. But one of the best headlines, just to give you an example, was three days after Jennifer Levin's death, when the *Daily News* ran on their cover, "How Jennifer Courted Death."

The trouble with these habits of coverage is not only that they are racist, classist and sexist, but that they are terribly inaccurate. They lead the press into perpetuating lies about who rapes and who gets raped, and they lead the press to ignore what rape really is. Most rapes do not happen between famous people, between races or even between strangers. Victims of rape are not virgins or vamps, but ordinary women with virtues and faults, just like all of us. And rapists are not all Black, lower-class or crazy. In fact, they are numerically more likely to be white. They come from all classes. They are usually known to the victim and, as I said, they have the most normal psychological profiles of any criminals.

To conclude, let me get back to one of the subjects of this panel: Are women depicted too often as victims? I would say yes, but not because the press covers the subject of rape or sex crimes too much, but because it covers these subjects in the wrong way. It tends to look at the victims—the women—instead of looking at the criminals—the men. To really cover rape, the press should be looking at why rape is so persistent and so prevalent in our society. It should be looking at sexism, and that's what the mainstream press is utterly failing to do at the moment.

Helen Benedict is the author of Virgin or Vamp: How the Press Covers Sex Crimes.

December 11, 1993

Rhymes With Bitch

Laura Flanders and Veena Cabreros-Sud

Politically sound readers will not, we're sure, be sending their loved ones forth this Hallowe'en wrapped in the garb of a wicked witch. Not unless their child is prepared to subvert misogynist stereotypes. The witch-hating days are over, all correct-thinking folks agree. We know now that witches were healers, heiresses, lesbians and feminist fore-sisters. In this, the much touted Year of the Woman, your child better be ready to summon a bite-size Mary Daly quote. (A curt comment might be "A specifically Western and Christian manifestation of the androcratic State of Atrocity...was the witch craze"). If not, cloak your minor in a cartoon turtle or a killer cockroach suit.

Feminist revisionists have put an end to witch-hate. Or so one would like to think.

In fact, the "w" word lives on. Applied most recently to Imelda Marcos, Leona Helmsley and Hillary Clinton, the term still stings. A *New York Times* piece, "Regarding Bill" by Richard Ben Cramer, looked at the Clintons' partnership and the unwilling cookie-cooker this way: "Clinton gave sleazy state business to his wife's law firm. Of course, she ran him. Hard as nails she was. Wouldn't make cookies. She was a witch."

At Bush/Quayle headquarters, according to the *Houston Chronicle*, deputy campaign manager Mary Matalin conjures up her candidate's game-plan beneath a photo of Hillary scrawled with the unattributed bubble, "I will get you my pretty, and your little dog too." Apparently Matalin fancies herself as Dorothy and casts Clinton as the Wicked Witch of Arkansas. Is Democratic campaign strategist and Matalin's sweetheart, James Carville, Toto, or the man without a brain? The public should be told.

Perhaps we are expecting too much to hope that age-old woman-hating would simply fade away. After all, it has only been 300 years.

The hangings stopped in Salem Village at the end of October 1692, when the local Governor's own wife, Lady Mary Phips, was accused of witchcraft by a person claiming to be possessed. The Governor called a halt to the hangings, but not before the witch panic had claimed the lives of 14 women and five men. Some 200 had been accused, 150 jailed. (More media mythology: the "witches" of Salem were hanged, not burned, but that's a different story.)

Given the slow pace of cultural change in the United States, we should be grateful that "witch-hunt" has come to bear some negative connotations. It's just picky, perhaps, to point out that while wicked witches are still women, the wickedly witch-hunted are mostly men.

James Webb, former Assistant Navy Secretary under Reagan, wailed of a "Witch Hunt in the Navy," in the October 6 *New York Times*. The botched internal investigation and the ongoing revelations of violence against women at a Gulf War celebration in Las Vegas last year have "left in their wake a witch hunt that threatens to swamp the entire naval service," he complained. He added "careers have been ruined."

The man appealing to witch-sympathizers for understanding has spawned an entire fraternity of woman-haters. It was James Webb who, on a visit to the Naval Academy several years ago, referred to female midshipmen as "thunder thighs." An informal group calling themselves "Webbites" now shamelessly practice bigotry in an effort to rid the Naval Academy of women.

The Tailhook investigation into the 1991 Naval Aviators' convention was "a witch hunt for senior officers who ignored lewd behavior," a Webb colleague, Navy Admiral Davis said this September after several admirals were disciplined and one civilian Secretary of the Navy dismissed. The investigation "would not solve the Navy's cultural problem," he explained.

Those who contend that Paula Coughlin, the lieutenant pilot and admiral's aide who was forced to run the Tailhooker's humiliating hotel gauntlet, was simply experiencing a "cultural problem," also dismiss the victims in the other popular witch-hunt of the 90s. Like the youth accusers of Salem and surrounding towns, children are being cast as witch-hunters; unlike them, their charges are often skeptically received.

Addressing statistics that suggest that as many as 1.2 million U.S. adults experienced sexual abuse as children, reporter Daniel Goleman asked in a "Science Desk" story for the *Times* July 21, "Is it Satan or is it Salem?" Citing disbelievers of survivors, Goleman continued, "These critics liken the wave of such cases to the hysteria and false accusations of the Salem witch trials."

Three hundred years ago, children's claims were enough to get a person hanged. Particularly, as scholar Carol Karlsen has pointed out, if the accused was a widow or a woman who controlled assets, interrupting the orderly transmission of property from one generation of males to another. Or if she enabled women to procure abortions or participated in "that filthie sinne of the Communitie of Woemen."

Three hundred years ago this month, opposition to the witch-hunts finally brought about a halt to killings in Salem. Dissidents at the time also focused not on women, who made up the majority of those accused, but on men: John Proctor, the husband of an accused woman, and George Burroughs, once a pastor of Salem Village whom they considered innocent. Then as now, it seems that witch-hunting is a nasty thing to do to men. With respect to women, the culture's still not sure. Better watch out, though. Spooks can come back to haunt you and your children. It's safer to dress up as a turtle.

Originally published in New York Perspectives
October 30, 1992

TAILHOOK'S "CASUALTY"

According to a Naval judge, Adm. Frank Kelso lied to investigators in an effort to cover up his role at the 1991 Tailhook convention, the Naval gathering where dozens of women were assaulted. The Navy responded to this charge by having Kelso retire two months early, with no reduction in rank or pension, with a letter of commendation saying he had done nothing wrong. Despite this golden parachute, Kelso was treated as a victim by some media: "The battle of the sexes in uniform claimed another casualty today," reported CBS News' David Martin (2/15/94), "when the chief of Naval Operations, Adm. Frank Kelso, announced he would step down in an effort to get the Tailhook scandal over with once and for all." Since no one will apparently be convicted of any of the assaults—and the female officer who brought the original charges has resigned from the Navy, citing continued abuse—it appears that the sexual harassment CBS refers to as the "battle of the sexes in uniform" will continue.

EXTRA!Update 4/94

Anti-Gay Violence

Off the *New York Times'* Agenda

The *New York Times* no longer prints the word "gay" only in quotation marks, but it still has a long way to go to represent gay and lesbian reality. On the issue of gay-bashing, *Times* coverage in recent months has shown a pattern of neglect and distortion.

"A Gay Protest Against Attacks Becomes Violent" was the headline of a June 18, 1990 *Times* article, obscuring the key fact that it was anti-gay hecklers who used violence against the protest. The march, co-sponsored by the gay and lesbian rights group Queer Nation and the AIDS Coalition To Unleash Power (ACT-UP), was held in Greenwich Village to protest a wave of assaults on gay and lesbian people. "Where were the media when the 50 queer-bashings took place in May? Nowhere," says Maxine Wolfe, a member of Queer Nation.

On July 16, when more than 100 members of Queer Nation protested outside of the homes of the alleged attackers of the march, all three New York tabloids ran stories on the demonstration. There was no mention in the *Times*.

This avoidance of the issue by the *Times* is not unusual. On May 11, all the New York papers fanfared Mayor David Dinkins's condemnation of racist and anti-Semitic attacks. His criticism of anti-gay violence in the same speech was not included in the *Times* report. In reporting on another rally less than a dozen days later, the *Times* again conspicuously omitted comments about anti-gay bias by Mayor Dinkins, New York Governor Mario Cuomo and lesbian activist Virginia Apuzzo.

"The *New York Times* only does the little it can get away with," says Stephen Miller of the Gay & Lesbian Alliance Against Defamation (GLAAD). The paper, for example, continues to print that James Zappalorti, a Staten Island man beaten and kicked to death for being gay, was killed by attackers "who perceived him to be gay," even after both of his parents have declared publicly that their son was homosexual and that that was the reason he was murdered.

Miller asked John Darnton, the *Times* metro editor, for a correction of the paper's report that Zappalorti's father denied that his son was gay. "He said he realized that every other news source quoted the father differently, but that the paper has to stand by its reporter," Miller said.

If *Times* editors wonder, as stated in a June 26 editorial, why gay and lesbian activists have to resort to radical confrontation ("a breakdown in sense and civility") to get their point across, they need only look at their own record.

"They just don't get it," said Maxine Wolfe after the killing of another gay man—hammered and stabbed to death outside a gay bar in Queens—also went unnoted in the *Times*: "If we don't act who will? The *Times* has shown it certainly won't."

July/August 1990

WILL EDITORS CONFRONT HOMOPHOBIA?

The *New York Times* had to virtually retract whole sections of an article, "Lesbian Partners Find the Means to be Parents" (1/30/89), after criticism from the National Gay and Lesbian Task Force and GLAAD. The groups were upset by parts of the article which contained un-named sources and baseless innuendos suggesting that lesbian parenting could damage children: "Some clinicians speculate that in the long term, girls might have difficulty in intimate relationships with men, boys might be uncomfortable with their roles as males. If lesbian parents are openly hostile towards men, these difficulties could be worsened."

In an editor's note, the *Times* (2/3/89) admitted that the offending comments "were added to the article during the editing" after reporter Gina Kolata had submitted it. "In the absence of evidence that hostility towards men is common among lesbian parents," the Times conceded, "the reference to such hostility was unwarranted. The article should have given lesbian parents a chance to respond."

EXTRA! Special Issue 1992

Femme, Fair, Fabulous

The Media's Lesbian Chic

We thought it was going to take a revolution but here we are. The magazines are wild for lesbians: *New York*: "Lesbian Chic", *Mademoiselle*: "Women in Love", a lesbian feature in June's *Vogue* and who knows what's coming out this summer (excuse the pun). For those who thought the mainstream would never get over its fear of dykes unless society reassessed its approach to heterosexuality, the good news is that lesbians are the new "hot subculture" (*Rolling Stone*). The bad news; the patriarchy is holding fast. Gay women are in the papers, but so is homophobia, and the revolution's nowhere in sight.

A decade ago it was easy to complain that the media stereotyped gays and lesbians to make them as unattractive to the straight world as they could. The butch dyke, the drag queen, the press rarely showed a homosexual that didn't fit that mold. Since then—a breakthrough—gay men and lesbians are the trendy topic of the media scene. *Vanity Fair* called these the "Gay Nineties:" "With a supportive president in the White House and an influx of openly gay people in the corridors of power in Washington, prosperous gays are climbing on board..." (*VF* 5/93).

In one respect, *Vanity Fair* writer Luisita Lopez Torregrosa got it right: prosperous gays are climbing. The question is, what happened to everyone else? An answer came in *New York* magazine's May issue, cover story "Lesbian Chic." What *New York* called "The Bold, Brave New World of Gay Women," was a universe of femme, fair, fabulous "new" lezzies, at least if you judge from the photos. From only diesel dykes, suddenly there are none.

"From what I see, we're not that different than we were ten years ago," said Elaine Romignoli, owner of Crazy Nannies, former owner of lesbian landmarks Bonnie & Clydes and The Cubby Hole. "Over 25 years in this business, my bars have always had a certain number of lipstick lesbians, working class lesbians and the androgenous types." It's just that some seem to have become invisible.

Crazy Nannies, on Manhattan's Seventh Ave. South, was visited by *New York*'s Jeanie Russell Kasindorf. Ellen Carton of GLAAD (the Gay & Lesbian Alliance Against Defamation) made sure the writer got a look at several lesbian joints downtown. "I guess it wasn't chic enough," said Carton. *NY*'s story mentioned only a (male-owned) "upscale lesbian bar" whose claim to fame is that under Romignoli's ownership, Madonna once dropped in. In fact, Madonna made it into Kasindorf's lead, no matter that she's not what you might call "technically gay." According to Carton, GLAAD recommended that *New York* use a collage of lesbian images for their cover. They chose kd lang instead.

"I understand the focus on stars," said Kathy Acey, Executive Director of ASTRAEA National Lesbian Action Foundation. Kathy got a call from Ms. Kasindorf too, and was interviewed for "Lesbian Chic." "But that's not me, I don't see me there." Sure enough, Acey never made it into *NY*'s "Bold, Brave New World." She didn't and neither did her issues.

Asked to define "the big lesbian issues," Torie Osborn of the National Gay and Lesbian Task Force (NGLTF) is quoted in *NY* as saying "Invisibility. Period. End of Sentence." The comment and the context speak to the question facing many lesbians looking at the coverage of the media's current trend of choice.

Ivy Young is Director of NGLTF's annual conference, Creating Change, "The mainstream media are still not seeing lesbians of color. They're not seeing what political history is here.. who we are politically, what our history of struggle has been," she said.

As Acey put it: "Lesbians, particularly lesbians of color, bring a broad agenda because you can't leave your community behind or your economics behind."

It would be hard to get a sense of that from the current slew of articles. *Mademoiselle*'s piece, aimed at younger women, painted "older sisters" as irrelevant. "Lesbians are becoming more visible as a new generation of gay women are coming out," wrote *Mademoi-*

selle's Elise Harris. "Unlike their more secretive predecessors, (they're) spending less time in the closet." As if no-one and nothing paved their way.

"It's a function of a particular segment of the media that they're more prone to talk about the interests of those who own and control the resources of this country," said Ivy Young. The result is what Young calls "invisibility inside invisibility." It's also a function of who is setting the agenda of the movement. The lesbian community doesn't have the financial resources that the gay men do. No lesbian music mogul, like the Campaign for Military Service's benefactor David Geffen, has established a multi-million dollar lesbian survival project highlighting for example, lesbians and cancer. The lesbian cancer project in Washington D.C. could do with a few $25,000 checks like the ones Geffen and Barry Diller each gave to start the Military Service campaign—and the attendant media visibility.

The *Village Voice*'s Robert Massa recently wrote about the decline of AIDS as a focus of the gay and lesbian movement. "As the momentum has built behind gays in the military and other gay causes, the epidemic has moved to a back burner." So too with the broad, social justice lesbian agenda. As Liz Hendrikson summed it up: "We have high profile, perfect professional people, people in business suits. But we don't have a definition of obscenity, our culture continues to be denigrated. One part of our community can get ahead. The rest is left behind."

The part that is being left behind is that part of the agenda that has to do with challenging gender roles. And the people being left behind are the ones who've always been out front doing that.

Chicago Times columnist Clarence Page estimated on *McNeil/Lehrer Newshour*, after the big lesbian and gay march on Washington April 25, that "80, 90 percent of homosexual America looks just like straight America." Perhaps that's because the mainstream media for the most part chose to cover the march on DC as a "coming of age" for the homosexual community—that is, a coming into mainstream media form. Those that didn't fit weren't in the picture. The historic Dyke March on DC, for example, where lesbians on bikes revved down the mall and fire-eaters did their thing in front of the White House, was barely visible in the mainstream news coverage. That march, a first, was organized by the Lesbian Avengers, a year-old group that attracted some 20,000 to the streets, April 24. Straight America is what put the "avenger" in the name.

The Avengers made it into the *New York* article, even a picture of their logo on a banner: the lit bomb. But the Avengers' agenda that goes beyond invisibility was omitted. Quoting Avenger Phyllis Lutsky on the group's activism in Queens, New York, writer Kasindorf didn't mention what was going on in that borough's school board [namely an attack on a pro-tolerance curriculum]. *NY* referred to the Colorado boycott twice, without saying what it is. [On the electoral ballot in 1992 was a measure preventing the state's anti-discrimination laws from covering discrimination on the basis of sexual orientation. The subject of national protests and a boycott, Colorado's Amendment 2 was declared unconstitutional by the Supreme Court in 1996.] "Lesbians are also trying to break down the doors of the television talk shows," Kasindorf leaves her readers knowing. What about breaking down gender stereotypes, bringing about women's liberation, ending oppression based on economic, physical, educational privilege...?

As ASTRAEA's Kathy Acey sees it, lesbians and gay men are at the beginning of the end of the process of getting legal rights in the U.S.A. "But legal rights have never meant anything in terms of social justice."

In a recent article, "It's the Grassroots, Stupid," journalist Donna Minkowitz criticized the vision of "gay liberation from the top down." It's a cruel fact that some gays and lesbians are gaining acceptability just as the community as a whole is under vicious attack. Minkowitz appeared recently on the *Jane Pratt* TV show. She's been invited to participate in numerous talk shows on lesbian themes recently: Jane Whitney, Maury Povich, Montel Williams. Meanwhile, our "supportive" President Clinton just invited a new Communications Director onto his staff: David Gergen, once a PBS commentator and an editor at *U.S. News & World Report*. In 1990, Gergen criticized gay performance artist, Tim Miller solely because he used his work "to encourage education, understanding and eventual acceptance" of the gay community. This, wrote Gergen (*USN&WR*, 7/30/90) was "wanton destruction of a nation's values." He called it "decadence and blasphemy." That's what's really in the corridors of power.

Originally published in New Directions for Women
June 2, 1993

"Feelings", reprinted from Dykes to Watch Out For: The Sequel, by Alison Bechdel,
Firebrand Books, Ithaca New York. Copyright © 1992, Alison Bechdel

Part IV

Ripe for the Right

For years, media professionals considered women "beyond the pale" of acceptable expertise, but in the 1990s conservative women became the belles of mainstream media's ball. It's useful to remember the origins of the phrase. In the 17th Century, "the Pale" was the area of Ireland under English control. Beyond "the Pale" was the remaining part that the British had not yet colonized.

The Pundit Spectrum

How Many Women—
and Which Ones?

The myth of the feminist dominatrix lives. When a handful of right-wing women founded the "Independent Women's Forum" in 1992, they did so because "they felt invisible in a media culture that tends to represent all professional women as liberal Democrats" and they wanted "to get conservative women's views heard in the media and on Capitol Hill" (*Village Voice*, 7/11/95).

Talk about setting achievable goals.

In 1992, television's most visible female pundits were former Reagan speechwriter Mona Charen and Reagan's Civil Rights Commissioner Linda Chavez. Female liberal Democrats were hardly controlling the culture; as for outspoken feminists, they were largely invisible then—as they are today.

For one thing, women of any kind have a hard time making news. In fact, according to the monitoring group Women, Men and Media, female participation in the reported news is down. The number of front-page references to and photographs of women dropped from January 1994 to January 1995, and the number of front-page articles or TV news stories reported by women showed meager gains or none at all.

Female sources were likely to be ignored by TV correspondents— even when those correspondents were women—and the absence couldn't be explained simply by sexism on the political scene. Prominent senators like Barbara Boxer (D-CA) and Carol Moseley Braun (D-IL) were close to invisible even in the newspapers in their hometowns.

What WMM is finding "amounts to a symbolic annihilation of women," declared co-chair Betty Friedan at the group's televised press conference in D.C. (CSPAN, 5/31/95). But as another participant in WMM's discussion commented, when the question "how many women" is followed by "which ones," it's clear that some women are more "symbolically annihilated" than others.

"The right wing has been very effective in bringing women's voices to the fore," said Betsey Wright, a former aide to President Clinton. "They dominate public opinion-shaping. Why aren't we hearing from feminists? Where are the progressive women columnists?"

We looked. Of 185 leading independent journalists and syndicated columnists listed in the Summer '95 *News Media Yellow Book*, a journalism directory, only 39 are women (21 percent). Of the females, almost half give advice: Following in the tradition of "Hints from Heloise" and Sonja Heinze's "Curious Shopper," 17 women columnists focus on topics like nutrition, interior decorating, sex and family psychology, recipes, travel tips or entertainment reviews.

In the tiny field of syndicated female political commentators, the right is well-represented by some ideological heavy hitters. At least three former Reagan administration women have syndicated columns: Charen, Chavez and former UN Ambassador Jeane Kirkpatrick. Other conservative women who appear regularly on the op-ed pages include Suzanne Fields, Georgie Anne Geyer and Debra Saunders.

Is the other side represented? It depends what you mean by the "other side." Ellen Goodman, Molly Ivins and Mary McGrory are all left-of-center female columnists with wide circulation. Goodman's and Ivins' columns are often as much about humor as about politics. None of the three is particularly radical—none seems comfortable challenging Bill Clinton from the left, as Charen and Kirkpatrick frequently did to Bush from the right.

But getting a hard-hitting, outspoken progressive feminist—a woman as wild for female freedom as Charen is crazy for free trade—into the front ranks of columnists will not be easy. Getting syndicated is harder than ever, John Brewer, president of the New York Times Syndicate, told the National Society of Newspaper Columnists this summer (*Editor & Publisher*, 7/8/95). "There are very few competitive markets left and fewer newspapers," Brewer noted. But there's still space for "certain kinds of features," he said—for instance, "conservative columns by minorities or women."

September/October 1995

QUOTA OF NONE

Op-ed pages lost their leading feminist voice when Anna Quindlen stepped down from her post at the *New York Times* at the end of 1994. Quindlen has remarked (*New York Times*, 11/22/90) that when it comes to women, many op-ed pages operate with a "quota of one." With the *Times*, it seems to be "one *at most*": After Quindlen's departure, it took the op-ed page six months to add another woman to the regular roster—former White House correspondent Maureen Dowd, who has shown little interest in feminist issues.

One might have thought that with seven men and no women writing regular columns during this period, the editors might have made an extra effort to seek out female guest columnists. Think again: Out of 330 op-eds by outside writers, 278, or 84 percent, were by men. All in all, during the first six months of 1995, men got to write 93 percent of all the columns on the nation's most prestigious op-ed page.

EXTRA! September/October 1995

The Sound of Silence

Where Are the Feminists in Talk Radio?

Radio relies heavily upon the imagination—the listener's and the speaker's. You can't see those of us in the business, we can't see you, and we can't see each other. So we make up what we call "the community of the air." As my colleagues and I sit down in front of our radio microphones, we hold our heads high, inhale as soundlessly as possible, and imagine. For my part, I picture that I am part of a rising tide of radio radicals, "speaking truth to power." I believe that the female audio warriors are out there, ranged against the bigots of Rush-radio. But that's not the reality.

I grew up listening to radio. My mother is an audio addict. In her London home, there's a radio in every room. Visiting New York this winter, she was trapped in a snowbound train, and what really drove her crazy was that her car was caught in a tunnel where her beloved pocket radio (always in her shopping bag) wouldn't function. "There was nothing but static to listen to," she lamented.

The radio of my childhood was replete with soft-spoken British hosts. The women I remember were mellifluous storytellers on *Listen with Mother*, a daily dose of Nanny England— and a ghastly show. But tuning in to afternoon programming stateside almost makes me homesick for Nanny. At least she didn't directly threaten your life. Here, the typical lineup features Bob Grant, the racist (African Americans are "savages"); Rush Limbaugh ("I like the women's movement—especially from behind"); and G. Gordon Liddy, whose only regret about Watergate is having been caught.

This isn't the community to which I want to belong; they're just the talkers who dominate the field. So, I wonder, does my community—neither Nazi nor Nanny—exist outside of my fantasies? Where are the women?

According to a 1993 Times Mirror Center for the People & the

Press poll, listeners to talk radio are predominantly white, conser-vative, and male. One theory to explain this is that women are put off by the combative talk on radio. "A lot of women deal with so much combat in their real lives that they don't want to engage in mock combat on the radio," says Washington, D. C., host Victoria Jones. Perhaps she's right. But it's not that simple. A 1995 poll of 500 *McCall's*, primarily female, readers found that 76 percent of them were listening to talk radio, including the most belligerent shows. Forty-one percent said they tuned in "very frequently," and 89 percent of the most frequent listeners said they liked what they heard. Some women get a kick out of listening in to what *McCall's* called the "biggest, baddest boys' club." "It's become this whole cult thing," said one respondent.

It's a cult that has an advantage: lack of competition. Women commentators barely have a toehold in this bad-boys club. We have always had to fight our way into the most lucrative areas of broad-casting. One early female broadcaster insisted that the problem was that male network heads didn't consider female voices sufficiently authoritative. Nowadays, women's "authority" seems to be relegated to nurturing: women as therapists are big on radio. "The only women who are generally accepted are helpers," complains Carole Hem-ingway, a feminist with 20 years' radio experience in Los Angeles and New York. "Helper is still the role that society feels women should be in, and commercial industry executives especially feel that way."

The most widely heard women talk show hosts in the U.S. are therapist-entertainers: psychologist Joy Browne and psychotherapist Laura Schlessinger are heard on between 150 and 300 stations each. Along with their shows, some of the most popular ones are those like Deborah Ray's *Here's to Your Health*, and the widely syndicated *Laura Lee Show*. Cheerleader-voiced, peppy Lee seeks to "ponder the human dilemma." She worries about MSG and hasn't done sugar for a long time.

"When people are putting radio shows together, they go where the money is," says Carol Nashe, executive vice president of the

National Association of Radio Talk Show Hosts (NARTSH). And health programs like Schlessinger's or Ray's promise easy money: knowing the listeners' interest, corporations can run aptly targeted advertising in a way they can't on more general shows.

About 5 percent of the members of NARTSH are women—or about 150 out of 2,000. "That seems like a lot to me. The number used to be very minor," says Nashe. Are these women wave-length warriors? (I feel like the fledgling in the kids' book *Are You My Mother?*) Are these people who could affect the ways that public opinions form? Not really. The women who are playing in the Limbaugh-land of nationally syndicated "power" talk shows can be counted on one hand. In 1995, of the top 25 "most important hosts" cataloged by the trade rag *Talkers Magazine*, only five were female: Gloria Allred, Joy Browne, Blanquita Cullum, Victoria Jones, and Laura Schlessinger. In 1996, 19 of the top 100 hosts were women, which just about the same ratio.

Along with Schlessinger and Browne, one of the "hottest properties in talk radio today" according to *Talkers* publisher Michael Harrison is Washington, D.C.'s Blanquita Cullum. "She's the ultimate package," he says. Cullum's a female audio warrior, for sure, but not quite the teammate I had in mind. Mexican-English and a single mother, Cullum broadcasts on 45 high-powered stations across the country and is considering a leap to TV, too. Charismatic and cheery, she uses listeners' calls mostly to keep her own chatty monologue rolling. Resolutely conservative, the *BQ View* is easy listening for those on the right. But Cullum flies not only because of her politics, but because she's vehement: forthright's more fun to listen to than fuzzy.

There are some liberals out there. At least three of the top 100 on the *Talkers* 1996 list considered themselves liberal—Allred of Los Angeles, Jones of Washington, D.C., and Lynn Samuels of New York. The only feminist on the 1995 list, Gloria Allred, who is a lawyer, lost her daily drive-time gig on KABC Los Angeles that year, six weeks after she staged a protest at the 1995 NARTSH convention when G. Gordon Liddy received the annual free-speech award.

She was replaced by a conservative man.

Judy Jarvis, based in Hartford, Connecticut, is the female host most often cited as Cullum's progressive counterpart. Jarvis is comfortable calling herself a feminist—she's proud to have a copy of the first issue of Ms. magazine. But her definition of feminism is a little different from the one I'm used to. Ask Jarvis about welfare and she says: "What helps kids is a little shame. Don't do it. Keep your legs crossed."

So must I give up my radio feminist fantasy? Not completely. Where programmers are insulated from the constant demands of commercial advertising, the picture is a bit less bleak. National Public Radio boasts 50 women on the air, working as anchors, hosts, and correspondents. Linda Wertheimer was there in NPR's first year (1971) and says that the network "didn't want our reporters to sound like the voice of God," perhaps making a difference for women's opportunities. But increasingly, NPR is dependent on corporate underwriters, and a study published in 1993 by Fairness and Accuracy in Reporting (FAIR), showed that the spectrum of opinion on the network barely differed from what you find in the commercial sphere. Few community-based or grassroots experts are invited to give regular commentary, and there's a growing skittishness about breaking ranks with the establishment.

The only network that rejects corporate underwriting is Pacifica Radio, where there are some genuine alternatives. In February 1996, Pacifica launched a new election and state-of-democracy program called Democracy Now!, hosted by the intrepid investigative reporter Amy Goodman. Goodman, of New York's WBAI, makes a habit of challenging conventional coverage of hot spots like Haiti and East Timor. Her program is entirely dependent on foundation funding and listener contributions, and it is "always a struggle to get funders" says Goodman. In 1994, Pacifica had started a daily news and discussion show hosted by economist Julianne Malveaux. But, according to Malveaux, the left-leaning network, rather than relishing some Limbaugh-like-fireworks, regularly asked her to "tone down" her manner of presentation. Ultimately the show was canceled, not because of differences in style, insists Mary Tilson, Pacifica station relations director, but for lack of funding.

Which brings us to economics. When it comes to feminists, the struggle is daunting in the extreme. For ten years, Frieda Werden has been producing a weekly women's news and current affairs program called *WINGS: Women's International News Gathering Service*, based in Austin, Texas. It's carried on approximately 60 community and college stations across the U.S., and more throughout the world. But *WINGS* survives on shoestrings and volunteers. None of the big women's foundations have funded sympathetic media. And that's the real reason I don't hear many soulmates on the air.

Blanquita Cullum was launched with help from Holland Coors, of the conservative beer-brewing family. Beverly LaHaye, president of Concerned Women for America (CWA), uses her syndicated radio show to sell *Family Voice*, her magazine, and fund-raise for her group. CWA now claims 600,000 members (nearly three times the official size of NOW). Couldn't feminist financiers do the same? Why aren't they out there supporting the programs we need and building networks at the same time?

Perhaps I'm dreaming. Recently, I woke up to my radio blaring— I'd fallen asleep listening to a talk show. Clearly I'm turning into my mother. And I'm worried: when I complete the inexorable metamorphosis into Mom, will there be anything but static to listen to?

Reprinted with permission from Ms.
Copyright © 1996

The "Stolen Feminism" Hoax

Anti-Feminist Attack
Based on Error-Filled Anecdotes

In her book, *Who Stole Feminism? How Women Have Betrayed Women*, Christina Hoff Sommers sounds the alarm. "American feminism is currently dominated by a group of women who seek to persuade the public that American women are not the free creatures we think we are," she writes. Such feminists have "alienated and silenced women and men alike." Where once there were Reds under the bed, now there is the Fem Menace by every blackboard: "These consciousness-raisers are driving out the scholars on many campuses."

Unlike the "well-adjusted" women of the 19th Century "first wave" of feminism, "gender feminists" (as Sommers calls the modern ones she doesn't like) are manipulating facts, squelching debate and running off with money and influence.

"The gender feminists have proved very adroit in getting financial support from governmental and private sources. They hold the keys to many bureaucratic fiefdoms," Sommers reports, without citing statistics. "It is now virtually impossible to be appointed to high administrative office in any university system without having passed muster with the gender feminists," she asserts.

Even as Sommers berates feminists for embracing "victimhood," she complains that classicists like herself are under personal attack: "To criticize feminist ideology is now hazardous in the extreme."

Sommers, an associate professor at Clark University, is entitled to her opinions. The problem is that her book, published this year by Simon & Schuster, claims to be about facts. The *National Review* (6/21/94) excerpted a portion under the headline "Why Feminism's Vital Statistics Are Always Wrong." Her book is filled with the same kind of errors, unsubstantiated charges and citations of "advocacy research" that she claims to find in the work of the feminists she takes to task.

Anti-Feminist Folktales

Reviewing the book in the *Wall Street Journal* (7/1/94), Melanie Kirkpatrick enthused: "One of the strengths of *Who Stole Feminism?* is its lack of a political agenda.... Ms. Sommers simply lines up her facts and shoots one bulls-eye after another."

In fact, like anti-"p.c." writers before her, Sommers relies heavily on a handful of oft-repeated anti-feminist anecdotes—or folktales. In *Who Stole Feminism?*, readers find again the tale told by Katie Roiphe (*The Morning After*) and Sarah Crichton of *Newsweek* (10/25/93) of the rape-on-campus study that included the question, "Have you had sexual intercourse when you didn't want to because a man gave you alcohol or drugs?" Like Roiphe and Crichton, Sommers exaggerates the importance of the question—she claims that "once you remove the positive responses to question eight, the finding that one in four college women is a victim of rape or attempted rape drops to one in nine."

Mary Koss, the study's author, explicitly writes in *Current Controversies in Family Violence* (a book Sommers makes reference to) that when answers to that question are removed, the victims of rape or attempted rape fall from one in four to one in five. The one in nine figure related to completed rapes alone, as reported in a newspaper story Sommers apparently misread.

Sommers also retells the story of the English professor at Pennsylvania State University who "took offense" at Goya's "The Naked Maja," a reproduction of which was hanging in her classroom. According to Sommers, who sources only the *Pottsville Republican*, the professor "filed formal harassment charges" and got the painting removed. The professor, Nancy Stumhofer, says she never objected to the painting but to male students' comments about it while she tried to teach. "I never claimed I had been sexually harassed by the painting," Stumhofer pointed out in *Democratic Culture* (Spring/94). Nor were formal charges ever filed.

In arguing against feminist claims that wife-beating was tolerated in English common law, Sommers quotes the 18th Century legal historian William Blackstone: "The husband was prohibited from using any violence to his wife...." The ellipsis conceals a Latin phrase that Sommers either didn't bother to translate or decided to ignore. In English it reads: "other than that which lawfully and reasonably belongs to the husband for the due government and correction of his wife" (Linda Hirshman, *L.A. Times* op-ed,7/31/94). In other words, the complete text says the exact opposite of Sommers' partial quotation.

Even when Sommers spots an authentic feminist foul-up, she makes errors of her own. Naomi Wolf, in her book *The Beauty Myth* claims that there are 150,000 deaths from anorexia a year. Sommers points out that this is actually an estimate of the number of cases of anorexia per year. Then she states that the actual number of deaths from anorexia is "less than 100 per year." This number is highly dubious, since it is based on a count of death certificates, which rarely list anorexia as a cause of death; anorexia-related deaths are usually listed as heart failure or suicide. Studies of anorexia suggest that the long-term fatality rate may be 15 percent or higher (*The Course of Eating Disorders*, Herzog et al, eds.).

As Sommers writes: "Where were the fact checkers, the editors, the skeptical journalists?" Naomi Wolf has long since admitted her error, as has Gloria Steinem who repeated it. Sommers herself seems to have a harder time facing facts and correcting her errors.

Sea of Credulity

In her account of a campaign sparked by FAIR to get NBC to play a 30-second public service announcement about domestic violence before its broadcast of the 1993 Super Bowl game, Sommers repeats uncritically one reporter's version of the incident, and adds fresh errors of her own.

Sommers writes that there wasn't "any basis for saying that there was a significant rise in domestic violence on Super Bowl Sunday." Her book suggests that she never read FAIR's Jan. 18, 1993 news release, which spelled out the grounds for addressing domestic violence on Super Bowl Sunday. That release stated: "The Super Bowl is one of the most widely viewed television events every year.

Unfortunately, women's shelters report that Super Bowl Sunday is also one of the worst days of the year for violence against women in the home." The release cited press reports (*New York Times*, 1/5/92, 1/22/92; *Chicago Tribune*, 1/27/91) based on the accounts of those who work with battered women.

In contrast to a "roiling sea of media credulity"—including at least one journalist who had been writing about the Super Bowl-related violence for years before FAIR's campaign—Sommers praises "a lone island of professional integrity": Ken Ringle, a *Washington Post* staff writer. Ringle is hardly to be held up as an ethical model: the *American Journalism Review* (5/93) found that, in his Super Bowl article (1/31/93), he appeared "to have twisted and used quotes selectively to support his thesis," and noted that the *Post's* ombudsman had acknowledged "inaccuracies and flaws" in his reporting. Sommers cites the *AJR* article in a footnote, but declines to quote it.

Sommers claims to be a skeptic who believes in going to the original source, but neither she nor Ringle ever called the national FAIR office in New York to check their stories or get copies of the materials that FAIR distributed. Nor did Sommers consult a calender: Her "chronology" put the Super Bowl on Jan. 30, which was actually a Saturday.

Sommers also claims that around the Super Bowl, "a very large mailing was sent by Dobisky Associates, FAIR's publicists, warning at risk women: 'Don't remain at home with him during the game.'" Had Sommers (or Ringle) called FAIR, s/he would have discovered that FAIR has never worked with Dobisky Associates—and had never heard of the firm before Ringle's piece.

In her account, Sommers uses quotes from a psychotherapist named Michael Lindsey that appeared in Ringle's piece. One of his comments she quotes twice, for emphasis. She doesn't mention that the *Post's* ombudsman had acknowledged that Lindsey's remarks had been taken out of context by Ringle.

Nor does Sommers mention that the views attributed to Lindsey by Ringle—critical of FAIR's Super Bowl efforts and of a link between football and domestic violence—were directly contradicted by accurate quotes from Lindsey in the same day's *New York Times* (1/31/93): "That PSA will save lives," said Lindsey. "It will give people the permission to call for help. The same way so much violence in football gives people permission to batter."

Right-Wing Feminism?

Sommers claims that she's a feminist, and journalists have largely taken her at her word. She has been identified as such on television, and many of the reviews of *Who Stole Feminism?* ran under headlines such as "Rebel in the Sisterhood" (*Boston Globe*, 6/16/94) or "A Feminist on the Outs" (*Time*, 8/1/94).

Yet Sommers was quoted in *Esquire* earlier this year (2/94), "There are a lot of homely women in women's studies. Preaching these anti-male, anti-sex sermons is a way for them to compensate for various heartaches—they're just mad at the beautiful girls." By that standard, Rush Limbaugh ("Feminism was established so as to allow unattractive women easier access to the mainstream of society"— *Limbaugh Letter*, 3/94) is a feminist.

Actually, Limbaugh—a proven font of disinformation—and Sommers—who portrays herself as a stickler for accuracy—have developed a mutual admiration society. Limbaugh repeatedly plugs her "brave and courageous book" (radio show, 6/14/94). "I'm proud that you like the book," Sommers wrote to Limbaugh in a letter he quoted on the air (7/26/94). "I'm asking you not to stop telling the public about it ."

Sommers claims that "in the outside world I'm a liberal" (*Boston Globe*, 11/14/94), although *Who Stole Feminism?* has mostly been lauded by the right. *Crossfire*'s Pat Buchanan (7/4/94) declared that "Ms. Sommers is right on the mark;" former Reagan speech writer Mona Charen called Sommers "a brave woman" (*Rocky Mountain News*, 6/2/94); *U.S. News* columnist John Leo commended her in a piece arguing that men are battered just as often as women (7/11/94). Professional feminist-baiter Camille Paglia praised Sommers' book to the *Boston Globe* (6/26/94): "It's so rich.... If someone tries to go against this now, they're really spitting in the wind."

It's no surprise that conservatives are enjoying the most recent attack on feminism, since right-wing foundations helped bring it to the public eye. Complaining that "it is not so easy to receive grants for a study that criticizes the feminist establishment for its errors and excesses," she cites the right-wing Olin, Bradley and Carthage foundations as supporters without whose "gracious and generous support...I could not have written this book." In fact, according to foundation records, these three right-wing groups gave her at least $164,000 between 1991 and 1993 to write her book—on top of a reported "six-figure" advance from Simon & Schuster (*Boston Globe*, 5/17/92).

Once published, *Who Stole Feminism?* was featured on the cover of the *National Review* (6/21/94), another Olin grantee. Sommers is scheduled to appear on the *McLaughlin Group* in September, a series that has also received Olin's support. *Newsweek*'s review (6/20/94) predicted that Sommers' *Who Stole Feminism?* was "likely to be the most talked about manifesto since Susan Faludi's *Backlash*." It's a pity reviewer Laura Shapiro did not investigate why.

The conservative foundations backing the book are hardly interested in promoting "a more representative and less doctrinaire feminism," which is how Sommers describes her mission. Olin, for example, was the foundation that backed Dinesh D'Souza's attack on progressive academics, *Illiberal Education*, and David Brock's scurrilous *The Real Anita Hill*.

Had a comparable book been funded by an alliance of ardently left-wing foundations, one might have expected mainstream reporters to use that fact as an excuse to discredit the book—or, more likely, to ignore it. If, on the other hand, mainstream media gave regular attention to debates within feminism, much of *Who Stole Feminism?* would have sounded old. There have always been differences within feminism—between those who blame women's oppression on biology and those who target social power relations, for example. And for more than a century, feminists have debated the pros and cons of "protective" legislation as it relates to sex-work and pornography. It's a testament to the media's failure, or bias, that Sommers' shallow look at this discussion has received more attention than, say, *Pleasure and Danger*, a compilation on the topic edited by Carole Vance, published a decade ago.

If audiences were used to televised discussions between a variety of women's rights advocates, Sommers' suggestion that anti-pornography lawyer Catharine MacKinnon and journalist Susan Faludi belong to the same camp of "gender feminists" would have struck viewers as patently absurd.

From P.C. to Feminazis

As it is, most outlets gave *Who Stole Feminism?* the same cursory scrutiny they usually devote to feminist themes. Writing in the *Chicago Sun-Times* (6/26/94), Delia O'Hare gave thanks for a book that "remind(s) us that unflagging skepticism is still a vital tool of good citizenship." She stated that only "one factual error turned up as I checked the facts."

O'Hare must not have been trying. Sommers's book is filled with errors, from repeatedly calling the National Organization for Women the National Organization *of* Women, to quoting one source assaying cultural relativism was a "goon" when she actually said it was a "boon."

Political books deserve more alert critics. They also need to be placed in a larger context. *Boston Globe* writer Barbara Carton (5/16/94) referred to Sommers' attack as part of an "internecine feminist conflict." In fact, Sommers work is of broader relevance. In 1984, William Bennett, then chair of the National Endowment for the Humanities, charged that higher education had to be reclaimed from curriculum reformers (*To Reclaim a Legacy*). Ten years later, Sommers is updating the charge, this time targeting "gender feminists."

The anti-"p.c." forces of the 1980s talked about how '60s radicals marginalized and silenced traditionalists, even as the NEA debates proved who had power to silence whom. Sommers, who replaces "'60s radicals" with "feminists," is connected to the p.c.-bashing crowd through her involvement in the National Association of Scholars (NAS). "Only one organization," writes Sommers, "has been openly expressing concern at what the transformationists are doing"—the NAS. She suggests the group is poorly funded and understaffed: "In contrast to the transformationists," she says, "the NAS operates entirely on its own."

She fails to note the NAS's high-placed supporters. Launched in 1987 with help from the Olin Foundation (*In These Times*, 5/27/92), NAS is supported by conservative funders like Olin, Bradley and Coors. Three of its members, appointed by President George Bush, sit on the board of the National Council on the Humanities. The NCH, which governs the National Endowment for the Humanities, is the federal agency with probably the greatest impact on research and curricula in the liberal arts.

Meanwhile, Sommers raises the spectre of "gender feminists" in the halls of power. She states that Donna Shalala, "no bit player in the misandrist game," "heads a department whose outlays are almost double that of the Department of Defense"—not mentioning that more than 95 percent of the Health and Human Services budget are non-discretionary items like Social Security, Medicare and Medicaid. Suggesting that Shalala's department wields more economic clout than the Pentagon is misleading, to say the least.

If mainstream media took debate about feminism seriously, one might have seen Sommers subjected to more investigative questioning. Instead, she appeared virtually unchallenged on CNBC's *Equal Time* (7/15/94) with journalist/host Susan King and co-host Linda Chavez, former Reagan civil rights commissioner—who seemed to agree that "feminazis" do indeed exist.

On CNN's *Crossfire* (7/4/94), Eleanor Smeal of the Fund for a Feminist Majority did have a brief opportunity to confront Sommers on her facts. "Smeal is only ever invited onto prime time to defend feminism against absurd attacks," said Fund press coordinator Colleen Demody. "She's never allowed to define the debate." The same can't be said, unfortunately, for Christina Hoff Sommers.

September/October 1994

Copyright © 1991 by Kirk Anderson

Why Read the Right?

A Feminist Perspective

One breezy October evening three weeks before the 1994 election, Ellen Messer-Davidow, an associate professor at the University of Minnesota, advised New York feminists to start reading the writings of the right. Because most progressives don't spend their time perusing conservative publications, she said, they usually don't notice right-wing arguments until they spread to the media's center stream.

Long before Christina Hoff Sommers published her attack on feminist scholarship, *Who Stole Feminism? How Women Have Betrayed Women*, for example, Carol Iannone, vice president of the National Association of Scholars (NAS), had authored "Feminism and Literature" (*New Criterion*, 11/85), "The Barbarism of Feminist Scholarship" (*Intercollegiate Review*, Fall/87) and "Analyzing the Feminist Whine" (*American Spectator*, 5/88).

Failing to cover the process by which certain arguments pass from the margins to the mainstream, news reporters have missed a vital story, said Davidow, and left the public dangerously ill-informed. Davidow, who is preparing a book on right-wing institutions, was invited by FAIR's Women's Desk and the Sister Fund to address feminist media activists at a briefing hosted by the *Ms.* Foundation in New York City. She began her research by reading academic works, she explained, then turned her attentions to journalism to track the traveling rhetoric of the right. Then in 1992-93, she spent time "undercover" at the landmark conservative think-tank, the Heritage Foundation, and at two conservative training programs for journalists.

At Heritage, she watched how ideologically driven research was used to influence national policy. In 1989, for example, when Heritage published a 127-page monograph calling for a "National Health System for America," under which prices would be set through "the market choices of those who can afford to buy their own health-care protection," the first step was to give an exclusive interview to the *Washington Post* (6/1/89). When the story appeared, Heritage marketers sent it to 40 syndicated columnists, 600 opinion page editors and 1,100 healthcare reporters at major dailies.

Local newspaper endorsements were brought to the attention of appropriate politicians. Another marketing division at the foundation targeted particular audiences like the elderly or people concerned about health care, and helped them build pressure for new laws. "Out of nowhere," Davidow told FAIR, "this monograph suddenly became a major contender for conservatives in Congress."

The National Journalism Center and the Leadership Institute train reporters, authors and activists: the catchers, one could say, for what think-tanks like Heritage pitch. The Leadership Institute runs nine schools that offer training in fund raising, organizing and broadcast journalism. Rep. Dick Armey (R-TX), now House Majority Leader, once wrote a fund-raising letter for the institute that began, "While you read this letter, left-wing journalism professors are preparing their new crop of media radicals."

The National Journalism Center runs free, six-week training programs four times a year for students, followed by internships that give them pseudo-credentials and experience in the job market. In 1990, NJC estimated that "500 alumni were working in media posts at AP, UPI, ABC, CBS, CNN, the *Washington Post, Wall Street Journal*, etc.," Davidow said.

In an article in *Social Text* (Fall/93), Ellen Messer-Davidow wrote that when "p.c." hit the newstands, progressive academics "limited by their training, came to the attack through texts and focused on its textual features—the rhetoric, the ideas, the validity of the claims."

Most people mistakenly assumed, wrote Davidow, "that the debate is the attack. The debate is only part of the attack." By the time conservative ideas about campus radicalism, welfare, health care or faulty feminist facts hit the headlines in a sympathetic or at best uncritical mainstream media, part of the right's social change program is "already a *fait accompli*."

At a time, for example, when the very notion of state protection for the vulnerable is being discussed in Congress, the effective destruction of feminist credibility is key. In the wake of Sommers and her allies, the details are forgotten, but many in the public and the media are left doubting statistics perceived to have come from feminist sources. A vast range of experts are cast into doubt: and they are the experts on precisely those issues, like poverty, the family and welfare, that are up for legislative debate.

March/April 1995

Conservative Women
Are Right for Media

Mainstream Media
Have Finally Found
Some Women to Love

After years of ignoring the expertise of women's organizations, the media spotlight is focussing on one women's group. Members of the conservative Independent Women's Forum aren't pigeon-holed in the arena of "women's issues"—you can find them critiquing the State of the Union address on *Charlie Rose* (PBS, 1/23/96), ridiculing liberalism on *Politically Incorrect* (Comedy Central, 12/4/95), and discussing prostitution on *Crossfire* (CNN, 7/13/95). They'll hold forth on human rights on *All Things Considered* (NPR, 9/4/95) and the *MacNeil/Lehrer NewsHour* (PBS, 9/19/95); they argue about everything from the budget to the V-chip on *CNN & Company*, where one of their members is a regular guest.

The IWF came together in 1992 to answer a need, says Anita Blair, the group's executive vice president. "We've heard from the media that it's hard to find views that are alternative to the feminists," she told the *Washington Times* (12/16/93). There certainly was a vacuum, but not because news outlets were crammed with advocates of women's rights. Throughout the '80s and early '90s, although key policy debates took place on traditionally female turf— over "social" questions of family, health, security, the rights and responsibilities of the individual and the state—mainstream media preferred to ignore women experts altogether than feature an actual feminist.

Nonetheless, popular pressure continued to demand a space for women in media discourse. When a group of conservative females came along, they were a convenient way to fill the media's gender gap.

Lip Service

The Independent Women's Forum calls its newsletter, *The Women's Quarterly*, an "intellectual antidote to *Ms.*," and claims to be a "non-partisan" group determined to take on the feminist "establishment." Conservative syndicated columnist Mona Charen (*Women's Quarterly*, Summer/95) recognizes her allies: She lauded IWF for refuting "feminist nonsense that is swallowed so uncritically by the mainstream press."

The mainstream, however, sometimes seems to have trouble discerning the group's perspective. According to the *Washington Post*'s Megan Rosenfeld (11/30/95), "It can be a challenge to sort out exactly where the IWFers sit on the political spectrum." The *New York Times* (11/20/95) has identified IWF neutrally as "a policy group."

A glance at the IWF's positions, however, reveals a consistent role—as the female lips for the Republican line. In 1995, IWF leaders testified in Congress against affirmative action and for defunding the Violence Against Women Act; they took an active stand against integration at the Virginia Military Institute, and came out in favor of tort reform. ("Women have been needlessly frightened by [silicone breast implant] scare stories," the IWF asserts—press release, 12/11/95.)

The IWF's Melinda Sidak testified (8/2/95) in support of denying tax funding to non-governmental organizations and non-profit groups, and she singled out the American Bar Association for vilification. No wonder. As a lawyer for the Tobacco Institute (the cigarette industry's lobbying organization), Sidak once asserted that "smoking has not been shown to cause cancer or any other disease" (*Adweek*, 5/28/90).

Echoing the far right's UN-panic, IWF Executive Director Barbara Ledeen urged Congress (7/18/95) to shun the Fourth World Conference on Women because participation was tantamount to permitting an "other entity to dictate this country's domestic policies." IWF's Blair promoted the papal line that the use of the word "gender" in the Beijing Conference Platform for Action would lead to a "sexual free-for-all" (*Washington Times*, 7/24/95).

No one seems to label this conservative rhetoric "strident." The *Washington Post's* Rosenfeld called it "provocative" when an article in the *Quarterly* promoted hiring more domestic servants as a solution for unemployment (11/30/95). In fact, an insider at CNN explained, IWF members are useful on panel discussions precisely because "they'll take a sharp line."

The Right Moves

CNN also likes Laura Ingraham and other IWFers because they "put out the Generation X look." But so do equally articulate young feminists like Susan Faludi, Rebecca Walker and Urvashi Vaid, who seldom find their way onto CNN. What has Ingraham got that they don't? Conservative credentials.

Ingraham got what she called her "first experience as an activist" at the new right's flagship campus publication, the *Dartmouth Review*. Following in the footsteps of her one-time fiancé, Dinesh D'Souza, she served as the paper's editor-in-chief; in line with the paper's bigotry-building tradition, Ingraham sent a writer to infiltrate Dartmouth's new Gay Students' Association, published transcripts of the meeting and sent secretly recorded tapes to the parents of the members of the group (*CounterPunch*, 9/95). She also did a stint at Princeton's *Prospect*, a magazine founded in 1972 by right-wing college alumni opposed to the opening of the university to female students.

Ingraham went from college to the White House, where she was a domestic policy adviser and speechwriter under Reagan. She participated in biweekly meetings of young "Third Wave" conservatives at the Heritage Foundation—which called her a "young conservative leader" to watch in a 1987 report.

Ingraham later clerked for Judge Clarence Thomas in his pre-Supreme Court days. Ingraham, like many IWF members, participated in Women for Judge Thomas, an ad-hoc group that attracted media attention for defense of Thomas against Anita Hill.

The *Boston Globe* (5/29/94) called the rise of anti-feminist groups like IWF an "insurgency," accepting the "anti-establishment" characterization that the IWF projects, but it's hard to get much closer to the establishment than these women. Sidak, another IWF honcho who participated in the Heritage Foundation's Third Wave meetings, was a special counsel at age 27 to then-Transportation Secretary Elizabeth Dole.

IWF officers include economist and would-be First Lady Wendy Lee Gramm; former NEH Director and arts-defunder Lynne Cheney (wife of Dick Cheney, Bush's Secretary of Defense); and Barbara Ledeen, whose husband is Reagan-era National Security Council consultant Michael Ledeen (who played an active role in the Iran-Contra scandal).

Media Splash

The *Washington Post's* Rosenfeld (11/30/95) expressed surprise at the IWF's success getting into the media: IWF members get published, quoted in news stories and invited on talk shows with "astonishing regularity."

The group's financial backing helps lessen the surprise: According to 1994 foundation records, IWF received $100,000 in start-up funds from the Carthage Foundation, and the Bradley Foundation gave the group $40,000 to produce a media directory of conservative women to distribute to media outlets nationwide. (The directory lists other Bradley grantees like Christina Hoff Sommers, who promotes a similar anti-feminist agenda.)

Conservative credentials and ready cash help to explain why a brand new group with roughly 550 members has managed to make a media splash. The *New York Times* published six opinion pieces by IWF leaders in 1995, the *Wall Street Journal* published five, the *Washington Post* three. But it doesn't explain why during that same period those same papers chose to publish *no* commentary on any subject by anyone from NOW (with 275,000 members) or the Feminist Majority Foundation (with more than 60,000).

Nor does the agility of conservative women explain why mainstream news outlets ignored two major demonstrations in Washington D.C. last fall (11/15/95, 12/15/95) protesting federal budget cuts organized by the feminist Women's Committee of 100. It may be "influence" that gets IWF included. It is politics, and a lack of journalistic integrity—that causes a coalition of groups representing close to one million women to be ignored.

March/April 1996

The *New York Times Magazine* featured Laura Ingraham as part of its cover story on conservatives from Generation X (2/12/95).

Hate on Tape

The Religious Right's Video Strategy

It was the military and the media that made *The Gay Agenda* popular, says Bill Horn, once a CBS sportscaster, now video maker for the Springs of Life charismatic Christian church that produced the tape.

"Since *The Gay Agenda* was featured on *Larry King Live* and ABC *World News Tonight*, calls have poured in on the 1-800 sales number requesting a copy," boast the producers. After appearing on Pat Robertson's *700 Club* with clips, Horn says he gets 500 requests a day.

The Gay Agenda poses as a teaching tape, revealing what Horn calls the "hidden" side of gay life. Using amateur footage from gay parades and demonstrations, the tape stars doctors and scholars and "recovered" homosexuals who recite lists of unsourced statistics on what they say are the unhealthy practices of gay men.

Ten thousand copies were distributed to voters in Colorado and Oregon last fall, in time to influence voting on anti-gay initiatives that were on the ballots in those states. In Colorado, where Amendment 2 was passed, a poll found that 70 percent of "yes" voters said they were influenced by the tape (*Rocky Mountain News*, 4/8/93).

Then in December 1993, Marine Commandant General Carl E. Mundy received a copy. "After viewing it, I reproduced copies for each of my fellow service chiefs, the chairman and the vice chairman of the Joint Chiefs of Staff," he told Rep. Pat Schroeder in a letter. "It appears to be extreme, but its message is vivid and, I believe, warrants a factual assessment."

By now, each senator and representative in Washington has received a copy, and Rev. Donald Wildmon of the American Family Association has distributed tapes to every legislator in the states of Washington, Maine, New Mexico and Montana, where voters face anti-gay initiatives in upcoming elections.

"Dueling Videos"

Yet Bill Horn is right when he says that *The Gay Agenda* received little or no media attention until the gay and lesbian community launched their response.

Though writers for the gay and lesbian press had reported on the use of *The Gay Agenda* in the campaigns of '92, and footage documenting the mass distribution of the tape was available from the award-winning filmmaking collective Testing The Limits, mainstream editors did not consider the religious right's anti-gay video a national story.

Only in February, when the Gay and Lesbian Emergency Media Coalition (GLEMC) launched its own video response, *Hate, Lies and Videotape*, did the mainstream media react. *Hate, Lies...* compares the religious right's anti-gay effort to crude KKK films attacking African Americans and Nazi propaganda vilifying Jews. With its release, the media had what *USA TODAY* (2/2/93) dubbed "A Videotape Duel" and ipso facto, a story.

"The dueling videos amount to a direct trade of volleys between the religious right and the gay rights movement, each now aggressively staking out its ground," reported the *Washington Post* (2/18/93). Quoting John Green, a monitor of grassroots movements, the *Post* suggested that the far right's tactics were reactive: "The gay-rights movement has become very organized and seems to be making strides, so they are a good target" for the religious right.

"Both sides in the [gays in the military] debate have been working hard trying to influence public opinion, using a variety of techniques," announced Diane Sawyer on *ABC World News Tonight* (3/26/93). "A battle of dueling videotapes," CNN declared that same day.

The fact that the video war, rather than the human war, attracted mainstream attention, exposes much of what is chronically wrong with the media's response to the anti-gay, anti-civil rights movement. *The Gay Agenda* is not a "volley" traded between equivalent players (as CNN put it on 3/26/93, "Gay Rights Vs. Religious Right"). This kind of "balance" equates vicious lies about gay and lesbian people (e.g., "92 percent of homosexuals engage in rimming.... You couldn't do it without some ingestion of feces") with the response to those lies.

Grassroots Camouflage

Presenting the tape as a new, grassroots response to an advancing gay movement is misleading and inaccurate. "To make local antihomosexual campaigns appear to be exclusively grassroots efforts when they are guided by major national organizations" has been one of the New Right's primary objectives, according to Jean Hardisty, director of Political Research Associates (*Public Eye*, 3/93). So too, the camouflaging of the religious content behind a secular, "defend the family" theme.

While magazines such as *Vanity Fair* (5/93) are writing about the "the Gay Nineties" and "an influx of openly gay people in the corridors of power," the media's focus on gay gains obscures the assault organized by the right and veils its sources.

The far right has been using video for decades. Don Black, a former Imperial Wizard, appears in the GLEMC tape lecturing on the prospects for VCRs and the need for Klan supporters to build "our own private network."

At the GLEMC press conference, Loretta Ross of the Center for Democratic Renewal, which researches hate groups, pointed out connections between the religious right and other far-right groups. For example, Billy McCormick, a founder of Pat Robertson's Christian Coalition, which is selling *The Gay Agenda* over a 900-number telephone line, is also a key supporter of David Duke.

The far right routinely capitalizes on public fears generated by AIDS, Ross said, as when a Georgia-based Klan leader claimed that "interracial couples are an open door to infecting white people."

Documenting the political and historical connections of the religious right's attacks would be valuable work for the mainstream media. Instead, even when *Larry King Live* showed parts of *The Gay Agenda*, the GLEMC video, *Hate, Lies and Videotape*, was not excerpted. Instead, stand-in host Frank Sesno played on the discomfort that exists around gay and lesbian images and behavior. After screening clips from *The Gay Agenda*, Sesno turned to Rachael Williams of GLEMC and asked, "Do you condone that kind of behavior? It seems a fair question."

"Our Own *700 Club*"

Jessea Greenman, co-chair of the San Francisco Bay Area chapter of GLAAD (Gay & Lesbian Alliance Against Defamation), helped to organize a community forum to discuss *The Gay Agenda*. "We have to learn a sense of entitlement," she says. "Whenever we get an article printed or a documentary produced, it is seen as advocacy and [conservatives] call up and complain."

Tongues Untied, a documentary on Black gay male culture produced by Marlon Riggs and aired on PBS after much controversy, was seen as pornographic, Greenman points out. "No one's saying *The Gay Agenda* is porn." On the other hand, its not very sexy to say that gay and lesbian lives are normal, and for that the gay community pays a price in the sex-obsessed media.

DeeDee Halleck of Deep Dish Television, an independent satellite distribution network, says that progressives need their own media. "Until we have our own *700 Club*, we'll continue to be the victims in the public theater of this society." GLEMC's new tape was distributed on the Deep Dish satellite in early May.

Meanwhile, *The Gay Agenda* has its clones. In New York, home of the world's largest gay and lesbian community, a Christian right group is circulating its own video, a 30-minute tape called *Why Parents Should Object to the Children of the Rainbow*. According to the *New York Observer* (3/8/93), the tape was shown at P.T.A. meetings and in private homes, in some cases with the approval of school principals, to mobilize parental opposition to Schools Chancellor Joseph Fernandez, who supported a pro-tolerance curriculum. Fueled by their success in ejecting Fernandez from office, the tape's makers, Concerned Parents for Educational Accountability, used the tape in similar meetings around the May 4 New York school board elections.

Bill Horn's sequel to *The Gay Agenda*, on "the gay agenda and the public schools," was scheduled for release in May.

"We have to begin to control the message," says Ann Northrop, once a producer for CBS TV, now the executive director of GLEMC. "They're way ahead."

June 1993

Copyright © 1993 Matt Wuerker

Merger Mania

(With no apologies whatever to Paul Cameron of the Family Research Council.)

Mainstream media hailed the 1996 Telecommunications Act as the harbinger of good things. It will increase competition in the communications industry, expert after expert assured the public. In fact, the law accelerated consolidation. By massively de-regulating the market, the Telcom Act permitted communications companies to buy one another up in a massive merger-spree. The trick in all this trade was that by the end of 1996, four giant, multi-billion dollar corporations controlled the national TV news networks of NBC, ABC, CBS and CNN. The number of women among the most senior executive officers of those four corporations? ZERO.

Sometimes you've got to laugh.

It's not that I'm against their affection for one another. It's the flaunting of their pathological relations on the front pages of this country's newspapers that I feel poses a real moral threat. In recent months, even publications that promote themselves as upstanding and respectable have subjected their readers to an unadulterated diet of gloating—over even illegal unions. We've read about men whose perverted liaisons have "quenched a personal thirst" (*New York Times* 8/1/95). "The Mouse that scored" roared the headline writers in the wake of the Disney purchase of ABC. And the pandering to the Hollywood homo-media lobby has only become worse this year.

Consider the so-called "marriage" between NYNEX and Bell Atlantic: Are photographs of affluent men in dizzy celebration of their newly state-sanctioned relationships really the sort of image we believe our innocent children should be exposed to on the front pages of the *New York Times*? The accompanying article went so far as to detail in distastefully graphic terms

Messrs. Smith and Seidenberg's sordid "urge to merge" (*New York Times* 4/25/96). This sort of thing has got to stop.

We must be clear. Defenders of these CEO's rights to marry assert that the Telecommunications Act promotes "diversity" but nothing could be further from the truth. Homogeneity is the inevitable consequence of collusion. Moreover, government-enforced acceptance of this type of corrupt behavior has implications for the health and well-being of children. It endorses attitudes and activity that directly challenge Christian ethics: for example, lying. GE does not bring good things to life and it has entirely failed to bring anything resembling life to news anchor Tom Brokaw.

The passage of the 1996 Telecommunications Act indicates that the insidious Media Agenda, so long in coming, is close to acquiring complete legitimacy. But the Democratic Administration's sinister condonation of same-system unions is nothing to which normal Americans should acquiesce. It is for this reason that I'd like to announce the launch of a new organization: The Coalition for the Protection of Non-Monogamy in the Media. For genuine diversity, debate and difference. Have an argument today.

May, 1996 (previously unpublished)

Promise Keepers,
Media Sleepers

It's easy to tell what makes folks in the establishment media nervous. When Black men came together in Washington, D.C. for 1995's Million Man March, most journalists scrutinized with healthy skepticism the political agenda fueling the Nation of Islam-led event. Many came down hard and heavy on the organizers' exclusion of women and whites.

When Pride rallies involving thousands of gay, lesbian, bisexual and transgendered people attracted national attention in the early 1990s, *ABC World News Tonight* and CNN's *Larry King Live* (both 3/26/93) played excerpts of a hate-filled videotape of the marches, made by homophobes and debated what the right called "The Gay Agenda" in earnest on national TV.

Every woman knows that a lot of men get the jitters when females meet "alone" in groups of two or more. In 1996, feminists couldn't convene a single day of networking without Robert Novak grilling NOW's Patricia Ireland about whether the so-called "Feminist Expo" was anti-men (*Crossfire*, 2/2/96).

Yet when an "out" homophobe and anti-feminist founds a movement to defend "traditional" (anti-equality) values, and he attracts a million men to a military-styled program called Promise Keepers, mainstream media don't seem to worry. In fact, they cut him acres of slack: "Full of Promise," gushed *Time* magazine (11/6/95). The *New York Times* (9/22/96) reported on the Promise Keepers' "manly devotion to spiritual yearnings."

In the case of the Million Man March, journalists distinguished between the leaders and the led. Most reporters agreed that the majority of marchers were well-intentioned but they played up the possibility, even probability, that a nefarious political program lay behind the facade of Rev. Louis Farrakhan's atonement day. But when more than 30,000 Promise Keepers filed into Shea Stadium to sign up to fight an explicitly sexist, implicitly racist culture "war," *New York Times* reporter Frank Bruni (9/22/26) saw only the bright veneer.

From Bruni's description—"The men listening raptly...were white, Black, Hispanic and Asian, reflecting the organization's call for interracial harmony"—readers would never have guessed that attendance at PK rallies is over 95 percent white (the *Nation*, 10/7/96). In his report from Shea, Bruni failed even to mention that the PK gathering kept women out. (That the event was for "men only" appeared only in the photo caption.)

The *Times* headline—"In an Arena of Faithful, Joyful Noise and Prayer"—also gave no indication that PK was political. "The program for Friday evening and yesterday involved sermons and sing-alongs, tearful testimonials and matter-of-fact discussions of current events," wrote Bruni. Nothing to get anxious about in that.

Bruni quoted no critics of Promise Keepers in his 28-paragraph story for the *Times*. But some were present, and to many, the speakers' political agenda was clear. House majority leader (and born-again Christian) Dick Armey (R.-TX), one of Newt Gingrich's closest House allies, was held up as a model congressman; a speaker announced that the PK rally was to be broadcast into Cuba, where it would "explode like a bomb."

Reporters don't have to venture inside most PK events to see the literature tables burdened with materials from explicitly conservative organizations. Focus on the Family, a $100 million religious right organization, publishes the books of PK founder Bill McCartney and helped bank-roll the group at the start. FOF's leader, social psychologist and radio commentator James Dobson, spent much of 1996 disparaging the current Republican Party for its "moderate" tilt. The Campus Crusade for Christ, the Christian Coalition and Exodus International (a group dedicated to "converting" homosexuals) generally pepper PK events with their representatives.

"We see what we want to see," feminist activist and writer Suzanne Pharr told FAIR's *CounterSpin* (9/27/96). "[The mainstream media] think this is something large and sort of trendy, something at best they might poke a little fun at, but not really take a deep look at or do some real analysis."

Easy-to-Read Program

Discerning the political proclivities of Promise Keepers hardly requires deep research.

Promise Keepers' founder, former University of Colorado football coach Bill McCartney, once defended two of his players accused of date rape by saying it's only rape "when real physical violence is involved." In 1992 he used his name and university affiliation to support Amendment Two, a statewide ballot measure (later struck down by the U.S. Supreme Court) blocking local anti-discrimination laws that protected gays and lesbians. He told a local press conference that homosexuality is "an abomination of almighty God." (The *New York Times* had reported those comments—3/15/92—but in 1996, its PK reporter apparently failed to check the file.)

Coach McCartney has been a featured speaker at meetings of the militant anti-feminist, anti-abortion outfit, Operation Rescue. Like some of his anti-abortion colleagues, he's keen on military language: "Many of you feel like you've been in a war a long time," McCartney told the crowd at a PK rally in Los Angeles in 1996. "The fiercest fighting is just ahead...It's war time." A videotape of several PK events, including this one, has been made available to the press by Sterling Research Associates in NYC.

PK literature is easy to read. In *Seven Promises of a Promise Keeper*, Dallas pastor Tony Evans, states the pro-patriarchal program plainly: "The first thing you do is sit down with your wife and say something like this: 'Honey, I've made a terrible mistake, I've given you my role. I gave up leading this family, and I forced you to take my place. Now I must reclaim that role.' Don't misunderstand what I'm saying here. I'm not suggesting that you ask for your role back, I'm urging you to take it back. If you simply ask for it, your wife is likely to [refuse]...Your wife's concerns may be justified. Unfortunately, however, there can be no compromise here." (Quoted in *Ms.*, 11-12/95.)

At one of the Promise Keeper rallies videotaped for Sterling Research, an unnamed woman appeared on a massive video screen to ask for forgiveness for females: "We ask you to forgive us for not showing you the respect that you deserve." Tens of thousands of men present roared.

The Christian Coalition's magazine *Christian American* profiled PK in April 1995 with an article titled "Real Men Are Back"; in the same month, the Coalition-linked TV show, *The 700 Club*, gave PK and McCartney a lengthy plug.

Reconciliation ≠ Justice

It's no surprise that right-wing media love McCartney, but it is still a tad surprising to see a right-wing demagogue get the same uncritical treatment from ABC's *World News Tonight*.

The week after Bill McCartney convened the country's largest-ever gathering of male clergy, Peter Jennings (2/16/96) dubbed McCartney "Person of the Week." Rather than researching PK himself, Jennings regurgitated what sounded like PK publicity handouts: "McCartney has been criticized by homosexuals who say that he discriminates. McCartney does take the traditional biblical view that homosexuality is a sin," Jennings said. Then he waxed lyrical about McCartney's achievements: "He has once again managed to inspire a large number of people to come together for what they regard as the common good."

In anticipation of the rally in Los Angeles, the *L.A. Times* (4/20/96) declared that the "Men's Group Strives for Racial Harmony," echoing slippery PK rhetoric about racial "reconciliation." But being reconciled is not the same as being equal. Indeed, PK President Randy Phillips was quoted in the Colorado Springs *Gazette Telegraph* as saying, "The goal is not integration" (*Nation*, 10/7/96).

Al Ross pointed out on *CounterSpin* (9/27/96) that if the economic agenda of PK and their allies was carried out, "the economic infrastructure of communities of color would be devastated."

"Ralph Reed used to say that the stealth candidates of the Christian Coalition had to fly beneath the radar of society to make inroads," Reflected Ross (*CounterSpin*, 9/27/96). "PK have been filling enormous football stadia with extreme right-wing activists and no one's noticed. Either there is no more radar, or someone's turned it off."

When critical pieces have appeared in commercial outlets, there has often been a sharp response. The *Gentlemen's Quarterly* (GQ) ran a strongly critical piece about PK in January 1996. (Author Scott Raab says that what PK offers men is "protection...from themselves.") The Christian Coalition immediately accused the magazine of "bigotry" and retaliated with a slew of press releases (*Freedom Writer*, 9/96).

Writing in the *Progressive* magazine (8/96), Nancy Novosad reports that when a domestic violence worker called Mary Pohutsky was quoted in a Michigan newspaper, voicing her qualms about PK, her organization was besieged with calls. Influential members of the local community threatened to withdraw their support from her organization. The newspaper, too, received an onslaught of calls which appeared to be part of a coordinated campaign. Perhaps it's that sort of PK power that is making the movement too hot for mainstream media to investigate.

Or perhaps the power press is simply not disturbed by PK's talk. We heard plenty of rhetoric just like it during the recent debates over affirmative action, gay and lesbian rights, welfare and crime. The mainstream media are very receptive to people who promote "individual responsibility," demonize "immoral" females and homosexuals and bemoan the "traditional" family's decline. Perhaps that's why PK's not scary. It's forthright talk about fairness and equality that makes establishment media squirm.

January/February 1997

WHEN THE RADAR IS ON

Reporters looking for in-depth reporting on Promise Keepers can read the alternative press: *On the Issues* (Spring/95), *Ms.* (11-12/95), *Sojourners* (9/96), *Freedom Writer* (9/96), *In These Times* (8/5/96) and the *Nation* (10/7/96) have all carried articles on PK.

As most media failed to do this research, some activists have tried to do it for them. In Portland Oregon, when PK came to town, Suzanne Pharr, with colleagues from the anti-domestic violence and gay and lesbian rights movement, distributed articles from the alternative media to reporters and held a teach-in. Having challenged the PK's right to exclude women from the state-funded stadium, Pharr's group won access for all—and ten women and ten men attended the rally. Then they reported back to activists and did interviews with mainstream and alternative press.

Sometimes simply by turning up to PK events, activists can affect the media spin. TJ Walker, a radio talkshow host turned organizer, showed up outside the ThunderDome in St. Petersburg when a PK rally was being held there in August 1995. His opposition to PK made it onto every local news channel and into the *St. Petersburg Times* (8/5/96).

"It's easy to shape local news coverage," says Walker, who now directs an organization called Equity Media Center in New York. "News media can't resist the conflict and confrontation aspect, yet almost everywhere PK goes there's no one there to talk to reporters."

Walker dogged PK in North Carolina and in New York City—and each time, he was interviewed by local reporters. Outside Shea Stadium, the cable news channel New York 1 (9/21/96) asked Walker's colleague, Rev. Wanda Gayle Logan, to respond to PK's "chivalrous" attitude to women: PK may put women on a pedestal, said Logan, "but that pedestal comes with a price…She doesn't have a vote—that's sexism."

"Rather than talking among ourselves, we need to be out there, at the event, to talk to the mass public [via mass media]," says Walker.

Equity Media Center offers media training workshops to people who would like to gain more facility with talking to the press. Other groups are offering similar workshops nation-wide—check with local media activists.

EXTRA! January/February 1997

Part V

Confiding in Corporations

It would be wrong to complain that there is too little reporting about medical issues. Hours of television and pages of print are devoted to the topic every week. But is the concern for women's health or for corporate wealth?

This is what Bonnie Erbe discovered when she launched *To the Contrary* (a weekly news analysis program featuring a panel of women). Erbe told *CounterSpin* that she approached "possibly a hundred corporations" before getting underwriting support from two.

"We came close with a number of companies," said Erbe. "But sponsors generally want to sponsor shows that carry a message that goes along with the things that they're trying to do, i.e., sell building materials or sell clothes, or sell perfumes, or sell telephones, what have you...You cannot get a TV or a radio show on the air in America these days unless it targets an audience that corporations are interested in targetting and unless it carries a message that is acceptable to corporations" (*CounterSpin*, 5/21/93).

Beware: P.R. Implants
in News Coverage

In 1985, Charlotte Mahlum received silicone breast implants manufactured by Dow Corning. One ruptured, leaking silicone into her breast, body and skin.

Ten years later, the 46-year-old former coffee-shop waitress wears diapers. She has been diagnosed with incontinence, hand tremors, atrophy in one foot and brain lesions. She can no longer work; her husband has to clean up after her. And on October 28, eight men and women voted unanimously in a Reno courtroom that Dow Chemical was at least partly responsible for her rapidly declining health.

For five weeks, the Nevada jurors listened to testimony showing that Dow Corning's colleagues at Dow Chemical had hidden what they knew about the hazards of liquid silicone. Dow Chemical didn't sell the implants, but they controlled a subsidiary that marketed Dow Corning's worldwide. Dow Chemical didn't test the implants, but they'd tested the fluid inside them. The plaintiff's lawyers produced documents showing that Dow Chemical had known since the 1950s that the silicone that makes up 85 percent of the liquid inside Dow Corning's implants could migrate to the liver, the lung, the brain. They knew the gel could affect the immune system and damage the nerves—but they didn't tell.

Dow produced medical studies in its defense, but under cross-examination it emerged that some had devastating flaws. Others had been abandoned or destroyed. A rheumatologist who recommended "aerobic conditioning" for Mahlum admitted receiving three-quarters of a million dollars from implant manufacturers during two and a half years. He testified as he had in five other cases—that breast implants were not making the plaintiff sick.

The jury believed otherwise, and ordered Dow Chemical to pay out $14.2 million in punitive damages. Mahlum said she hoped her victory would "send a message" to others about corporate responsibility. But the message that the media sent about the trial was very different.

Corporate Woes

When women implanted with silicone began to come forward with their health problems, manufacturers like Dow Corning faced a serious legal and financial threat. Although media reporting stressed the corporation's "woes" over the women's (see *EXTRA!*, 4-5/92), when the FDA declared a moratorium on most implants in 1992, the word got out that powerful companies had made profits from products that posed a risk to women's lives.

In the three years since, Dow Corning and the others have pumped millions into research and public relations—and they've turned all that around.

A massive advertising campaign and media effort promoted several myths. One was that rising numbers of breast implant cases were evidence—not of damaging products—but of greedy plaintiffs and their lawyers. "Implant Lawsuits Create a Medical Rush to Cash In," headlined a *New York Times* story by Gina Kolata (9/18/95). Kolata ignored the fact that, when nervous manufacturers agreed to a global settlement with implanted women in 1994, they set the shortest registration deadline they could get away with—hence the "rush" of women who wanted to join.

Another notion promoted by reporters was that corporations, not women, were in trouble. Dow Corning, the biggest corporation in the class-action implants case, filed for bankruptcy in May 1995—and in no time at all the manufacturers enjoyed "most favored victim" status in the press.

"A company has, I think, been driven out of business," Linda Chavez announced somberly on *CNN & Company* on the day of the filing (5/15/95). "All that's twisted about America's tort system was capsulized in a single moment...when Michigan's hugely successful Dow Corning Corp. filed for Chapter 11 bankruptcy protection," the

Detroit News, Dow Corning's local paper, editorialized ("The Triumph of Greed," 7/9/95).

On the verge of an effort to bust the paper's own unions, the *News* postured as the friend of the working family: The editorial featured a Dow Corning worker's son "who's taken to asking, 'Dad, are you gonna lose your job?'"

Actually, Dow Corning's profits were soaring. Shortly after the *News* editorial stories appeared, the company's CEO reassured investors (*Chemical Week*, 7/19/95): "Dow Corning recently completed the best quarter in the company's history and the demand for our silicone technology remains strong worldwide.... The Chapter 11 process is specifically designed to allow a company to conduct its normal business operations while it resolves its financial disputes."

A Defense Centerpiece

By far the biggest myth sold by the corporations to the media was the notion that scientific studies had disproved suffering women's claims.

In May 1995, Dow Corning took out full-page ads in a dozen national papers. Two years after discontinuing the product but just as several implant trials—including the Mahlum trial—were due to start, Dow Corning's ad promised: "Here's what some people don't want you to know about breast implants." Studies at "prestigious medical institutions" like Harvard Medical School, the Mayo Clinic, the University of Michigan and Emory University showed "no link between breast implants and disease."

What Dow Corning failed to mention was that implant manufacturers had funded several of the studies. In fact, Dow Corning's general counsel testified in the company's bankruptcy case that Dow Corning bankrolled implant research solely "to provide the epidemiological data necessary to defend against allegations of breast implant plaintiffs." As the counsel put it, "These studies were intended to be a centerpiece of Dow Corning's generic defense."

Some studies, like the ones at Emory University and at Michigan, were directly funded by Dow Corning. Others, like the Mayo Clinic study, were made possible by grants from a foundation whose chair has admitted that it acted as a "facilitator" delivering the manufacturers' funds (*Legal Intelligencer*, 10/30/95).

As of 1995, Dow Corning had donated $5 million to $7 million to Brigham and Women's Hospital (Harvard's partner in its research), and three of the Harvard study's six authors were either paid by implant manufacturers for other research or had agreed to act as experts in litigation on the company's behalf.

The manufacturers' influence over the research was not so subtle—Dow Corning was given a chance to "review" at least some of Harvard's study questionnaires before they were mailed to participants. And according to Dow Corning's General Counsel, "Each external scientific study that Dow Corning funded was only after consulting with legal counsel to determine its impact on the breast implant litigation."

Limited Research

The Harvard and Mayo studies didn't assess whether women with silicone implants were healthy. Instead, they looked at groups of women with and without implants, and compared the incidence of certain connective tissue diseases, like rheumatoid arthritis and lupus, because connective tissue-type symptoms kept cropping up in court.

In her story (6/13/95), Gina Kolata quoted a consumer advocate, Dr. Sydney Wolfe of Public Citizen's Health Action Group: "Wolfe says these studies are tainted by the money of their corporate sponsors and are too small in scope to be definitive." But she didn't tell her readers about the specifics of the funding. And she didn't mention that the studies' authors themselves shared Wolfe's concerns.

The Mayo and the Harvard study authors write clearly about the limitations of their research. The "classic" connective tissue diseases they were looking for usually occur in only 2 to 4 people per 100,000. Of the 87,501 registered nurses studied by Harvard, only 1 percent had silicone breast implants. In the Mahlum trial it emerged that only 11 of those had been sent the one set of questions that permitted them to register an array of undiagnosed symptoms and signs.

The bally-hooed Mayo results amounted to no more than that, of 749 women with breast implants and 1,498 without, a "specified connective tissue disease was diagnosed" in five implanted women and ten controls—an identical rate. During the research period, Mayo changed their "specifications" to include an extremely rare inherited disease that had shown up in the control group only. Without those three cases, women with implants would have had a 43 percent higher rate of the specified diseases.

The National Institute of Health finds that it takes seven to fifteen years or more for silicone-related diseases to show up. Since Mayo's subject sample had implants for a mean of seven years, at least half of them were well within this latency period. Harvard claimed, impossibly, to have included women with 40-year-old implants (silicone implants were not marketed before 1962) and the statistics were skewed by the inclusion of women whose implants had been in place for as little as 30 days.

The researchers at Mayo concluded (*New England Journal of Medicine*, 6/16/94), "We had limited power to detect an increased risk of rare connective tissue diseases.... Our results cannot be considered definitive proof of the absence of an association between breast implants and connective tissue disease."

"In all epidemiological studies of rheumatic diseases, diagnosis is a major problem," the Harvard team pointed out (*New England Journal of Medicine*, 6/22/95). "Our study cannot be considered definitively negative," they wrote.

But just as the research had been designed to boost the manufacturers' case, only the results that served their agenda were promoted to the press.

A second, larger study funded by Dow Corning found a 45 percent to 59 percent increased risk of rheumatoid arthritis, but the research appears to have been abandoned in the preliminary stage and the results—marked "strictly confidential"—emerged only in court.

P.R. Echoes

The science notwithstanding, in the wake of their ad and out-reach campaign, a slew of stories echoed Dow Corning's claims. Alongside their "no link" claims about the studies, Dow Corning's advertisements said that "plaintiffs attorneys have spawned a whole new industry from suing implant manufacturers," and the development of "lifesaving devices" like "heart pacemakers...and hydrocephalus shunts" was being "slowed down" by lawsuits. The corporations also charged that "plaintiffs' attorneys" were funding "state and local candidates, including judges." The ads announced a toll-free number for readers to call for corroborating material. Sure enough, within weeks, their claims were being reprinted—for free this time—by a willing press.

The *New York Times*' Gina Kolata (6/13/95) penned "A Case Of Justice Or a Total Travesty? Researchers Say Bad Science Won the Day in Breast Implant Battle," in which she gave pride of place to sources who charged that "a legal juggernaut can take on a life of its own, independent of hard evidence and bring a large and thriving company to its knees."

Two weeks later, the *Los Angeles Times* editorialized (6/28/95): "Tort lawyers have managed to use anecdotal evidence...to persuade juries that there is a causative link." The *Times* claimed (wrongly) that the Harvard and Brigham and Women's Hospital study "monitored" 87,501 nurses. (Neither Harvard's nor Mayo's researchers examined anyone. The research was retrospective, based on questionnaires.)

"Judges and juries have often overlooked rational evidence," claimed the *Los Angeles Times* editors. "Avaricious lawyers, like bees swarming over a honey pot," were threatening to destroy the women's chances for compensation from the manufacturers' global fund. The price of "crucial medical devices" was being inflated by the lawsuits.

"Lawsuits Feed Implant Hysteria," headlined the *Detroit News* over a Kolata-citing op-ed by Cathy Young (6/27/95): "Every week it seems there's more news about studies that find no link between the breast implants and any of the ailments." Young wrote that Harvard "did not get one penny from implant manufacturers"—not mentioning the millions that went to Harvard's co-sponsoring institution, or the money paid to individual researchers.

Two Texas judges called mistrials in pending implant cases when the ads appeared, because they were concerned that Dow Corning's accusations had unfairly prejudiced their juries. Some reporters appeared not only to be prejudiced by the ads and the materials that accompanied them—but willing to quote almost directly from the text.

Dow Corning's package of corroborating documents includes a Manhattan Institute "Research Memorandum" in which writer David E. Bernstein cites a Supreme Court ruling calling on judges to serve as "gatekeepers" forbidding plaintiffs from presenting certain scientific evidence. In breast implant cases, "some judges have been loath to exercise their gatekeeper role," concludes Bernstein.

The phrase echoes through the pages of the press. "It is incumbent...on judges to take a more active role as *gatekeepers*," editorialized the *L.A. Times* (6/28/95). "The presumption of innocence simply doesn't apply to corporate America," wrote the *Detroit News* (7/9/95): Jurors "tend to act on emotion," and "many judges remain reluctant to exercise their *gatekeeping* authority" (7/10/95). Writing about the Mahlum trial in November, the *Wall Street Journal* editorialists concluded (11/8/95): "The judge refused to act as a *gatekeeper* against pseudo-scientific testimony."

In *The New Republic* ("Tempest in a C-Cup: Are Breast Implants Actually OK?" 9/11/95), *New England Journal of Medicine* executive editor Marcia Angell restoked fears that an embargo on silicone implants posed a "threat to all medical devices." The *Journal*, which published the Harvard and Mayo studies, is cram-packed with advertisements by medical suppliers (including Dow Corning). The litigation surrounding implants, wrote Angell, "will probably affect a wide variety of silicone-containing devices," such as pacemakers and hydrocephalus shunts.

Changed Landscape

"The companies funded science to change the legal landscape," said plaintiff attorney Geoff White. And it worked, thanks to the press. On one occasion when it didn't, the flaks at Dow were outraged.

"We are extremely disappointed that *Redbook* decided against all our urging to the contrary to run Amanda Spake's article, 'Do Breast Implants Harm Babies?'" the principal of the manufacturer-funded Dilenschneider Group wrote, complaining that the author had gone ahead despite receiving their materials. "When presented with this same type of evidence and expressions of concern, another news organization, *20/20*, elected to abandon its story even though it was well into production. You had ample time to do the same."

For the most part, reporters did prefer the corporation's hand-outs to the reality of what was happening in courtrooms, or in the streets. When hundreds of women who believe their silicone breast implants made them ill gathered in Washington D.C. to call for a consumer boycott of products made by the implant-makers, the *New York Times* ran a picture of one of the women (9/19/95)—no story—and an 85-paragraph special report (9/18/95) on fortune-hunting lawyers who've made millions of dollars egging on not-very-sick women to bankrupt thriving companies.

And although *Court TV* considered Charlotte Mahlum's case in Nevada worthy of live coverage, hardly an article appeared in the national print press until the trial was at an end. Reporters shunned the documents dug up by Mahlum's lawyers, and ignored the testimony that had convinced the jurors. Instead, news wire stories focused on the money awarded and its likely impact on Dow Chemical and future litigation.

Soon, editorials began to condemn the jury, the plaintiff's lawyers, the law—even the judge. Anyone but Dow.

Mahlum's lawyers "persuaded the jury to punish Dow Chemical," editorialized the *San Diego Union-Tribune* (11/2/95). The *Washington Post* bemoaned the "Silicone Wars" (11/3/95): Ignoring the medical science, the *Post* wrote in an editorial, the Nevada jury "is reported to have expressed distrust of studies and to have relied more on its impressions of who was lying."

Dow's relationship to Corning was merely "that of a large stock-holder," claimed *Fortune* editor Joseph Nocera in a widely distributed column ("What Did Dow Chemical Do?" *New York Times*, 11/1/95). Nocera's lead was jocular: "The first thing we do...let's kill all the plaintiff's lawyers." The breast implant litigation, he argued, "has always been about the ability of hundreds of plaintiffs' lawyers, acting in concert, to use the threat of never-ending lawsuits to make the companies plead for mercy."

Nocera appeared on National Public Radio's *Weekend Edition* (11/4/95), where Scott Simon suggested that Dow Corning might be suffering because of its past "reputation." (Dow Corning is part of the conglomerate that manufactured napalm and Agent Orange, and spent years covering up evidence of the latter's effects.) "That's right," agreed Nocera. "You have this automatic assumption that's kind of cultural and it comes out of the '60s and the anti-war movement that they do bad things."

To the editors of the *Wall Street Journal* (11/8/95), the fact that the jury came to their decision after hearing weeks of evidence was irrelevant. In "Junk Science and Judges," the *Journal* writers charged that trial judges were "aiding and abetting the plaintiffs" to force companies to pay out "billions in damages despite a mountain of evidence they didn't do anything wrong." No *Journal* reporter attended the trial; Dow Chemical's attorney, Mary Terzino, was the only individual quoted, and the plaintiff's perspective was never mentioned in the piece.

The editorial went on to imply that plaintiffs' trial lawyers' political contributions were keeping "plaintiff-friendly" judges in place. (Nevada's state counsel wrote a scathing response, but no letter to the editor has so far appeared in print.)

Milking the Press

Instead of sparking public outrage at evidence of a 30-year corporate coverup, media reports on Mahlum's victory used the case to fuel a political drive for tort reform. Out of startling defeat, Dow

Chemical was able to snatch what could amount to an invaluable victory if liability law is changed. As Geoffrey White, one of Mahlum's lawyers put it: "The verdict is nothing in comparison to the positive publicity the companies are getting. They're milking this for all it's worth."

And the press is the cow.

"The press have bought hook, line and sinker the notion that there's no evidence," said Wes Wagnon, an attorney who's been prosecuting medical product liability cases including implants since 1977. "In fact, every time they go into court there's plenty of evidence."

By failing to examine the court records, and the evidence they reveal, journalists have become captives of corporate P.R. They accept the corporate-funded research as the only "real" science, and adopt the implant manufacturer's preferred framing of the story: The question for most journalists covering the story is not whether women's health is at risk, but whether a corporation is being treated unfairly. Businesses like Dow benefit from a "presumption of innocence;" there is no media presumption that a product ought to be proven safe before it is put into a woman's body.

Dow Corning is not the first instance of a wealthy company seeking refuge from litigation in bankruptcy court; the strategy emerged in the 1980s, when Johns Manville evaded asbestos claims and A.H. Robins escaped responsibility for damage caused by the Dalkon Shield intrauterine device. And products like the Dalkon Shield, the drug DES and toxic shock-inducing tampons show that there is also a history of corporations profiting from products that damage women. (It remains to be seen whether the silicon-based Norplant contraceptive will join this list.)

The FDA took silicone implants off the market in 1992 because the manufacturers could not establish that they were safe. Now journalists, spoon-fed corporate "fake facts," have tried to vindicate the "victim" corporations—possibly convincing millions of women in the process that silicone implants pose no threat. That's not "science" that's junk journalism.

January/February 1996

WHOSE NEWS?

Issues like abortion and breast surgery concern and affect millions of women in the U.S., but media rarely cover these issues from the perspective of women. More common are headlines like this one (*New York Times*, 1/22/92): "New Worry for Bush: Possibility of Supreme Court Decision On Abortion Poses Campaign Risk." The idea that a reversal of Roe v. Wade might be a worry or a risk for women was not explored. Similarly, a *Wall Street Journal* headline on the same day read, "Several Firms Face Breast-Implant Woes"—extending sympathy to the corporations, not to women who received dangerous implants.

EXTRA! 3/92

The Doctor's Case Against the Pill

Interview with Barbara Seaman

Barbara Seaman has been called the "Nader of women's health," the "first prophet of the women's health movement," and other names besides. One Philadelphia paper said, "She is to the Pill what Rachel Carson was to pesticides and Jessica Mitford to the funeral industry." When her book, The Doctor's Case Against the Pill, *came out in 1969, the* Library Journal *said, "Her book should be in every medical library." But even then, her research was too hot for some publications to handle. The* New York Times *said her book contained "almost nothing of solid substance," and she's had a rough ride with the mainstream media ever since. The newly released re-issue of* The Doctor's Case Against the Pill *includes a new foreword by Claudia Dreyfus who says, "If there are DES daughters today who can afford the expensive testing it takes to stay healthy, they owe a debt to Barbara Seaman. If there are women who give birth in pleasant birthing rooms with their husbands present during labor, they owe Barbara Seaman. If young women find patient package inserts with their contraceptive pills, they definitely owe Barbara." Why does she say that?*

I don't know if they should be grateful to me. Maybe they hate me. Those PPIs (patient package inserts) aren't very well written. They're kind of hellish to read.

Why did you start writing about the medical establishment?

I found myself very alarmed about the authoritarianism of the male gynecological and obstetrics profession at the time that my first child was born in 1957. At that time these brilliant obstetricians had been convinced that infant formula was superior to mother's milk. I told my obstetrician that I planned to breast-feed. He said, "You wouldn't be a good cow." And he went ahead and gave me a laxative.

You wouldn't be a good cow?

He thought that settled the matter. So he gave me a laxative that went right into the milk and my son became very sick. After that I became very suspicious of the therapies of doctors. After my daughter was born, I wrote my first article, for a magazine called *Mother's Manual*. It was on how to subvert the breast-feeding practices of hospitals. I told new moms how to palm the pills and ointments the nurses brought around. That article was enormously popular. Apparently there were loads of women out there who under their seeming compliance in the doctors' offices and the hospitals really wanted informed consent. They wanted straight information on which they could base their own decisions. So I started writing in that vein. Before long I was a very popular magazine columnist. I was doing my own column in *Ladies Home Journal*, one co-authored with my physician husband in *Brides*, another one ghostwritten for a celebrity in *Good Housekeeping*. I was reaching 18 or 20 million women a month. One of the main hot topics was the new contraception and the sexual revolution. We're talking about the early, middle and late sixties. Every time I wrote something about a side effect of the Pill, I was deluged with mail. Over and over my readers would say, "This is the first I've heard that this is a side effect. I've told my doctor I believed my stroke was a side effect, my depression was a side effect, my blood clot," whatever it was.

This is what people would write and say?

Yes. And he said, "No, it can't be from the Pill. The Pill is perfectly safe." So as time went on I really wanted to write a whole book about it, but I didn't have a degree. It still was not the age when ordinary lay people commonly wrote medical books of any sort. So I got a fellowship at the Carnegie Journalism School, an advanced science writing scholarship. I studied epidemiology. I really learned how to tell a good study from a bad study, which I discovered very few doctors knew how to do. Then I felt prepared to do this book. I found that the good studies exactly confirmed what my women's magazine readers were telling me. Of course there were bad studies funded by the drug industry and constantly placed before the doctors, which disbelieved that these were the side effects, but they were very weak studies. So I wrote this book. A doctor named Elizabeth Connell, who worked at Planned Parenthood, purloined a set of galleys, raised $100,000 from the pharmaceutical industry, and attempted to stop publication of the book. A particular young doctor whom she had persuaded to claim that he'd been misquoted, because I had taped my interview with him and everything was on the tape, had to drop the suit and the book came out. Then the Searle Company, which was the largest manufacturer of birth control pills at that time ...

G.D. Searle in Chicago.

They were the developer of the first pill, which incidentally had ten times the amount of progestin and five to eight times the amount of estrogen that's needed for contraception. I was running around saying, "These pills are a massive overdose." They never even established their lowest possible effective dose. Of course all the obstetricians and gynecologists and medical spokespeople, as well as the pharmaceutical spokespeople, were saying that I was a maniac and would be responsible for millions of unwanted, illegitimate children because I was scaring women into giving up this wonderful drug. Now these same doctors—it's very funny, they have a short memory, because they say, "Oh, yeah." In fact, ACOG [the American College of Obstetrics and Gynecology], with a grant from Ortho, which is now the largest pill manufacturer in the country, has been celebrating the 35th birthday of the Pill with a campaign on the safety benefits of the Pill. They don't tell anybody, they have not released the fact that they have a grant from Ortho to do this campaign, but one thing that the president of ACOG keeps saying these days is, "Oh, yes, the old pills were bad, but those were the old pills. Now they're really safe." He never remembers that his predecessor president of ACOG said the pills were perfectly safe in the old days.

We refer to that as "Now it can be told." The type of discussion that you're referring to is something we talk about often here when it comes to the media, that the media, too, will allow a CEO to say something today that contradicts directly what they had reported a CEO had said years before, and never bring out the contradiction. Tell us a little bit about the publishing response and the media response to the publication in 1969. What happened to you in your own magazines, Ladies Home Journal *and elsewhere?*

The book probably would have been ignored except that the G.D. Searle Company made the mistake of putting out a letter to book review editors saying, "Don't review this book because it's unscientific"—the same things that the same people are still saying. The letter was passed on to the science writers. The science writers read the book carefully and decided that it was a sound book. It got wonderful reviews all over the country. It came to the attention of Gaylord Nelson, a wonderful review in the *Washington Post*. He let me plan the hearings with his staff guy, Van Gordon, because he was planning Earth Day. Earth Day took place about one month after the Nelson pill hearings closed.

This is Senator Gaylord Nelson and the hearing that took place in 1970?

January through March. So we did the hearings, and in the midst of it I was very controversial, but the FDA Commissioner announced that he was going to put a patient package insert in the pills, that I had convinced him that doctors were not giving their patients enough information to make an informed choice, and suddenly I was relieved of my magazine jobs.

You'd think you'd be more of a catch than ever.

I was very surprised, because I thought I was bringing prestige to the magazine. Controversy always sells copies. But what happened, according to one of my editors, was the publisher, at least at this magazine, but presumably something similar happened at others, was taken to lunch by someone at an advertising agency who said, "We're planning a new campaign for our new whatever-it-was—diaper rash ointment, in one of the women's magazines. We think that your magazine is probably the best place to launch the campaign. But on the other hand, we're also considering *McCall's*, and we have a little problem with your magazine. One of your columnists, a contributing editor, is really so nasty about one of our leading prescription drugs." That was all they had to say. I was fired and the magazine got this big advertising campaign. Many of the pharmaceutical companies are divisions of very large companies with huge advertiser clout.

Let's come up to the present. In 1995 two articles appeared featuring you, one in In These Times, *one in* Science. *The* Science *article is quite clearly impressed and very laudatory. In* In These Times, *however, it's quite clear that in mainstream media you are what they refer to as a "pill pariah." What's the story?*

As my friend Lee Townsend, who used to be the editor of CBS *Evening News*, puts it, I've been "Naderized." I just learned that term from him this week.

What does it mean exactly?

Did you know that in the 1960s there was a terrible case where General Motors came after Ralph Nader and tried to discredit him?

He turned around and sued them and more or less got his reputation back.

But not his place in the media.

No. I don't think he ever got his place in the media back fully. So that's what Lee means by the term. First I lost my regular outlets in the magazines, except for Ms. (Now of course Ms. takes no advertising.) I was going along writing books and doing a lot of media discussions and then suddenly in the middle 1980s the TV and radio stuff just dried up in kind of a weird way. Actually, Lee Townsend was still at CBS the first time it happened. The same woman doctor, Elizabeth Connell, who had tried to prevent publication of *The Doctor's Case Against the Pill*, had refused always to appear in any public debate with me because she knew I would say to her, "Who gave you the money for your injunction?" Up until about 1985, if some show discussing a woman's health issue wanted to book us both on to debate, if she refused to appear with me they would get another doctor. Suddenly it changed. The first time it changed was on the CBS morning news. After booking me on they called me back with some flimsy excuse about why they couldn't have me. Then lo and behold, Dr. Connell was the doctor. After that, this became the pattern on all of the morning news programs. Really, all of the network and syndicated important talk shows. ABC was really disgusting. ABC for years—I don't know if they're still doing it—had a whole Women's Health Month. Every day they had 15 minutes on women's health. They trotted hundreds of people through their studios claiming to be health feminists. They were very carefully screened to give the appearance of there being a real discussion when there wasn't. I do absolutely believe that I'm blacklisted. But one more thing. I said, I'm getting old. I'm getting fat. Maybe they're just tired of me. But then it happens that, as you may know, I'm active in domestic violence and in divorce law reform. All of a sudden I started getting booked on network shows again, but only to discuss domestic violence or divorce law reform.

That was all right. So the blacklist only applied to the things I really know about.

In June 1995 the twenty-fifth anniversary edition of The Doctor's Case Against the Pill *was published by Hunter House; it's distributed by Publishers West.*

11/4/95

BREAST-FEEDING BACKLASH

To some journalists, all women's problems seem to be the fault of feminists. According to a *New York Times* story headlined "Nursing Becomes a Feminist Battlefield" (10/10/93), feminists are now to blame for making new mothers feel guilty: "Some activist feminists insist that breast-feeding is just another male trick to keep women at home," Susan Chira writes. "Others insist that it is a way for women to regain control over their bodies, showing men that breasts are more than just sex objects." No feminists were quoted "insisting" that new mothers do anything at all. And not mentioned at all was a more real source of coercion for new mothers: companies that dispense free samples of baby formula, knowing that if the mother doesn't nurse for more than a few days, her milk will dry up.

EXTRA! 12/93

Is It Real...Or Is It Astroturf?

PR Firm Finds "Grassroots" Support for Breast Implants

It's no small thing to win a public relations fight. A corporation under pressure benefits from the biases of the profit-making news media, but the pro-corporate leanings of commercial journalism don't guarantee favorable coverage. What you need are propaganda-generating troops, and if you have the money, you can buy some.

In the late 1980s, the pressure on silicone breast-implant manufacturers was mounting. After years of private lawsuits in which successful plaintiffs were silenced by gag orders imposed in court, sick women started appearing on television in December 1990, claiming that unscrupulous corporations were knowingly making money from implants that made women ill. As the FDA prepared to hold hearings on the breast implant controversy, Dow Corning Corp. (DCC) and other manufacturers of silicone products got busy.

"The issue of cover-up is going well," Dow Corning CEO Dan Hayes wrote in a 1991 internal memo (provided to FAIR by anti-Dow breast implant activists). "Obviously, this is the largest single issue on our platter because it affects not only the next 2-3 years profitability of DCC, but also ultimately has a big impact on the long-term ethics and believability issues.... What is at risk here is somewhere between $50 million and $500 million."

To counter concern stirred up by public-interest activists like those working with Ralph Nader's Public Citizen Health Research Group, DCC's P.R. campaign linked corporate-friendly science to pseudo-grassroots organizing.

"I have started to initiate surgeon contact," wrote Hayes. "The place we have the biggest hole still missing...is in this whole arena of getting the patient grassroots movement going....I'm very worried."

Dow Corning was in good hands—those of Burson-Marsteller,

the world's largest public relations firm. Burson-Marsteller has expertise in developing the phony grassroots organizations that professionals call "astroturf": industry-generated "citizens" groups who can be relied upon to lobby government and speak eloquently to media. (See John Stauber and Sheldon Rampton's *Toxic Sludge Is Good for You.*)

According to a confidential letter excerpted in Stauber and Rampton's *PR Watch* (First Quarter/96), Burson-Marsteller's strategy for DCC involved identifying patients who could be trained as spokespeople, making corporate grants to appropriate organizations, providing "day-to-day media support for the group....these women (including celebrities) will be trained and testimony will be written for them to deliver before Congressional committees."

The public relations goal was to get "women angry about having the right to make their own decision about implants taken away from them....We also want to place regional, and if possible, national media stories on the need for keeping this option open."

For those who've followed the breast implant debate, the argument above will sound familiar. One of the most often cited spokespeople for this point of view is Sharon Green, the executive director of the national breast cancer organization Y-ME. Her group participated in a partly DCC-funded "fly in" of women to Washington in the run up to the FDA's 1991 hearings.

In August 1995, Green testified in Congress: "We believe that women must be part of their health care choices and this included accepting the risks associated with those choices....Silicone gel implants provided the easiest, most inexpensive method of breast reconstruction with some of the best cosmetic results, yet they are no longer a viable option for women with breast cancer. What silicone product will be the next to go?"

Two months later, Y-ME's Green made another plug for implants on the *Oprah Winfrey Show* (9/27/95), arguing that without the implant option, women would be scared to go for mammograms.

The March/April 96 issue of *Ms.* magazine quoted Green as "the country's most vocal advocate for 'choice' as it concerns silicone implants" and listed Y-ME among the groups to contact "If You Need Help."

What neither *Ms.* nor *Oprah* mentioned was that Dow Corning and Bristol Myers Squibb (two of the silicone implant manufacturers) and Plastic Surgeons Associated are among the high-powered (and financially interested) funders of the Y-ME organization.

Media outlets have often failed to investigate the corporate sponsorship of astroturf organizations. Mary Ann Childers, a reporter for CBS in Chicago, went even further. Childers chose to interview Sharon Green for a segment (WBBM-TV, 2/2/96) on contemporary science and breast implants—even though she herself is on the honorary board of Y-ME.

"In the spirit of honest disclosure," Childers admitted her relationship to the group at the end of the segment, but she didn't think Y-ME's funding by Dow warranted any mention. "Years ago, they got support for their hotline, but they'll take money from anyone," she told *EXTRA!*

Burson-Marsteller, Dow Corning and their friends depend on groups that will "take money from anyone"—and on an uncaring media machine.

July/August 1996

The Politics of Health

The Menopause Industry

Interview with Sandra Coney

I don't know about you, but I have to say that I rather fondly look towards being an age when I'm no longer expected to be having children, when I've finally been around long enough to be accorded some authority on my own account, not as someone who's solely seen in relation to another person, usually an existing or non-existing male partner. I have to say that as a girl I'd always thought that that time would come when I was older. It seemed to me that older women in theater were always given the more powerful roles. I'm thinking of Lady Macbeth, people like that. And in politics, as women got older, you could see them as queens and prime ministers and so forth. That was all before I started reading about menopause. Now it seems as if just at that moment of coming into a certain kind of power, women, to judge by the media, are instead collapsing into hot flashes, depression, broken bones, at least if you read the popular magazines. So instead of freedom, maturity is apparently a time of total dependence on estrogen replacement drugs and other therapies, and getting older as a woman now sounds as scary as being young. With us today is a very special guest, Sandra Coney, who is on her first trip to the U.S. after a long career in feminist journalism in New Zealand. She is the founder of the landmark women's magazine Broadsheet, *which started in the same month and year as* Ms. *magazine here in the States. She's a long-time activist on women's health issues and the media. Sandra Coney's latest book is* The Menopause Industry: How the Medical Establishment Exploits Women.

Welcome, Sandra. To begin with, the "menopause industry": What do you mean exactly? You're not suggesting that menopause is a cultural creation, are you?

I am, rather. The title was to convey the idea that menopause was marketed to women and profits were made from that. So in fact a market has been created around menopause, or an industry, which doesn't necessarily benefit women but benefits the drug companies and indeed benefits a lot of doctors, because women who buy into this will visit the doctor a lot more often and have more tests and more interventions than women who don't bother and do it on their own.

You suggest regularly throughout the book that menopause, which is a normal biological event or process, has been turned into a disease. Give us an example. Osteoporosis, for example. That is a genuine problem that a lot of older women face, right?

It's a genuine problem for older men *and* older women, but I tried to trace the process by which the pharmaceutical industry, having created the product—estrogen—in a form that could be cheaply manufactured, set about creating the disease state for which the drug could be used. That process really began in the early sixties. As it's gone on from then, and we're now into thirty years of that, the drug companies have appropriated other diseases. So like, okay, first of all, it started off with hot flashes and menopausal symptoms. A lot of women stopped using estrogen in the late 1970s, when it was found there were increased rates of endometrial cancer in estrogen users. Then they re-marketed it in a very skillful campaign in the mid-1980s as a prevention for osteoporosis. It was at that stage that they turned osteoporosis from a disease state that men and women could both get into a menopausal symptom, a disease of women that could be treated by estrogen. Later on, in the 1990s, they've also added in heart disease, so it's now seen as a prevention for heart disease, and even in the latest literature they're starting to talk about it as a preventor for Alzheimer's disease. So it's been a very skillful marketing campaign. There are now basically no women who they're saying wouldn't benefit from hormones.

So you have a useful and easily marketed drug and then you find a good cause for it and a place to market it. Does all of this just coincidentally target one of the largest and most quickly growing sections of the market?

I think there are all sorts of reasons why this particular group was seen as a suitable market for intervention. It is easier, I think, to sell mass interventions to women. Women have an existing relationship with the medical profession, the health sector, through the control of their reproduction, the use of contraception, childbirth has been medicalized, so that women from quite a young age go to doctors and use the medical profession for these normal life events. Medicalizing a later life event becomes something that looks as if it could be more readily accomplished.

Some of the examples that you have in your book, The Menopause Industry, *of advertisements that are clearly targeting women at an age of menopause really exemplify what you're talking about. "Menrium treats the menopausal symptoms that bother him most." That's one advertisement. "Adolescence all over again?" The woman looks incredibly concerned. "When she's past the pill." "Helps you take the misery out of menopause." What message is being conveyed along with simply the advertising one?*

Those are among the early advertisements. It was really that this time in a woman's life is a time of loss and grieving when women felt useless and that their reproductive and sexual attractiveness had come to an end. So it initially picked up on a lot of the ideas borrowed from the way that Freudians had depicted menopause, which was as a time of loss and trauma for women because they had lost their major function in life, which was their reproductive ability.

So much for Lady Macbeth and Hamlet's mother.

Oh, yes. But nowadays I think a lot of it really plays on the idea of the aging, exploiting women's fears about aging, and also the idea of the corporate successful women, so that you will get slogans like

"The age of confidence," and you get these very serene, beautifully-groomed looking women. Another slogan that is used: "So a woman can continue to enjoy being a woman," as if in fact she ceases to be a woman when she becomes menopausal. So I think subtly the advertisements do prey on these fears of aging and suggest that the woman on hormones is a sophisticated, modern woman in control of her life. I think a lot of this picks up on the kind of women we're talking about who have grown up with the woman's movement who *do* expect to be more in control of their lives. This is targeted mainly at white, middle-class women.

I was going to ask you about that. All the pictures in the advertisements that you include in the book, at least all that I have in front of me, are of white women. Is there a racial coding here, too?

Absolutely. I think it's socio-economic, and it is obviously racial insofar as white women tend to have more money. I think that the youth culture has been a white culture and not so great as far as women are concerned. The very attractive young women that we have held up to us most of the time tend to be young, white women, the sort of Brooke Shields-y image. So I think all the statistics show that the major users are white women in high socio-economic groups. Those are the women in whom these fears of aging can be really preyed upon. But also they have the money to go to the doctor. They have the money to pay for the interventions.

So while the stereotype of the old African-American woman is one who can manage everything and look after everybody and doesn't need any care or attention, of the white woman it's this very delicate, dependent, nervous and prone-to-anxiety female.

And it's also very individualistic. These advertisements are always of the woman kind of isolated, not in a social situation. You never see the energies of women in the workplace or in a family situation. It's very much like the woman staring in the mirror, a very individualized image. In fact, the research into menopause in other cultures shows that in many cultures it's not ... we construct menopause according to the meaning of our culture, and in Western cultures that tends to be as a time of deterioration and loss of status, whereas in a lot of indigenous people's cultures or other ethnic groups, sometimes women do gain more status as they age, and they wouldn't, I don't think, be as susceptible to the messages of hormone replacement therapy.

What's your impression of the way this story is handled in the United States? Is it different from what you see in New Zealand?

It's quite hard in New Zealand, too, but we have a public health system, and I've really been struck since I've been here by the culture of the health system in America. You have a health market, so health is a commodity. So people provide health services for profit. That's their motivation. In a country with a public health system, the government has a number of motivations. Those are to get universal health coverage, to contain costs, but also to improve the health status of the population. So it's actually a more rational approach. The profit motive is not strong in public health systems. I've been really struck by that difference since I've been here in the way that an intervention like hormone replacement therapy seems more normal and acceptable in a health market than it does in countries with a public health system. I think women are a bit more questioning and they don't expect to be able to buy health and buy a fix in the same way as American women, to some extent, believe they can.

Sandra Coney's book The Menopause Industry: How the Medical Establishment Exploits Women, *is available from Hunter House publishers in Alameda, California.*

December 17, 1994

Clean and Cogent

Interview with Lucy Gwinn

Labor Day weekend in the U.S. means parades, picnics and the Jerry Lewis Telethon. The Telethon is supposed to raise money for the Muscular Dystrophy Association, but many disability rights advocates say that what it really does is to present a media image of disabled people as pathetic victims who, until they can be cured, need the charity and the pity of the able-bodied. Our next guest does more than criticize that depiction, not just at Telethon time but throughout the year. She counters it directly with a magazine called Mouth: The Voice of Disability Rights. *Lucy Gwinn is the editor of* Mouth.*

There's a very simple rule of journalism that says you should follow the money. In this case we find that there are whole industries that profit from the disabled. You have a particular problem with the rehabilitation industry. Why don't you tell us a little bit about your work in that area and then about your experiences with media in publicizing your concerns?*

I woke up from a coma in a nursing home. A drunk driver hit me. I didn't remember anything about that. A drunk driver hit me head-on. There I was, slapped away in a nursing home, and they would not let me leave. Nursing homes are a multi-billion dollar industry. They're all very well connected with Congress under the American Health Care Association, they call themselves. They have huge PAC funds to spend. I imagine they spend some of it on taking reporters to lunch and talking about "those poor pitiful people we take care of." There's nobody—I have not met more than five people in my life who want to be in a nursing home. Yet there are 1.9 million of us stranded in there, because it's big bucks. It's a whole lot cheaper to let us live free. I had to escape to get free myself, literally escape. They had security guards to keep us in. I escaped, got past the security guards and got out of there. But a lot of people aren't able to do that, if they're in wheelchairs or using walkers they're not going to get out. It was called a "rehab" where I was. They're like nursing homes, but sometimes they call themselves "rehabs" so they can get more money per day out of you or out of your insurance company. When I got out of there I made it my business, for about five years, to bring this to the attention of the public and get it stopped. We had Congressional hearings. I worked with a lot of reporters then.

Recently I got a call from *Sixty Minutes*. Andy Court, a producer there, called me up and said, "I hear you know something about this rehab industry and how it's getting out of control." I said, "Of course I do, because I have file cabinets full of it and specific documents." He said, "Find a couple of institutions in the country where they're doing this, they're robbing the taxpayer and the insurance companies. Find me five or six 'clean, cogent cases,'" he called it. This is a *Sixty Minutes* producer. I was very surprised. He said, "I want them to be presentable." I know what that means. That's a code word for "non-disabled." Nobody was in those places unless they were disabled. No, he didn't want to talk to them. I said, What about a woman who can't speak very well? "No, no, no." What about somebody in a wheelchair? "Well, we could shoot around that," he said. I had so much faith in *Sixty Minutes* until that moment.

I did try for about a week to find "clean, cogent, presentable" cases for him, because the story needs to get out. But then I faxed him and said, "Hey, Andy, I feel like I'm an escaped slave from the South and here I got up North and got the top-rated news program producer talking to me and he says, 'I'd love to expose the institution of slavery. How about if you find me some white slaves?'" He didn't think that was funny.

So the story went nowhere.

It's dead.

Lucy Gwinn is the editor of Mouth

September 9, 1995

Part VI

Media Minority

Until 1955, women were banned from the National Press Club, whose luncheon speeches by headline-getters often made the next day's news. Until 1971, women were allowed to watch Club events from the balcony but they were forbidden to eat or speak. Today, thanks to women who brought suit against nearly every major outlet, females are no longer confined to the media's balcony, but the struggle to eat and speak goes on. If you are a reporter, a lot depends on your attitude to the hand that feeds you, and what you want to say.

How Alternative Is It?

Feminist Media Activists Take Aim at the Progressive Press

Around 300 journalists, activists and critics crowded into a room at the Media & Democracy Congress in San Francisco on March 1, 1996, to discuss the coverage of issues related to gender. For once, alternative and progressive media came under as much fire as the commercial mainstream.

Nation columnist Katha Pollitt recalled that in 1995 she had written a column decrying the absence of African Americans in the progressive press. "I could have written almost the same article about the issue of gender," she told the Congress. "If you look at the mastheads of most left-wing magazines, they are dominated by men...white men."

And the problem, Pollitt said, goes beyond who's on the top of the masthead: "It's who writes and what do they write." The space for the "woman columnist" is almost as tightly confined in left media as it is in the mainstream press, she charged: "There's a certain amount of either sincere or lip-service acknowledgment of the culture of feminism." But the space that has been opened for feminist themes "never spills over—it's like a little river that's concrete on all sides," she said. "The discourse of feminism totally drops out when the subject isn't feminism itself." (On the other hand, if you're a woman, "you can be asked to talk about anything having to do with women, whether you know anything about it at all," Pollitt remarked.)

If progressive journalists had done a better job of integrating gender-consciousness into their analysis, they might have mounted a more effective response to the right's assault on traditionally "women's" or "feminist" issues. Instead, the right's attack on abortion, divorce and sexual diversity stimulated, at best, ambivalence. When the right vilifies divorce, Pollitt pointed out, the left responds by saying, "'We're against breaking up families....' You don't hear anyone saying, 'Hey—divorce, we need it.'" Those voices are seldom heard in mainstream media—and the silence is similar in the "alternatives."

"Separate media, Separate Movements"

Meanwhile, "feminist" publications that do air such views are frequently not on left journalism's radar. Feminists who gave up fighting to get women's issues into the pages of the male-dominated progressive media and went off to make media of their own now find themselves in "separate media, separate movements," commented Helen Zia of *Ms.* magazine.

The stories they cover are often ignored for years—not just by mainstream editors and writers, but also in the outlets of the left. Stories that appear for the first time in so-called "feminist" or "women's" outlets just don't get "buzzed about" as much as comparable stories elsewhere, said John Stoltenberg, managing editor at the women's quarterly *On The Issues.* But especially in the contemporary political climate, "Editors have a responsibility to pay attention to the feminist press and to echo it... It's not a female ghetto that you can afford to ignore."

When both mainstream and "progressive" media fail to look beyond the traditional "inside the Beltway" news frame, not only media consumers but also activists pay a price. "We need research that's useful to our movements," said Rinku Sen of the San Francisco-based Center for Third World Organizing. "And documentation of the very good organizing that exists...so that other people can see it and do the same thing." Otherwise, even important victories can be eroded through lack of nurture and attention.

Both Sen and Tara Roberts of *Essence* made the point that the concerns of young women, poor women and women of color have been under-reported in mainstream and alternative media alike. Yet those women make up the majority most affected by contemporary social and economic policy. Asking for a shift in focus is not asking for special favors from reporters, but simply calling on them to do their jobs.

"The media gets very enamored of its own reflection," commented Urvashi Vaid, author of *Virtual Equality: The Mainstreaming of Gay & Lesbian Liberation*. "And that extends to our own media as well as mainstream media.... If I hear another story in the gay press about [media mogul and gay philanthropist] David Geffen I'll vomit," Vaid declared. "We need a shift in the content...to cover working people's lives."

Women Aren't the Only Gender

The left's approach to gender itself reveals the narrow frame of much progressive debate. "Within the queer movement we've had debates about gender for years," pointed out Vaid. Yet that analysis—done by people who challenge standard models of "masculinity" and "femininity"—has been overwhelmingly ignored in the left press.

Part of the problem is that in left media, "gender issues" are still interpreted as "women's issues," commented Jackson Katz, of the Massachussetts-based group Real Men. "Focusing solely on women when it comes to gender gives men an excuse not to pay attention. Yet men are precisely the ones who have to take on these issues."

The progressive media is one place we have to discuss these issues, yet it doesn't often happen, Katz and his colleague, videomaker and educator Byron Hurt, complained. "A lot of men have never had another man challenge them on their sexism or their expression of masculinity," said Hurt—not in life, and not in media of any kind.

"We can talk for a long time about the challenges of integrating issues of gender and race into mainstream media," concluded Donna Edwards of the D.C.-based Center for a New Democracy. "But I'd like to talk about the challenge of integrating those issues into the progressive media so that...when there are hot-button issues that come up that then get pitched into the mainstream media, there is a foundation of understanding that has been laid."

As Edwards put it, the coverage of the O.J. Simpson trial was illustrative. "When it comes to a point that an issue [like domestic violence] is thrust in the mainstream media, not having laid that framework costs us dearly.... I would have liked to have had an opportunity before the last two years to lay out the issues in a way that's responsible, so that when the mainstream media is ready to pounce on an issue we're not blindsided."

Outreach to women in mainstream media might help build connections, suggested Susan Faludi, author of *Backlash*. "Things have gotten to such a pass that [activists] rein themselves in from even approaching women working in the mainstream, who may be open and at the same time feeling very isolated."

"The reaching out is critical," agreed Vaid, along with more factual analysis of how women, people of color, and lesbians and gays are advancing in mainstream and alternative media. "We also need a self-defense mechanism to respond to the right-wing's attacks on individuals and groups."

May/June 1996

Defending Our Lives

Interview with Margaret Lazarus

Defending Our Lives *is a documentary film about domestic violence. It won 1994's Academy Award for short documentaries. Despite that credential and the importance and timeliness of the issues it addresses, PBS has refused to air the film. Their explanation? The film transgresses PBS's editorial guidelines because it was co-produced by a group—Battered Women Fighting Back—that has a vested interest in its subject matter—battered women. That explanation didn't fly with media critics and activists, who have heard this kind of thing from PBS before, or with the film's producers. We have with us the film's producer, Margaret Lazarus. Why don't you tell us a little bit about the film* Defending Our Lives?

We began to make *Defending Our Lives* four years ago. Our aim was to make a film that showed the magnitude and the severity of domestic violence. It's been a problem that's been identified for a long time, but I think it's very hard for people to understand how severe and how serious a problem it is. We thought a film could visualize that in a way that would be hard to forget and hard to put out of your mind. So that was our aim.

And the film was very successful. You won an Academy Award, after all. Did you think it would kind of be a natural that PBS would pick it up?

That was our hope. Particularly because it's been identified as such an important social issue right now, an issue of great concern to everyone in this country. It's been my understanding that PBS has somewhat of a mandate to deal with things that are of interest and an issue to people in the U.S. at this time and that where other stations could perhaps focus more on entertainment, that it was the responsibility of our public airwaves to deal responsibly and face issues that are of concern to people.

So when PBS sent you their initial rejection of the film, did you immediately follow up with them?

Yes. I wrote them a letter back and said, "This is kind of crazy." Their rejection was based on what I consider an extremely erroneous assumption that this was an "advocacy" film, when in fact it was a film that was made and paid for exclusively by Cambridge Documentary Film. One of the producers that we worked with began as one of the counselors inside a prison, starting a group of nine people who were working against domestic violence. She later started an organization that worked for human rights which defined domestic violence as a human rights problem. It was hardly an "advocacy film." I don't think that advocacy films should be banned from PBS. But even under their very own definition we were not an advocacy film. So we were kind of astounded.

Their official response, at least part of it, was that there was a "conflict of interest" because one of the producers represented an organization which was also represented in the film. Is that correct?

I don't know if there was a conflict. They said there was "direct self-interest" on the part of one of the producers. And as I mentioned, this is a person who worked free for the film. The organization that she was involved in when we were making the film was literally a prison group with nine members. Later on she did found a community-based organization which included the very women in our film, but it seems to me that "direct self-interest" is defined as economic interest. Any legal opinion that we've asked says that's what that means. That's so far from what happened. Let's just even assume that she gets some money from the rental of the film, which doesn't happen, but let's assume it did, to support her community aims. The aims are to end domestic violence. It seems a specious reason for rejecting something, particularly when they underwrite shows from major corporations. But that isn't even what happened in our case. I think that was just the nearest and easiest and handiest excuse.

There's clearly no interest to be gained from this, and the only thing this film was designed to do is make people aware of what a big problem domestic violence is. If that's the "self-interest" of the group, then that's again laughable. Why should that not be a righteous aim?

July 30, 1994

PBS REJECTS
ANOTHER
OSCAR-WINNING DOCUMENTARY

PBS is refusing to run yet another Academy Award-winning documentary. This year it's *Defending Our Lives*, a film about battered women, that has been denied access to the leading national outlet for independent documentaries. Mary Jane McKinven, director of news and public affairs for PBS, rejected the film on the grounds that a co-producer of the film, Stacey Kabat, was a leader of Battered Women Fight Back, a women's advocacy group. "In order to protect the integrity of public television programming," McKinven wrote in a letter to the film's executive producer Margaret Lazarus, "the content of such programming must be free from the control of parties with a direct self-interest in that content.

PBS has often invoked such "principles" in the past—for example, when rejecting another Oscar-winning documentary, *Deadly Deception*, and when discouraging labor support for programming about working people. But such guidelines seem to be ignored when the interested party is not a public interest group or a labor union, but a for profit corporation. A few examples:

• PBS broadcast *James Reston: The Man Millions Read*, a documentary about the *New York Times'* most famous pundit, which was funded by and produced "in association with" the *Times*. The director and producer, Susan Dryfoos, is a member of the

Sulzberger family which owns the paper, and the daughter of a former *Times* publisher. Unsurprisingly, the documentary treated Reston with "admiration and respect," according to the *Times'* own review (1/8/93).

- PBS's *The Prize: The Epic Quest for Oil, Money and Power*, an eight-part, multi-million-dollar series on oil, was funded by Paine Webber, a corporation with investments in oil exploration and production. The series was based on a book by and featured as its main analyst Daniel Yergin, president of Cambridge Energy Research Associates, a consultant to major oil companies and OPEC governments. Almost every expert featured in the series was a defender of the oil industry (*EXTRA!*, 9-10/93).

- PBS ran *Living Against the Odds*, a special on risk assessment funded by the petrochemical company Chevron (*EXTRA!*, 5-6/91). Chevron must have been pleased with the program's contention that "we have to stop pointing the finger at industry for every environmental hazard."

- PBS distributes *Wall $treet Week*, a show underwritten by financial companies like Prudential Securities, Travelers and Massachusetts Financial Services—all of which have a clear interest in news about Wall Street. PBS operates under the assumption that it is acceptable for businesses to fund programs about business, but unacceptable for labor to fund programs about labor (*EXTRA!*, Summer/90).

PBS's letter said that the "perception" that shows are being "created to advance the aims of [a] group" is "as important as the fact." The *fact* is that powerful corporations often underwrite PBS shows that serve their interests. It's just non-profit public interests groups, like the battered women's group that helped make *Defending Our Lives*, that can't get their voices heard on PBS.

EXTRA! July/August 1994

Grappling with Gingrich

Interview with Amy Goodman of Democracy Now

When a reporter among the press corps disobeys the unspoken rules of Capitol Hill's media establishment, it highlights just how rarely journalists ever break ranks to confront, rather than curry favor with, people in power. Pacifica Radio's Amy Goodman broke from the pack and caused a stir. Covering Newt Gingrich's daily Speaker's Conference, she called him to account for his attack on Hillary Clinton—and the angry outburst that followed made it into the next day's news.

You've experienced the Speaker's Conference. How does that work?

It's quite a phenomenon. The former Speaker, Tom Foley, did not allow in cameras. Newt Gingrich, being a master of the mass media, decided to allow in cameras. Very often, both CNN and C-Span run it live. That is Newt Gingrich's twenty minutes in the spotlight, in the sun, every day. It's almost as if he's a conductor of symphony. It has gone very well for him. In fact, I was there at the fifty-day mark when he was evaluating all the things that the Republicans had accomplished. He ended by saying, "And I look at this institution right here and I feel the Speaker's Conference"—that's the Speaker's press conference—"has gone very well, and we'll continue it as long as it does." There we were in the Speaker's Conference, and I felt there was a feeling the journalists had of being very proud that this was working. Now they could get their sound bites for their editors and they could say they themselves asked the Speaker a question. I considered it a great insult that this institution was working so well for Newt Gingrich that he wanted to continue it. This is an insult for reporters that they are playing right along. I do not think it's worth the price that is paid to have that kind of access, to continue to be truly like props for this play that is being staged every day.

It was at the Speaker's Conference that you asked Newt Gingrich about his alleged comment calling Hillary Clinton a "bitch." Many people may have heard the sound bite, but here's the full exchange:

Amy: I have a question about tone. You were talking about that earlier. Many people are talking about what's going on in the House as a war on women, that most of the poor are women, the whole issue about reproductive rights that keeps getting raised. But this is a question not about legislation. Some say you really fired the opening salvo against women when you didn't apologize to American women for calling the First lady a bitch. Why haven't you apologized?

Gingrich: I never agreed to say anything about that. And I can't imagine you're asking this question.

Amy: Have you apologized for it?

Gingrich: I've talked to Mrs. Clinton. She understands exactly where we're at.

Amy: Why haven't you apologized to American women? Because it goes beyond calling ...

Gingrich: I never said ... I never said ... To the best of my knowledge I never said what you just said.

Amy: You're calling your mother a liar, then?

Gingrich: I'm calling you a remarkably foolish person for having that kind of a conversation here, and I am very sorry you have cared to bring what Connie Chung did back into the public arena.

You took some criticism for that question, so why don't you tell us what your thinking was behind it.

Let me put it in the context of the week. What happened in the week leading up to this, the Tuesday, Wednesday and Thursday leading up to the Friday of the Speaker's Conference? One day the Ways and Means Committee late at night was debating the issue of [welfare funding to the states], finally deciding that they would take "illegitimate" births plus the increase in abortion rate in a state, put that over live births, and if that number increased, in other words, if the abortion rate increased or the "illegitimate" births increased, that state would not get a bonus. You had this overwhelming group of white men debating how women get pregnant, particularly young women who were poor. I was very struck by this discussion with very few women involved. That was one night. Again, it was late at night. It hardly got coverage in the press the next day because it was very complicated and also it happened so late at night. This again as the press was hailing this as, so many decisions are getting passed every day, the premium seemed to be on the speed rather than on the content of what was happening. That was one day.

The next day there was a conference called in the Senate swamp, which is an area outside of the Senate, by two of the at that time 29 women who have charged Senator Bob Packwood with sexual harassment and assault, who said that it ranged from jumping them to, in several cases, ripping women's clothes off. The women were quite explicit. They were out there carrying 4,000 letters from Oregonians to the majority leader, Bob Dole, saying, "Why haven't there been Senate ethics hearing in the case of Robert Packwood?" These women risked their livelihoods, many of them Republicans working for Packwood or Republican fundraisers, risked their livelihoods in coming forward. And here the only thing they had seen was that Bob Packwood in the last two years got promoted to be head of the Senate Finance Committee, which is one of the most powerful positions in the Senate. This got almost no coverage. Also, a couple of weeks before when Gloria Steinem and the head of NOW, Patricia Ireland, put out a challenge to the Congress—If welfare is so cushy, live on a welfare check for a week! This also got almost no coverage.

Then the next day I was watching the House Appropriations Committee make their final proposals to the floor. There again, it was 8:00 at night, the debate was over an amendment, put forward by Congressman Istook from Oklahoma, saying that women should not be able to get abortions paid by Medicaid even if they've been victims of rape or incest. Anita Lowey of New York stood up and said, "You're sending this message to the country that you must have your rapist's child. You're sending this message to the country: You must have your father's child." With that, they passed the amendment. This kind of atmosphere I felt overall was just not being conveyed to the American people, no matter what the committee was. These are committees that you wouldn't think they would be talking about women, but day after day, everywhere we went, they were talking about women. So this was the setting for that question.

I did go on talk shows after that around the country. They played this interaction. But they didn't play the first two sentences. My point was, while Gingrich had been referring to "tone" earlier in the Speaker's Conference, that while you heard the question and it was, "Many are saying there's a war on women going on in Washington." The whole discussion of the poor, and most of the poor are women, the whole discussion about reproductive rights. But I didn't want to address that issue, because at a rational level I didn't think the Speaker's Conference actually is about reason. It hits people on a gut level, and it's about control. Who is controlling the discussion? I didn't want to give Newt Gingrich a chance to just hold forth, as he always did. I felt he had to be challenged at each point, and that's what a journalist's job is, not to be there as props to provide that platform. That's why I went back and forth. Some called that "badgering." I simply called that "answer the question."

Amy Goodman hosts Pacifica Radio's daily program Democracy Now.

April 4, 1995

Volunteer Slavery

Interview with Jill Nelson

*Jill Nelson is a free-lance writer whose stories appeared in the Vil-
lage* Voice *and* Essence *magazine, among others. In 1986 she took a
job at the* Washington Post. *Her experiences at the* Post *as the first
Black woman to write for their Sunday magazine became the subject of
Nelson's first book,* Volunteer Slavery: My Authentic Negro Experience. *How did you expect working in a big mainstream institution to
be different from your free-lancing and from the alternative publications
you'd worked for?*

I expected to be paid more, and that was an expectation that was
realized. I think in many ways I didn't know what to expect. I had
never done it before. It was my first real job job. But I was recruited
by the *Post*, and strongly recruited. I'm smart and have a lot of opinions, so I asked a lot of questions. I really felt when I went there
that we had all laid our cards out on the table. They knew where I
was coming from and knew who I was, and I would be treated with
respect.

*You mentioned a sense, which I think many people have had, that it
was enough for you to be there and that they didn't necessarily expect you
to do anything.*

I think that was a very clear sense that I had. As I say in the book,
I don't mind being a token. I just don't want to be an unused one. I
think that for African-American people and people of color and
women what often happens with us is when we are hired we are told
that we are being done a favor and that when white men are hired
we are told that it is a meritocracy. I think everybody is hired because
of who they are, including white guys, and I think that's fine. I think
the real issue for me and for workers in general is: Are we allowed

and encouraged to do the work we can do and are hired to do once we're in the institution? I don't want to sit around.

The very first issue of the Washington Post's *much-lauded Sunday magazine was in fact deeply problematic on a number of levels. Many people may remember, our D.C. listeners in particular, that the cover of that first issue featured a very menacing-looking figure of a Black male rapper. There was the story that went with that. What was your response to that initial issue?*

Put my couch on my back, put my daughter on the couch and get out of town. It really was. I come from a family where we were read *The Little Engine That Could* every night and "If at first you don't succeed, try, try, again." I was shocked and appalled. I thought that the paper and the editors just absolutely dropped the ball and blew it. This protest was begun the day the magazine came out, September 7th. It went on until December 9th. So it was extremely difficult for me. I was new to the city. I had people telling me, "I don't want to be interviewed by you until the controversy is resolved." Or, "You can interview me but you can't publish it until the controversy is resolved." It was really an odd feeling. I'm much more someone who is outside demonstrating against something than inside being demonstrated against. So it was tough. It was very tough. I think it had a chilling effect definitely on the magazine, and still does.

And what comes out so interestingly in the book is the way that even though that was the first issue and you are the first Black woman to be on the staff here, the community somehow sees you as somehow being accountable for the product of the Washington Post.

I think there's a real tendency for us to make individual people, Black people, responsible for all ills. It makes me crazy. You can't do it. I think it's as offensive as people who say to me, "What do Black people think about Louis Farrakhan or Jesse Jackson?" How the hell do I know what Black people think about anything? I know what I think as a thinking Black person who might think about some of these issues. But I think it's a real difficult position to be in, because you are betwixt and between your loyalties to your community, your loyalties to your job, and then the loyalties that are most important, which I believe is to yourself and your sense of integrity and dignity.

A lot of our listeners are media activists. I think they'd like to hear what sorts of protests do these outlets respond to?

I think they really respond to letters. I don't think it matters if the letter is typed and printed on a laser computer or written on a greasy sandwich bag. They have these statistics where each letter represents X number of people, so it's important to write a letter. If you don't want to do that you should call. I think it's important that people understand the structure of these institutions. You can't go up against an institution unless you understand how the institution is structured and how it functions. I think also people need to realize that often significant numbers of people who work in these institutions are supportive, are sympathetic and might even be willing to be Deep Throats.

Jill Nelson's first book, Volunteer Slavery, *is out in paperback now.*

June 25, 1994

TOO BAD TO BE TRUE

"Janet Cooke seemed too good to be true: a smart, young black woman who could write up a storm."

—Lawrence J. Goodrich, staff writer
Christian Science Monitor (12/6/95)

Virtual Equality

Interview with Urvashi Vaid

Our next guest's new book is called Virtual Equality. *There's a difference, she says, between media visibility and institutional equality, and in the pursuit of the first the strategy to get the second can get pretty confused. Urvashi Vaid has been a community organizer and an attorney for fifteen years. From 1986 to 1992 she served as public information director and then executive director of NGLTF, the National Gay and Lesbian Task Force. In 1994 she was named one of* Time *magazine's "Fifty for the Future," and now she's an author. Her new book,* Virtual Equality, *came out this month from Anchor*

In your book you sum up the idea of virtual equality. You talk about the landmark meeting that lesbian and gay political activists had with President Clinton in March of 1993. You say, "We got to sit with the President of the United States, but we were not able to prevent his cutting a deal that bargained away our civil rights." A similar sort of situation exists in mainstream media coverage. It's something that we talk about often here on CounterSpin. *Would you say that gay and lesbian people have virtual equality in the press?*

Yes. I think that we certainly have visibility in the media today to a greater extent than we did, although that tends to ebb and flow depending on the particular person in charge of the editorial content of whatever paper. But it's virtual equality, because I still don't think the straight press is covering the gay movement, gay issues, with any kind of complexity or depth. It's a kind of episodic coverage which appears whenever a particular gay person is so visibly discriminated against that they can't help but notice. But the daily reality of discrimination and violence and stigmatization and the daily grind that is our lives in the course of the AIDS epidemic is no longer being covered, quite frankly.

You make two points in Virtual Equality. *One, you go back over the history of how hard it was to get AIDS covered, the old story that we talked about on* CounterSpin *before, about how between 1981 and 1982 there were 6 stories about AIDS but 54 about contaminated Tylenol capsules. But later in the book you quote somebody saying it was much easier to get AIDS covered in fact than gay or lesbian issues covered. Where does that leave us now?*

I think both statements are in fact true. We had a heck of a time trying to get the media to notice an epidemic that was affecting poor people, Black people and gay men. Once they noticed it, they didn't want to acknowledge the fact that homophobia and racism and economic issues or poverty played a role in the epidemic and the way it was spreading. So I think both statements are true. Where it leaves us now is that there are continuing realities that come up with AIDS. The fact is that it's an epidemic that continues unabated in certain populations. We don't hear any coverage about how the Medicaid cutbacks and the welfare cutbacks are going to affect people with AIDS, which is something I'd like to know about. We don't even hear that from the gay organizations or the AIDS organizations, much less the media.

You mentioned two different approaches: legitimation and liberation. Could you define those terms? What's the difference?

Sure. The terms refer to different strategies that the gay political movement has followed. The legitimation approach argues that gay people just seek only a place at the table. The liberation approach argues that we actually want to rebuild the table and create a new society that is more democratic and more fair based on race, gender and economic situation. Legitimationists in our movement are basically pursuing a gay-rights single-issue movement strategy. The liberationists see gay and lesbian equality as intimately connected to the equality of people of color and the end of racial prejudice and the full equality of women. So that in a nutshell is the difference.

If you were to look for an alternative to the straight press, you might look to the gay and lesbian media, but you might also look to the progressive press, the Nation, Z, *the* Progressive *and so on. How do you think those magazines have done in avoiding niche coverage, or what we sometimes call "wildlife coverage"?*

I think the—if you could call it "progressive"—media, like much of the left, has been very uncomfortable with gay issues. I don't feel that the *Nation* has done that much great coverage. Andy Kopkind [a gay man] was responsible for most of the great coverage that they did. I think the *Progressive* is doing excellent coverage and integrating it into the magazine on a regular basis. But the sad thing about the progressive media is that there are fewer and fewer outlets. I think that is a huge problem as we try to rebuild a progressive movement in this country, which I think some of us are trying to do.

The gay press has moved away from seeing itself as an advocacy press and now sees itself mirroring fashion journalism, *Vanity Fair* and so on. (That's what *Out* magazine is doing. They want to be the gay *Vanity Fair*. I think that's pathetic, and they're doing a tremendous disservice to educating the country.) Or the gay presses I see, the weekly newspapers in Boston and Washington or Chicago, they're being like clipping services for the Associated Press wires. They're not doing a lot of investigative reporting. They're actually profitable enterprises. They're not really serving the community by asking hard questions, digging beneath the press releases that they get from gay organizations to write original stories. Very, very few papers do that. What I hoped to achieve with this book was to open up discussion of progressive ideas inside the gay and lesbian movement and to give non-gay people, who have only heard one kind of conservative critique from gay activists, to give progressive non-gay people the news that there is a progressive lesbian and gay community out there.

Urvashi Vaid's, new book, Virtual Equality: The Mainstreaming of Gay and Lesbian Liberation, *is available now from Anchor Books. Don't forget to check out the fly cover as well as the contents.*

BE LIKE CLINT

"Homosexuals should not be portrayed at all on TV. If young males need to identify with someone, they should identify with Clint Eastwood."

—Lou Sheldon of the
Traditional Values Coalition
(Los Angeles Times, 11/3/94)

Ask, We'll Tell

Gay and Lesbian
Independent Film and Video

*This article was commissioned by Media Network, the sponsors of a
series of films and videos by gay and lesbian filmmakers. Information can
be obtained from Media Network in NYC.*

It would be hard to find a clearer expression of the need for queer
film and video than the admonition Don't Ask, Don't Tell. The
Clinton administration's recommendation to the military for dealing with homosexuals exposes precisely the establishment's fear and
its object. Gay people can enlist, the formula allows, and continue
to participate in the armed forces as they have, as long as they don't
speak out about their sexuality.

Senator Nunn explained to a witness during the hearings on the
military's ban the difference between the showers he takes in the
gym and the ones dousing servicemen on base. The difference is,
he said, that the men in his gym "don't broadcast their sexuality."
The fearsome prospect apparently, is not conduct, but communication. Hence the power in speech, and the need for projects like those
sponsored this year by Media Network, asking and telling about gay
and lesbian lives.

The fear behind Don't Ask, Don't Tell is deeply rooted and, from
the perspective of the status-quo, well founded. After all, that's how
we got this far — by asking and telling. People of color, women,
survivors, gays... our experience is the reality that the white,
nuclear, painless social picture belies. Like the prostitute on Capitol Hill, we're in on some serious secrets involving famous folks.
Our primary power is the truth about our lives. But only if we ask,
only if we tell.

From the pamphleteers of the 18th Century to the consciousness-
raising groups of the 20th, history has jerked forward on the fuel of

provocative speech. Why else the soap box? Why else the political rally? Why else the First Amendment?

Around the world, language itself has been deemed seditious. Invading English in Ireland banned the speaking of Gaelic; Officers in British jails in Ireland still stop prisoners communicating in their own tongue. A major New York publisher once told Palestinian professor Edward Said that an Egyptian book was inappropriate for the U.S. market because Arabic was a "controversial language."

Like language, so speech: calling things by their name. World War II Philippine and Korean "comfort women" were given Japanese first names to claim them; slaves, like married women, are renamed. In this respect, gay speech—daring to talk about "the love that dare not speak its name"—has particular significance.

In straight society, most people are assumed to be heterosexual unless they say otherwise. Existing socially as queer has a lot to do with saying it. Because simply saying it breaks social assumptions, gay self-identification becomes a kind of political act; not just conveying a message, it is one. As First Amendment lawyer Nan Hunter has written in a forthcoming article, "to be openly gay, when the closet is an option, is to function as an advocate as well as a symbol." From the 1950s to the current day, the state's regulation of sexuality has always been accompanied by debate about speech.

Post World War II expulsions of gay "subversives" from federal institutions and from the nation via immigration were defended on the basis of national security. The existence of gay men and women in the armed forces, in education, in government jobs, was seen to pose a threat because the gay identity was "perversion". The illness metaphor expressed the belief that gayness was, in itself, contagious, dangerous, with or without the gay person saying or doing anything at all. "Perverts" could pollute, period. The formulation expressed the government's view that homosexual identity was synonymous with homosexual acts.

The gay movement's response ranged from fury and a demand for social change — to self-hatred and a call for tolerance. As Martin

Duberman's new book, *Stonewall*, describes, heated debates raged in the early Mattachine society over the 1950s homophile movement's goals: the changed society called for by radicals, or just a version of the same that let us in.

Through its fiscal agency program, Media Network has been able to provide non-profit status to many independent producers. MN's sponsorship of a series of works focussing on lesbian and gay lives speaks to the on-going debate over the political meaning of queer personal life. Some of the tapes recount the history of our community, like Polly Thistlethwaite's video project on the Lesbian Herstory Archive. Taking viewers back to the days when lesbians were arrested for failing to wear three mandatory pieces of clothing, the tape recalls the historic contortions into which this state has gone in an effort to control sexuality.

Some efforts, like the dress code, belong to the same tradition of absurdity as Don't Ask Don't Tell. (Don't dress, don't think?) Other episodes, like the battle over gay bars and butch-femme style, hinted at the fight to come.

For those whose goal is tolerance, gays and lesbians retain responsibility for our own acceptability — the behavior of some can threaten the treatment of the class. At the very first pickets protesting the exclusion of homosexuals from federal employment, Martin Duberman quotes Franklyn Kameny explaining in 1964 to Mattachine members: "If we want to be employed by the Federal Government, we have to look employable to the Federal Government...Clean-scrubbed demonstrations will get us ahead."

The dangerous fault outlining "acceptability" had its roots in compromise. Liberals in government and pro-tolerance homophiles found agreement on the shaky turf of "privacy." Anticipating the ridiculous Don't Ask, Don't Tell, this analysis neither condoned behavior, nor outlawed it, it simply restricted it to the private sphere. The "whatever you do in the privacy of your own home" approach. The freedom conveyed is the freedom to stay invisible and mute.

"Negative liberty," writes Hunter in reference to the privacy principle, "with its barrier between the individual and the state, coexists easily with silence."

Establishing rights on individual, rather than collective ground leaves some on safer territory than others. As with the battle over abortion, which culminated in Roe v Wade and also affirmed only those rights associated with privacy, those with safer "individual" space survive better than those who have less personal privilege (access/protection). Some gay people, like some women, don't have as many options as others—including the option of silence. "Screaming Queers" don't have to open their mouths. Butch dykes don't have to do anything. Gay bars perched awkwardly on the fence between private and public. As long as security depended on invisibility, bars' rights to operate as "private" space left patrons no protection against police raids that publicly exposed them.

Tami Gold's tape *Juggling Gender* looks at personal/political issues through the study of one woman's relationship to her identity as a woman with a beard. The juggler, Jennifer Miller's, personal story expresses something of the experience of the movement.

"I grew up not wanting to be defined as other," says Miller. Gradually she changed her mind. "I am other." And there's power in that.

"My having a beard has given me cause to be radical and courageous, and I think that's really what it takes," says Miller, in *Juggling Gender*. Piercing the illusion that freedom can be based on privacy, Jennifer talks of the power she finds — the "power from having no secrets." Like Miller, the movement has moved beyond tolerance-at-a-personal-price.

Speaking about our lives can save them. In this respect, series like the Lesbian & Gay Film Festival, the Lesbian and Gay Experimental Film Festival, films like those distributed by Women Make Movies, or the projects sponsored by Media Network are more than educational or entertaining.

Queer visibility, through "coming out," has permanently changed the world. As recently as 1987, *Parade* magazine (12/6/87) was reminiscing: "The '50s, viewed through the rosy prism of nostalgia, were the good old days... Homosexuals stayed in the closet, not on the front pages." Unfortunately for *Parade*, the closets are jammed open. And they got that way in the struggle to save gay lives.

Withheld information has always cost queer life. Nor are homosexuals the first to learn that telling our stories can save us. Consider slave narratives, the men and women who countered the notion that Black people feel duller pain than whites; the raped woman who names the father of her child. Consider the sex-worker who refuses to accept her john's version of her worth. Remember Anita Hill under oath, testifying against the president's man. Civil Rights nominee, Lani Guinier, was not allowed to ask or tell.

Heather McDonald's interviews with isolated Kiev queers in her tape, *Kiev Blue* remind us how our worlds have been changed by knowing someone out and gay and strong. And if this wasn't clear before, the deadly line between free speech and health got drawn out sharply in the 1980s effort to respond to AIDS.

In January 1986, the Reagan Administration's Centers for Disease Control declared that federally-funded educational materials produced by GMHC (Gay Men's Health Crisis) and similar AIDS service groups must use "inoffensive" language (sic). In so doing, government restrictions on safe-sex materials literally put a human price on speech. Sen. Jesse Helms took it further, with an amendment forbidding the use of any CDC funds to "provide AIDS education, information, or prevention materials and activities that promote or encourage homosexual sexual activities."

In the same year that Bowers v Hardwick confirmed states' rights to outlaw same-sex intercourse but not their right to scrutinize gay private life, Helms' amendment recommended the withdrawal of public funding from service providers who did more than advocate abstention. If gay sex could not be uniformly prohibited, he seemed to be arguing, at least the affirming of the right to enjoy it could.

The 1980s queer community's response was to come out loud. Our silence, to paraphrase the ACT-UP slogan, will lead us quietly to our death. Today, Testing the Limits, a project sponsored by Media Network, uses video to combat homophobia and increase awareness of AIDS. Testing the Limits' new series, *Rights and Reactions* tells stories—of lesbians and gay men fighting daily, for their survival. *Green on Thursdays*, a documentary by Dean Bushala and Deidre Heaslip, asks and tells about gay-bashing in Chicago.

Projects like Seeing Through AIDS talk about coming out as a health act. Media Network's Seeing Through AIDS is a series of workshops funded by Astraea, The Sister Fund, North Star and the NYC Department of Health, that take videotapes into community settings to teach strategies for educating and counselling on AIDS. Tailored for specific constituencies, women of color, lesbians and care-providers, these video workshops address empowerment and safe-sex talk as agents of social change.

Television's first monthly gay and lesbian magazine, *In The Life*, produced by John Scagliotti and sponsored by Media Network, conveys the same message. "This show is all about coming out," said Kate Clinton the first week. "Where gays and lesbians are free to be themselves, openly, honestly and without guilt," said co-host, Karen Williams. Scagliotti's first film, *Before Stonewall*, is part of a film/lecture series curated by Alan Hertzberg in association with the Donnell Public Library in New York. "Pride and Prejudice," as Hertzberg describes it: "was designed to be used as a prototype by media librarians across the country as a means of spurring interest in the subject of homosexuality while combatting the lack of information, the bigotry and the various attacks in Washington and in the media."

Attacks in the media are no news to the gay community. Groups like GLAAD (The Gay & Lesbian Alliance Against Defamation) have brought to public attention the slander of popular talk show hosts, like those on the ABC Radio network who broadcast to millions their hatred of gays and lesbians. Opinion pages around the country have long offered homophobes a platform. Horrible homosexuals have dominated Patrick Buchanan's columns: "Homosexuality involves sexual acts most men consider not only immoral, but filthy," he wrote in his widely syndicated column, (*New York Post*, 9/3/89). A year later he was claiming that "our promiscuous homosexuals appear literally hellbent on Satanism and Suicide" (10/17/90).

Condemnation in the media has accompanied assaults on media itself, and on expression. Around the same time as the CDC campaign, attacks on the National Endowment for the Arts (NEA) and PBS began focusing on queer artists and filmmakers who got federal funds. Like Helms's successful strategy, at the NEA the expression of gay identity was connected to "promotion" of homosexuality.

In 1990, Nixon speech-writer, then PBS pundit and *U.S. News & World Report* editor, David Gergen, criticized the work of NEA-funded artist Tim Miller solely because he used his work "to encourage education, understanding and eventual acceptance" of the gay community. This, in Gergen's words, amounted to "wanton destruction of a nation's values" and "decadence and blasphemy." (*USN&WR*, 7/30/90). President Clinton, May 30, 1993, announced that he had selected David Gergen to serve as his Communications Consultant. The choice says something loud about the administration's real commitment to Don't Ask, Don't Tell.

At the same time that gays and lesbians have made gains, the onslaught against us has escalated. And no wonder, quiet folk don't disturb the peace like loud ones do. In the run up to the 1992 presidential elections, the battle was declared on video. From the religious right a videotape, called *The Gay Agenda*, started playing in people's homes. Posing as a teaching tape, revealing what its producer, Bill Horn (once a CBS sportscaster), calls the "hidden" side of gay life, *The Gay Agenda* uses amateur footage from gay parades and demonstrations to bring into "America's living rooms" (Horn's target), flashy images of "scandalous" gay pride. In December, 1992, Marine Commandant General Carl E. Mundy made sure *The Gay Agenda* got distributed to every member of the Joint Chiefs of Staff. Donald Wildmon, of the American Family Association, got copies of *The Gay Agenda* to every legislator in every state that is facing anti-gay initiatives in upcoming elections. By now each senator and representative in Washington has a copy.

Playing on the discomfort that exists around gay and lesbian images and behavior, *The Gay Agenda* taps an old and delicate source. Frank Kameny's appeal for "clean-scrubbed demonstrations" thought we could avoid precisely this. But the establishment has never believed in a distinction between "being" and "doing" gay. The "in the privacy of our homes" defense simply drew the line at the living room door. Gay pride parades post *Stonewall* stormed that line from one side; Bill Horn and Co. are ramming it from the other.

Scott Nakagawa, organizer with the National Lesbian and Gay Task Force (NGLTF) makes a memorable appearance in The Gay and Lesbian Emergency Media Campaign's new tape, *Sacred Lies, Civil Truths*. Nakagawa is interviewed on the road, where he is working in states like Oregon and Colorado, Washington, Maine, New Mexico, Montana, Florida to combat anti-gay initiatives that exploit public fear of gays. The goal of the religious right is not simply to put gays back in the closet. The goal, says Nakagawa is "to dismantle the gains of the civil rights movement and the women's movement... to recreate society in the form of traditional family values...racism, sexism, neglect of the poor." The attack on gays and lesbians, as Urvashi Vaid put it to the gathered (more than the reported 300—) thousands April 25 in Washington D.C., is not about morality, but power, and equal rights.

So too, the genuine gay agenda. Speaking out as visible, audible, multiple, diverse and gay has always been about more than defending private sexual activities. The radical part was always about broad, social change. The "true civil rights coalition," that Nakagawa tells GLEMC the lesbian and gay community must build, must establish that "human equality is not something that can be compromised, voted on, discussed or debated." The founding men and women of Mattachine said the same.

Confronting homosexuality in all its public significance makes us uncomfortable for the same reason coming out is hard. For his appearance on *In The Life*, playwright and actor David Drake chose an excerpt from his play "The Night Larry Kramer Kissed Me" that made the point. His parents, once he told them he felt gay, were quick to offer their condolences: "We don't care, We don't care." They freaked out when he said "I do."

Poet Muriel Rukeyser once wrote that a woman telling her story would be "a world split open." In an African language "Gamba Adisa"—"to make her meaning known," means warrior. No wonder that the Clinton crew and the religious right would rather we didn't ask or tell. No wonder poet Audre Lorde took Gamba Adisa for her name.

Heather McDonald's tape, *Kiev Blue*, paints a picture of Ukraine gay ("blue") life shortly before the repeal of Article 121, outlawing male homosexuality. (Russia repealed its 1960 anti-homosexual ban 5/28/93.) Now comes "the hard part," Ukrainian Eddie writes to Heather, "Finding within ourselves some sense of personal freedom."

In this country too, the hard part is confronting the habit of apologizing that makes us nervous when the "flamboyant" queers go by (or get shown on video next door). Self hatred has taught us to be thankful to be allowed to live a quiet life. It does split the world when we are more than apologetic. If we were truly to believe that each life was equal to each and every other, we'd be forced as a society, and as individuals, to make some serious change.

"One of the most damaging things gay and lesbian people can do is not let the world know who we are," says Donna Redwing, of Oregon No on 9, the civil rights coalition that defeated an anti-gay initiative in that state November, '92. Series like Media Network's new set of sponsored projects show that it's too late for Don't Ask, Don't Tell. Today, it's the religious right who are fielding "stealth" candidates; who advocate hiding who they are.

Someone should tell them it doesn't work. Ask, we'll tell.

Reprinted by permission of ImMEDIAte Impact

May 31, 1993

Part VII

Real Majority

Reporting on the world as if women matter is not only right—it's good journalism. When women talk, they tend to open a door to the heart of the story. Besides, as the Red Queen told Alice: "It's ridiculous to leave all the conversation to the pudding." (*Through the Looking Glass*)

Hard Cases and Human Rights

With Catharine MacKinnon
in the City of Freud

Catharine MacKinnon fit in perfectly at the United Nations World Conference on Human Rights this June. The historic gathering in Vienna cultivated precisely the kind of panic-mode polemics in which the U.S. antiporn litigator excels. "Catharine MacKinnon Will Speak" is all the fliers in the corridor said, and roughly 500 people turned up to hear her take on the violation of women's human rights in Bosnia and Herzegovina. When she left, so did her mostly U.S. and European audience. No one from MacKinnon's crowd stayed on afterward to listen to the women from southern Sudan, whose workshop followed. "Please stay," the two African speakers pleaded from the platform. "We have a story of rape too." But as they started their presentation, only a handful of Sudanese supporters remained behind.

Getting an audience in Vienna was no small feat. Twenty-five years after the last such event, the conference was besieged by more than 2,000 human rights groups all battling to have a say in the world's definition of right and wrong. Their targets were the delegates from 160 countries who were mustered to draft a 1990s addendum to the UN's canon on human rights.

The UN authorities grudgingly made facilities available to the nongovernmental organizations (N.G.O.s), but those who produced the show decided early on that these unofficial players would get only bit parts. The first week was dominated by talk of who was to be physically allowed into the conference center (not the Dalai Lama, not the Committee for the Defense of Human Rights in Iran), where they could go (upstairs with the governments or only downstairs with the N.G.O.s) and what they could say to whom (no naming of abusive states permitted).

Almost immediately, the conference Drafting Committee voted

to eject N.G.O.s, and the press, from "sensitive" meetings. A complex system of colored I.D. cards separated the cool N.G.O.s from the uncool. And even downstairs, where nonprofit groups were crammed tight, attendance at the rights conference guaranteed no right whatsoever to be heard.

As a result, high drama won. Activists plastered every inch of the hall's wall space with propaganda. Nowhere could the eye alight without being assaulted by the image of a body in pain. One man took to trudging the corridors with an enlarged color photograph of someone he said had been boiled alive. Another display detailed the procedure for removing a prisoner's toenail. Suffering became a commodity to contrast and compare.

Against this backdrop women made some remarkable gains. With day-long hearings, strategy meetings and demonstrations, women's groups succeeded in getting their voices amplified above the din. Nearly every official speaker felt called upon to tip his (mostly his) hat in acknowledgment of women's rights, and many of the demands of the N.G.O. Women's Caucus, an ad hoc committee that organized to make recommendations to the conference, were integrated into the official Vienna Declaration. Even the *New York Times* hailed women as "easily the strongest and most effective lobby" at the meeting.

The strength of the women lay in their advance planning. More than two years ago an international coalition came together to strategize for Vienna. Having succeeded in getting women's rights on the official agenda, the tactic at the conference was pressure— enough to get articles particularizing women's rights adopted by the government delegates. To that end, an all-day tribunal on violence against women was organized. In the presence of four judges, more than two dozen women gave personal testimony about abuse at the hands of their husbands and boyfriends, their governments, their legal systems, national armies, guerrilla groups and their fathers.

"When I heard Bok Dong Kim, I felt a terrible void in my soul because what happened to the Korean 'comfort women' during

World War II is still happening to women today," said Fadil Mesmis-ervic, a Croatian.

"Consider a regime that institutionalizes the size of the stone that one should use to kill women...That's what we're up against," exclaimed Khalida Messaoudi from Algeria.

One of the more devastating testimonies came from a young New Jersey woman whose stepfather had systematically raped her for four years, saying that she required "special treatment" or she would die.

The event began with Charlotte Bunch, director of the Center for Women's Global Leadership (based at Rutgers University) and coordinator of the women's coalition, dropping hundreds of pages of signatures symbolically at the feet of the UN officials upstairs. The petition, in twenty-one languages and sponsored by 950 organizations worldwide, bore 500,000 names, all calling for the UN dignitaries to pay attention to women's rights.

"Women are tearing down the wall of silence that has prevented the world from recognizing our human rights," she said. Tear it down they did, or at least they tried. As one of the tribunal's judges, Ed Broadbent, a former Canadian M.P. turned human rights and development leader, pointed out, echoing something women have known for generations, when women speak, men mostly leave the room. During the tribunal the auditorium was predictably packed with women, but few men.

If that was standard, another aspect of the event was exceptional. The tribunal was one of the few meetings in Vienna in which there seemed to be no ranking of oppressions. One woman's horror was heard at equal volume to the next: All these things have occurred, are occurring, have elicited these responses...The quality of the consensus did not drown out the differences.

Bunch says that the focus on violence against women was chosen with this specifically in mind. Speaking to *UNIFEM News*, the newsletter of the UN development fund for women, she traced her global strategy back more than ten years—to the 1980 Copenhagen World Conference for Women. "There I was struck by the fact that in the workshops dealing with violence against women, there was little conflict between women from the North and the South," she said. "I had the strongest sense that women shared a common experience around violation in their lives."

But there is beauty and a beast in making violence a unifying theme. In a global women's movement rent by class, race, age and national divisions, the experience of violence provides powerful common ground. It's also sexy: sexier than labor rights, illiteracy, self-determination or poverty. The Vienna conference certainly demanded a clear, preferably dramatic, profile. If the story's gruesome enough, the mainstream media may come along. What bleeds, as the familiar press maxim has it, leads. And if you can target sex and violence together, you might just get the cover.

Kathleen Barry, who worked with Bunch a decade ago (they split in the mid-1980s), has long understood the impact and political utility of organizing around sexual abuse. The author of *Female Sexual Slavery*, Barry hosted her own day-long event on the topic "Sexual Exploitation of Women: A Violation of Human Rights." It was sponsored by the Coalition Against Trafficking in Women (which Barry directs), the Third World Movement Against Sexual Exploitation of Women, the International Abolitionist Federation, several others, and UNESCO.

"We're moving away from the traditional, patriarchal distinctions between free and forced prostitution," Barry declared to the press. In recent decades, she said, increases in global prostitution have been accompanied by intensive campaigns to legitimize it by promoting these "false distinctions."

The purpose of Barry's hearing was to introduce a "Convention on the Elimination of All Forms of Sexual Exploitation" for consideration by the UN General Assembly. It states, "The sexual exploitation of any woman is the sexual degradation of all women," and its Article 6(d) predictably holds liable "the producers, sellers, and distributors of pornography."

Fear of the sex industry is no new trend in feminism. The International Abolitionist Federation, for instance, has made its living from social purity drives dating back to the days when "white slavery" was the theme. Anima Basak, president of today's I.A.F., expressed her group's Victorian approach when she exclaimed that poverty—while "certainly one of the main causes"—is "not the only cause" of prostitution. We also have to talk, she said, about "morality and values."

Shocking testimony about sexual trafficking and sexual slavery came off Barry's stage in an uninterrupted flow. Asian and Pacific women were particularly moving in their description of systematic abuses. But there was no debate on Barry's central thesis. Nor was there any interjection from the floor voicing concern that some women should seek to proscribe what some others call their choices; no one from Feminists for Freedom of Expression or any other defender of free speech.

Dorchen Leidholdt, co-author of *The Sexual Liberals and the Attack on Feminism*, associate director of the Coalition Against Trafficking in Women, announced "a great victory for this movement" after the Women's Working Group revised its recommendations and eliminated the term "forced prostitution," replacing it with "sexual exploitation" (a change that occurred with no discussion). The words "sexual exploitation" were duly integrated into the official Vienna Declaration.

To have stood up and challenged the direction of Barry and her colleagues' rhetoric would have taken some Amazonian strong will. It's hard to talk in critical yet subtle terms to a panel made up largely of Third World sex-trade victims, older nuns and moral champions.

It was the same way with MacKinnon. In her fly-by appearance in Vienna, she told her rapt listeners about a fax she said she received last year. "There are news reports and pictures here," she read from the fax, which came to her from Croatia, "of Serbian tanks plastered with pornography...Some massacres in villages as well as rapes and/or executions in camps are being videotaped as they are happening." The systematic rape of women in the war in Bosnia and Herzegovina is, MacKinnon said, "a violation of women's humanity of unprecedented visibility and priority." On that she's right, particularly with respect to visibility. (Her article "Turning Rape Into

Pornography: Postmodern Genocide" got the cover of *Ms.* this summer.) Those who attended her presentation appeared to concur. The Bangladeshi women didn't stir even when she said that rape for forced pregnancy and detention camps for pregnant Bosnian women were "unprecedented" in world history. Yet Pakistani men raped Bangladeshi women in the early 1970s and forced their pregnancies, holding them in detention camps to give birth to "true Muslims."

Perhaps people grow silent in the presence of MacKinnon because her technique is to terrorize. If you're not with her, you're against her—part of what she calls, in relation to Bosnia and Herzegovina, "the feminist whitewash." The whitewashers are those who have failed, she says, to emphasize sufficiently the specifically Serbian atrocities. "The cluck-clucking about abuses on all sides," she said in Vienna, "reminds me of the way that women are blamed for getting ourselves raped."

There was not, one can assume, a person in the room who wasn't desperately concerned about the situation in Bosnia and Herzegovina. Yet MacKinnon's hyperbole cast all those who took a different approach from hers as blamers of the victim. Her style is effective because it combines force with drama and an immediate solution. The Bosnian and Croatian groups she has chosen to work with reflect that style: Militant, patriotic Zagreb-based groups that refused, for example, to engage in a discussion of joint Croatian/Serbian violations, at that point just coming to light. She is bringing a criminal case against Bosnian Serb strongman Radovan Karadzic.

In one N.G.O. workshop, women were driven to tears. Members of Bosnian and Croatian women's organizations fresh from the war zone barely a half-hour's flight from Vienna repeatedly called for "action now to close down the rape camps and stop the genocide." Several troubled Northern Europeans involved in peace and justice work finally asked the speakers to clarify: What sort of action? By whom? "If we call for intervention, what shall we tell our sisters in Somalia, in El Salvador?" asked Ellen Diederich of the German Women's Peace Archive. Katya Gattin from Zagreb's Kareta Feminist Group (one of MacKinnon's clients) replied, equally frustrated,

"You have your dilemmas about feminism and pacifism; discuss it at home, your safe home. Our lives are at stake and we don't see any point in asking who, why, what."

The strategy and tactics of those women's groups that lobbied in Vienna paid off. The Vienna Declaration of June 25 includes nine paragraphs on "The Equal Status and Human Rights of Women." But the conference had an easier time with women's human rights than it did with equal status. Of the recommendations from the Women's Caucus, those that addressed violence mostly got accepted. Those that dealt with poverty and development did not. The Women's Caucus asked for the appointment of a special rapporteur to investigate "violence and its causes;" the world conference recommended one on violence. Moreover, the caucus made a special point of requesting that women's rights and concern for gender-based discrimination be woven into the fabric of the Vienna Declaration throughout. In almost every case, those suggestions were ignored.

Given a choice between humanity and equality, the world conference gulped down humanity (it was force-fed). But getting women recognized as victims was never the hardest part. Equality is the sourer to swallow—for women activists as well as the (mostly) men upstairs. (Which is not to say that even all forms of violence were recognized: Declaration drafters rejected the suggestion that wife-beating, for example, should be judged a harmful customary practice.)

The anti-permissive, pro-control, pro-action-now approach of the new Victorian feminists seems suited to the dominant current in international affairs. its one-woman-equals-all, for-us-or-against-us ideology translates well into potentially global codes—far better than the feminism that emphasizes education above control and social mobilization over social regulation. The universe of the first group is finite: right versus wrong. There's not much space for difference. Even raising questions can get one characterized as enemy, pimp or rapist. That way lies feminist fundamentalism, and possibly more.

The world conference delegates talked of human rights and saving lives as they passed TV monitors broadcasting footage of the U.S. airstrike on Mogadishu. The irony barely surfaced as teatime talk. Today's UN is not an impartial register of global horror and good intentions. Post-Soviet Union, post-Iraq, the potency of the single-superpower UN has a lot of people worried. In that context, it was not just unfortunate that to be seen and heard at the world conference demanded the simplest, most dramatic picture human rights groups could find. It was scary. As was the absence of the full diversity of the women's movement. And if women really came to the city of Freud to address his famous question "What do women want?" some of their answers were equally disturbing.

Reprinted with permission from the Nation *magazine.*
Copyright © 1993

J'Accuse!

The woman in the tight, red kerchief opens her eyes wide and spreads her palms across the kneecaps of the women sitting by her side. "Since the Thursday before the arrival, I didn't sleep," she says. In the days after the restoration of ousted president Jean Bertrand Aristide, Haitians talk of "the arrival" like the Second Coming: no need to clarify who has arrived. "I didn't expect to eat better or be healthier suddenly, but he'd be back," the kerchiefed woman explains. "It's like my dead brother, or my dead father or a whole dead generation returning." Another woman describes the arrival of President Aristide as a birthing: "As I watched TV and waited, I put a belt around my stomach to stop my insides coming out. It felt like labor."

The women are speaking with U.S. visitors in a bright yellow-tiled room in northern Port-au-Prince. Brought together by one of Haiti's largest women's groups, Solidarite Fanm Ayisyèn (SOFA), they are talking about the future for women in wake of the arrival. Their visitors, myself included, are here with MADRE, a 20,000-strong U.S. women's group that has been sending aid to SOFA for the past 12 months.

The Haitians are old and young, from fifteen years of age to over sixty; political activists and friends of activists, market traders, domestic workers, peasants, professionals, daughters, wives; they are fifty of the hundreds of women who were raped by anti-Aristide terrorists in the last months of their country's most recent military regime. It wouldn't be unreasonable to measure the success of the U.S. intervention by the extent to which these women's abusers are brought to justice. But right now, the woman in the kerchief and her friends are celebrating.

A young market trader in a blue-check dress describes taunting an anti-Aristide thug who lives in her neighborhood on the day of the president's return. She dug out of hiding all the photographs of

Aristide never found by the Macoutes (a generic term for the agents of the dictators). "I was surprised I was still alive," she said. "But now I told him: You can kill me but you can't scare me because my husband is coming."

The impossible has happened in Haiti: President Aristide has come home. And like the tiny, wrinkled photos of the ousted president that people here have somehow perilously preserved, the dream of justice that successive military regimes have tried to eradicate is back and, miraculously, alive.

"Our first goal is to bring the men who attacked us to trial," said one of the raped women. "The next is to make sure it never happens again."

SOFA was founded eight years ago. At their last public meeting, they estimate that 3,000 women from all over Haiti were represented. Since the coup, they've had to work more discreetly, but they've worked. SOFA members in Port-au-Prince help market vendors establish credit collectives. In the countryside, the group tries to offer health care and literacy and political education sessions in the privacy of people's houses, out of sight.

The last time I was in Haiti was in early 1993. Then, the streets were hushed and atypically empty. From my bed, I could hear shooting. Twice in a week the morning revealed dead bodies in the hotel drive.

On this trip, things are different. Just one week to the day after Aristide flew into Port-au-Prince, the streets of the capital are teeming with recent returnees. Beneath almost every tree, skinny street vendors hawk fruit, fish, shoe leather, or sugar cane. Exiles from the city are gradually reappearing, and after dark, where recently there were only gunshots and their results, now there are young people laughing and bent-over women walking slowly hand in hand.

There's a sense of the extraordinary having happened, a sort of suspension of disbelief. But as the days pass, reality re-emerges. In a reference to a coup official's comment that the ousted president could no more return to Haiti that a laid egg could be put back inside a chicken, the city walls have paintings of large eggs being inserted into chickens; sometimes the hand doing the inserting is covered with stars and stripes. It's not an image many women would have come up with, but it's a statement about the restoration. Everyone knows the egg can't go back into the chicken, but people are clear there's been a miracle.

In his first public address, delivered from behind a three-inch-thick bullet-proof shield on the steps of the presidential palace, Aristide called the women of Haiti "real women," and "queens." "Given all the tribulations of life," said Aristide, "the women of Haiti are always there." The crowd—those crushed against the palace gates to hear, and those watching on TVs dragged into dusty neighborhood streets—sent up a cheer. One of those cheering was a powerful, dark-skinned woman in a brilliant blue shiny dress who attended our meeting. In her enthusiasm, she says, she picked up a neighbor and twirled her in the air. "When I heard Aristide talk about the Haitian women, I felt huge inside. I said to myself, yes, we are the Haitian women. We are beautiful and we are strong."

The woman in blue, we'll call her Geraldine, also knows about tribulation. Early in the morning of February 4, 1994, when she was sleeping with her husband, seven men knocked on the door. Two of the raiders appeared to be civilians, but three were dressed in army uniform, and two more wore the blue outfits of the Haitian police. In front of her husband and four of her kids, the soldiers raped her and then raped her daughters. "They put guns to their ears and forced them to lie down...." Among the weapons the men were carrying, she remembers an Israeli Uzi, several U.S. AK47 rifles and some 45s. "My tongue was filling up my mouth, I was spitting blood, mute."

Geraldine is not mute now. She talks about her 31-year-old niece, a guest, who scrambled out a window when the gang arrived. The young woman's body turned up three weeks later in a common dumping ground. Geraldine's husband has been disabled ever since that night. The beating he received caused permanent damage to his kidneys. But Geraldine is talking about the need for justice. So is the woman in the red kerchief, and the woman in the blue-check dress. Along with the other women of SOFA, the women in the rape group are clear that individual empowerment needs to be followed by social change.

"We feel better, but we're not actually better off," one woman said. "Aristide is a leader and an inspiration," says another. "But he cannot be everywhere. We need to be our own Aristides."

Achieving Justice

One of the priorities for the women in the room is bringing their abusers to trial. Another is changing Haitian law. At present, explained Evelyn, a third-year law school student and one of SOFA's coordinators, "We have no structure for justice for rape." By current law, the punishment for rape is compensation: Offenders are usually required to pay a fine. An alternative is an offer of marriage to their victims. "Rape is still treated as an honor crime," said Evelyn.

In the wake of recent history, it was hoped that Haitian offenders could be tried under an international code. A few years ago the world's attention was drawn to Bosnia, where horrific tales of systematic rape inspired some women to call for war crimes tribunals. At that time, the commander of the Bosnian Serbs, Radovan Karadjic, was charged with international offenses including mass rape because, it was argued, the crimes were committed under his authority and with his implicit consent. More recently, Korean so-called "comfort women" won compensation from the Japanese government, whom they charged with responsibility for the mass rape and forced prostitution of Korean women during World War II.

Nancy Kelly, part of the MADRE delegation, is a lawyer with the Immigration and Refugee program at Harvard Law School. "If we can get an international body to recognize rape as an act of torture, that could change things for women all over the world." So far, there has been no action in the Bosnian case. In the case of Haiti, a new initiative has been launched.

On September 26, a formal "Country Conditions Complaint" about Haiti was presented to the Inter-American Commission of Human Rights of the Organization of American States (OAS) by MADRE, the International Women's Human Rights Law Clinic at the City University of New York Law School, the Haitian Women's Advocacy Network, the Center for Constitutional Rights, and the Immigration and Refugee Program at Harvard Law School, among others.

"What we found, compiling the research of very many groups," said Nancy Kelly, "is a consistent pattern of abuse by members of the Haitian military, the police and armed auxiliaries." Women of all sorts were targeted "because they were politically involved themselves, or because members of their family were, or because they were working with women, sustaining civilian life. Others were attacked simply because they were women."

Between February and July of 1994, UN-OAS human rights monitors reported 77 cases of rape, 55 of which involved female activists or close relatives of male activists. Some women's organizations in Haiti reported counting as many as 18 rapes in a single day. The OAS complaint contains the testimony of over 100 women, some of whom were forced to witness the rape or murder of their children before being raped themselves. In one case, a fifteen-year-old boy was forced to rape his mother.

A favorable decision at the OAS regarding rape in the case of Haiti could have tremendous repercussions in the legal world. Unfortunately for the women of Haiti, it seems unlikely the OAS will consider the case anytime soon.

But there are, as we go to press, approximately 20,000 U.S. troops in Haiti. It wasn't totally unrealistic for some women to expect that the armed forces would be used to apprehend abusers. After all, President Clinton did emphasize rape when he addressed the public in a televised speech intended to convince Americans of the need for U.S. military action, after months in which his administration downplayed human rights reports.

"Haiti's dictators, led by General Raoul Cédras, control the most violent regime in our hemisphere," declared the president. "International observers discovered a terrifying pattern of soldiers and policemen raping the wives and daughters of suspected political dissidents."

The "New" Old Police

But a month after U.S. troops descended on Haiti, the women of SOFA see no evidence that the young GIs are intent on bringing murderers and rapists to trial. When the troops first arrived, "the people were very brave and the Macoutes were running scared," explained Anne Marie Coriolon, one of SOFA's directors. "Gradually though, there's been a change. People are beginning to realize that the Macoutes still have arms and they're not about to be disbanded."

"The people turn criminals over to the U.S. troops, and then we see them back on the streets in three days or less," said another woman. "We were told the U.S. troops were here to disarm the criminals, but that's not what's going on."

Spokespeople for the U.S. armed forces acknowledge holding only between 30 and 40 men in detention during the period immediately following the Aristide restoration. "It's not our responsibility to judge who's guilty," one young GI from California explained. "We're just here to keep the peace, not to get involved. Unless we see someone committing a crime in front of us, or doing something to threaten U.S. security, we've been told to leave them alone."

Lunching in a restaurant in Petionville, the wealthy district of Port-au-Prince, we witnessed a crowd growing in front of a nearby police station. An American military police lieutenant, sitting patiently in the cab of a dusty armored transport vehicle, explained that his unit was choosing policemen who were considered eligible for retraining. Under the U.S. plan, the current Haitian army, which includes the police, is to be replaced by an armed force of about 1,500 and a police corps of 7,000 to 10,000. But many men will be the same. A new academy has been established for retraining the "old" police, "professionalizing" them through the U.S. International Criminal Investigations Training Assistance Program (a project funded by the FBI). The "new" police will then be returned to their old neighborhoods.

How many of the Petionville police had been selected for retraining? "Them all," according to the lieutenant. "It will be easy enough to re-integrate the rest," he said. "I've seen them walking in their neighborhoods, smiling and shaking hands with people. I don't think there'll be any trouble."

The SOFA women were not surprised. On the day of Aristide's return a young boy spotted the thug who had forced him to rape his mother and, with the help of a crowd, turned the accused man over to U.S. troops, SOFA's Anne Marie Coriolon remembered. There is no guarantee that man will be held. "If he's released, then what?" asks Coriolon. "That little boy's life is in danger." So far, none of the women in the rape support group coordinated by SOFA has dared come forward to identify their assailants to the U.S. troops.

Another option is to hold the leaders of the anti-Aristide regime accountable for the actions of their men. According to the women who met with MADRE, most of the assailants came masked, but the thugs usually wore recognizable uniforms, or they announced they were with the Front for Haitian Progress and Advancement (FRAPH), a right-wing paramilitary group. "They wanted us to know who they were," one woman explained. "That was part of the point."

But the likelihood of any of the paramilitary leaders being brought to trial in connection with the rapes is slim. On October 5, the U.S. forces organized a press conference for FRAPH's leader, Emmanuel Constant. "They gave him the sound system, brought him in a U.S. vehicle, protected him while he spoke and drove him away at the end," said Coriolon. A reporter from *Haiti Info*, a Port-au-Prince-based newsletter, asked U.S. embassy spokesman Stanley Schrager how he (and Clinton) could call FRAPH "terrorist" and "anti-democratic" one day and protect their leader the next? "Life's bizarre...things change all the time," said Schrager, explaining that the U.S. now considers FRAPH a legitimate political party. The October 24 issue of the *Nation* was more enlightening: It revealed that the CIA had been instrumental in setting up the paramilitary group and that Constant was on their payroll at the time of the coup.

Business As Usual?

As the news crews started leaving Haiti, businessmen began arriving. At the airport on October 21, an English engineer was heard explaining to a customs official that his company had plans for him to stay six months. "Haiti's open for business," announced the *Miami Herald* less than a month after October 15. Haitian commerce minister Louis Dejoie assured U.S. executives that "Haiti is going to roll out the red carpet," at a conference in Miami.

To the women of SOFA, the revival of business as usual in Haiti means a return for women (the majority of industrial workers) to the sub-poverty Haitian wage ($.14/hr.). Plans from Aristide's first term in office to double the minimum wage have been abandoned. According to the *Multinational Monitor*, Aristide's administration gave in to pressure from the World Bank and the International Monetary Fund on that issue before August of 1994. Now an estimated $800 million in multilateral (mostly U.S.) aid has been promised to Haiti, and local people suspect there are some strings attached. To Jane Regan of *Haiti Info*, the massive influx of money slated for "elections assistance" and "stability" is tantamount to an "invisible invasion." "The intent of many of these programs," writes Regan, "is to counter the democratic and popular movement's demands for radical economic change and social justice."

"It's our responsibility," says Vivian Stromberg, "to not let the U.S. presence redirect Haitian democracy. If we're serious about meeting the needs of people, we have to be serious about supporting the organizations they themselves have set up to respond to those needs. We have to listen to the Haitians."

Listening Up

The day before the MADRE group returned to New York, they listened. At the appointed site for testimony collection, a kindergarten in a popular neighborhood called Martissant, MADRE workers were greeted by dozens of small children in blue-bib uniforms. As they walked into the whitewashed building, Nancy Kelly said she was expecting to see a handful of women, perhaps five or six, inside. But behind the classroom door, on tiny kiddie-chairs, their knees bent almost to their ears, 23 women sat waiting.

Kelly reminded the Haitians, again, there was no insurance that adding their testimonies to the OAS complaint would have any direct result. "It's especially unlikely that any damages or compensation would ever come your way....But the Haitian women have a lot to teach. Women have played a key role here and could play a key role internationally if your cases convince the OAS to recognize the severity of rape."

Despite the risks, the women testified in detail, describing their attackers, streets, dates, times of day. Some had been raped in front of their children, some alone; some in their own homes, some in abandoned shacks. Some had been forced to submit in order to protect their kids. Geraldine told her story, angry but confident that change was on its way. The woman in the kerchief told hers: she hadn't been political, she said, but everyone knew she supported Aristide, "because I talked about him all the time." The last testimony came from a fifteen-year-old with the family name of "Darling"—a tiny, stick-boned child clutching a piece of chalk in her right hand. Her mother, big eyes welling in a smooth, walnut-colored face, leaned towards her, hands reaching out for her daughter's. By the end, both mother and daughter, and also translator, reporter, and all the women from MADRE were in tears. The tragedy of the tale was one thing; more moving even than the stories was the women's courage to talk.

Reprinted with permission of ON THE ISSUES:
The Progressive Woman's Quarterly, *Spring 1995,*
copyright ©1995 by Choices Women's Medical Center, Inc.
To subscribe to ON THE ISSUES, *call 1-800-783-4903, M-F 9am-8pm*

Fruit of the Loom's Seedy Deal

Irish Labor Ripe for Picking

Maquiladora—there's no Gaelic equivalent for the Spanish word yet, but the idea is translating into Irish just fine for U.S. corporations looking for a foothold in the European market.

Crouched on the bayshore of northern Donegal, the entry to Buncrana is marked by a municipal welcome sign which boasts that this small Irish town is twinned with Campbellsville, Kentucky.

Along with small-town solidarity, what the two communities share is an intimate relationship with the garment maker Fruit of the Loom. On St. Patrick's Day this year, a huge truck pulled out of the low-lying Buncrana plant and lumbered into town. Small girls in traditional dress danced gingerly on the flatbed. To their left, Irish flags fluttered green and gold; to the right, stars and stripes. Above the girls, their audience, and the waiting traffic, the bold apple-and grape logo stood out, familiar to underwear-wearers around the world.

Fruit of the Loom set up shop in Buncrana five years before Western Europe opened up as a free-trade zone. The company bought a local outfit, enlarged the site, and opened a manufacturing plant to spin yarn imported from the United States into underwear and other clothing. A few years later, the company announced plans to pair its southern Irish operation with a couple of spinning plants in the British-controlled North. Now yarn for the manufacturing shop in Buncrana comes directly from Derry ("Londonderry" to the British) less than thirty miles away across the border.

"We have no doubt that as in Donegal, we will find people in Northern Ireland who are equally good at adapting to our production processes," declared William Farley, company chair, in 1990. "I also have no doubt that our investment in Northern Ireland will achieve the same success as our plants in the Republic of Ireland."

He was not wrong. Since 1989, Fruit of the Loom's international sales of "active wear" have almost tripled, according to the company's 1993 year-end report. By acquiring local facilities and building new plants within the European trade zone, Fruit of the Loom reached 350 million potential buyers and got local taxpayers' money to do it. Because of the dismal employment situation in both places, the Irish Republic and the British government wooed Fruit of the Loom with grants for employee training and the acquisition of property and equipment.

"When it was announced that Fruit of the Loom were to open a factory, there was great rejoicing," says journalist and veteran organizer Eamonn McCann, over a pint glass filled with water in Derry's popular Dungloe pub. "Now that we have the factory open and it's in production, if you go and talk to the workers at Fruit of the Loom, you will find that many of them want out of the factory. They don't like working there because they're not treated with any dignity there. They're not treated with any dignity there because the Fruit of the Loom company was given to understand that if they came to Derry, so grateful would the people of this area be for their presence, that they could treat us any way at all."

Workers were too nervous about reprisals to permit themselves to be identified, but they say the situation in the Derry plants is dire. "Women are leaving every week," says one. "Just getting up and going." Approximately 2,000 workers, most of them female, are paid according to how much they produce. "You have to do 100 per cent of the quota before you get paid in full," one worker says. A similar situation exists in the Irish Republic. Some employees reported being kept after hours, unpaid, until they met their quota. Starting pay is eighty-nine pounds (about $148) a week, with percentage increases based on piece work. "It's a company union," a long-time employee shrugged. "Nothing's been done for us by them."

In fact, according to McCann, the Dublin-based union that represents Fruit of the Loom employees (SIPTU, the Service, Industrial, Professional, and Technical Union), signed a contract with

Farley Industries before the plants in Derry were even built. The workers discovered that they were members when they saw a dues deduction taken from their wage.

"This is a top-down agreement of a classic and most vicious sort," says McCann, who claims the contract contains a no-strike clause. When asked about the deal, SIPTU officials in Derry recommended that reporters "talk to management."

The Northern Irish situation is peculiar because of the particular political problems the region faces, but in broad outline, it's familiar. Troubles or no troubles, Northern Ireland is increasingly being promoted as a place where international corporations can find cheap labor and a disciplined and docile work force.

"I think it's perfectly possible that we will have a political settlement here that will leave behind a great mass of economic and human-rights problems," says McCann. "Indeed, I think that's what political establishments all around are aiming at."

Richard Needham, Northern Irish Minister for the Economy, met Fruit of the Loom chairman William Farley on an airplane during a trip to the United States and talked the Chicago businessman into coming to war-wounded Northern Ireland. "It was his salesmanship that persuaded us," says Farley. That, and a handful of cash. As of December 31, 1993, Fruit of the Loom acknowledged receiving about $43.5 million in grants from the Republic and $42.1 million from the United Kingdom. In return, approximately 2,700 workers in Donegal and Derry got low-paying jobs, and British bureaucrats got a glimpse of what they're calling the "peace dividend"—the economic investment some believe will flow into the North once the political conflict there is calmed.

"Derry's a place where U.S. firms can have a foothold in Europe with certain advantages," explained John Keanie, Derry City town clerk and chief executive of the city council. He lists the selling points: a common language, the availability and price of land for development, and the low cost of labor. As municipal public-relations man, Keanie seeks international investment, and Fruit of the Loom is a coup he calls "delightful." From his oak-paneled room surrounded by the stained-glass windows of Derry's historic City Hall, he gushes about the future.

"I know it sounds like a bit of jargon, but we love to talk here about the peace dividend, and I think the peace dividend for the people here in the North would be more and more jobs."

Keanie goes further: "We're not going to wait until peace happens; we're working on it now." What's great about Fruit of the Loom, he says, is that it straddles the North/South divide, helping Derry establish itself as a regional power.

"We're all in the European Union now," says Keanie. "While the border is a political reality, of course, economically it's just not a big feature anymore."

It's not quite what civil-rights activists in Derry had in mind when they marched on the same City Hall in 1968 and 1969. The injustices then were clear, says Eamonn McCann. Then, the problems had to do with a British-backed system that deprived most Catholics of good housing, jobs, and any say in local power. One of the big triggers was discrimination in hiring and the domination of trade unions by powerful, anti-Catholic conservative blocs.

Today, in terms of housing distribution and quality, Northern Ireland has seen vast improvements. Although neighborhoods are as segregated as ever, people on both sides of the political divide live in better housing stock than they did in 1968. For more than two decades, all voting-age citizens have had equal rights at the polls. Well-armed British troops and a battery of "emergency" legislation still make political involvement dangerous, but plenty of people here have been able to ascend to the middle class and flee violent neighborhoods.

If peace were to come tomorrow, says McCann, the injustices would be different. Discrimination in employment is still obvious. Catholic men are two-and-a half times more likely to be unemployed than their Protestant counterparts. (The disparity for women is slightly less.) In 1991, half of all Catholic households had annual incomes of less than 6,000 pounds ($10,000), compared with 42 per cent of Protestant households.

The bigger picture is that Northern Irish households as a whole have lower average weekly incomes and endure greater poverty than any other part of the United Kingdom. This March, unemployment was estimated at 13.2 per cent of the population. According to government statistics, 76 per cent of nondependent individuals receive below the average regional income (compared with 59 per cent in England). Meanwhile, some people on both sides of the political divide have been making money. In 1993, a Rowntree Foundation report declared that more inequality now exists *within* respective communities, (Catholic, Protestant) then between them.

McCann, who is chairman of Derry's local trade-union council, hears about these inequalities every day. "They want peace, so everyone will say, 'Peace in Northern Ireland, the problem's over,'" he says. "The problem will not be over."

Since the prime ministers of Britain and Ireland signed an agreement in December 1993, the topic for discussion in Northern Ireland has been peace. Sinn Fein leader Gerry Adams was permitted a one-night stand in New York in February, and the pundits couldn't resist comparing Adams to Yasir Arafat. If change could happen in Palestine, why not Northern Ireland?

"It depends whose peace. It's not our peace that's on the agenda," says Marie Mulholland, a feminist activist who works with women looking for employment in Derry City. Mulholland has helped women find work and training at Fruit of the Loom and some other resident companies such as DuPont, the chemical manufacturers, and Seagate, a Silicon Valley firm that recently set up shop nearby. Now Derry is Seagate's European headquarters for computer-chip research and development. The firm found the conditions here more attractive than at sixteen other sites in Asia, the Americas, and Europe.

"The peace we want is about enshrining fundamental basic principles and rights…What we've got on the table is a situation where now the British and Irish governments combined are telling us what's best for us," says Mulholland.

A constitutional settlement is hardly around the corner. Protestant defenders of British rule have promised to fight to the death before they'll give in to any semblance of unification with the South. Derry City Councilor Gerry Campbell represents a Protestant constituency staunchly opposed to the current Irish-English negotiations.

"I don't think there would be a peace dividend, in fact probably the reverse," if the Downing Street Accord were implemented, he says. "There would be the potential for a massive Armageddon on the scale that we haven't seen the likes of in the past twenty-five years."

But on the industrial estates just outside Campbell's district, business in the North is looking more like business in the Irish Republic. The options for workers are the same: rotten jobs or no jobs. And religious discrimination is of little interest to far-off foreign employers except to the extent that a divided work force tends to enhance corporate profits.

On the bright side, at least workers in Ireland, North and south, have a tradition of trade-union organizing. As of 1993, the Irish plants are almost the only Fruit of the Loom operations covered by collective-bargaining agreements. SIPTU sent letters of encouragement to workers at Fruit of the Loom in Harlingen, Texas, this July. In Harlingen, near the border with Mexico, Fruit of the Loom has pulled out all the stops to derail an organizing effort by the Amalgamated Clothing and Textile Workers Union.

"In the past two weeks, they've broken every law," says Sam Luebke, a union organizer who had managed to sign up 80 per cent of the 15,000 workers he met with at the integrated cotton mill. In the run-up to an August vote on union membership, Fruit of the Loom representatives tried to discourage workers from signing up with the union. "They told people who were applying for green cards that the INS would come for them if they supported the union," says Luebke. They told others that they'd lose their food stamps if they joined. Like the Irish, the taxpayers of Harlingen paid dearly for Fruit of the Loom to come to their town. The city paid $7 million to build a water-purification plant for bleaching and dying yarn, though residents often complain about the quality of their tap water, which could be improved by just such a modern purification facility.

To fight the union, Fruit of the Loom sent out the message that the company could easily close, or relocate.

"Three months ago, supporting the union meant you cared about workers' rights. Now it's come to mean that you want to close the factory," says Luebke.

Irish critics of free trade face a similar problem. No one wants to seem to be against the "peace dividend."

Reprinted with permission from the Progressive *magazine*

Copyright © 1994

Building the Resistance

One month ago, travelers on the coastal road between Beirut and Tyre were playing chicken with Israeli gunboats. Sea-borne snipers pummeled the highway from Hetz-class battleships moored a mile offshore. Bomb craters and the remains of incinerated cars show where the shells missed the macadam, but today the roadside merchants are back in business. Along the seashore, Lebanese potters have erected fragile stacks of just-fired earthenware as if in a delicate defiance of the attacks they have survived.

The clay pots are back, just like the people. By six o'clock on the evening of the April 27 cease-fire, Beiruti women bringing food to refugees from the south found the makeshift shelters erected in the capital empty. Four hundred thousand southerners had sped back home, and no wonder. On the outskirts of the city lie refugee camps housing Palestinians who once also evacuated their villages in fear. The Palestinians believed they too would soon return home—that was almost 50 years ago.

Nabatiyeh was not always a frontier town. The official border with Israel is over 10 miles away, but in 1978 Israeli troops invaded southern Lebanon. Now a whole generation has grown up in Nabatiyeh with an occupying army only two miles away. Ali Jawad Meli stands by the foot-high pile of rubble that is all that is left of a two-story house he built a few years back. From its hilltop encampments, the Israeli army fires its U.S.-made howitzers so regularly at Nabatiyeh that even modest homes like Meli's have a bomb shelter. But on April 18, seven children and their mother were killed in a bombardment here.

"The Americans have given the Israelis the bombs to destroy our houses," says Meli. "Tell them to give them even bigger bombs, more destructive weapons, and we're going to stay here. No matter what happens, we're not leaving."

Five minutes' drive away, Hassan Dahler, a successful businessman who spent 30 years making money in Africa, looks at the wreck-age of his newly completed townhouse, also destroyed by Israeli bombs. "Is this civilization?" he asks. "Is this terrorism to ask for your land? Peace is very far away because my children are growing up to hate Israel because of this. This will shatter all the dreams of peace."

In Qana, a furious grandfather sits by the roadside. He hasn't eaten or left the United Nations base since more than 100 refugees were killed there by Israeli guided bombing on April 18. Between her tears, a Shiite grandmother draped in black says that she's so mad, she'd join Hezbollah herself rather than watch more members of her family die. Politicians and the press generally present a phony, simplified picture of Hezbollah as cold-blooded men with foreign funders. In fact, in Qana, trying to distinguish the guerrillas from the villagers is like trying to set aside the yeast in bread.

It has been over two months since President Clinton convened an emergency conference at Sharm el Sheikh and pledged unqual-ified support for Israel against Hamas, Islamic Jihad, and the Lebanese Hezbollah. But the war against "terrorism" is not going well. The *Jerusalem Post* reports that between April 11 to 27, Hezbol-lah fired more than 700 Katyushas, and Israel fired more than 18,000 shells back. No Israelis died, but 170 to 200 Lebanese did. On May 12, one U.S.-brokered cease-fire and an expensive package of Amer-ican aid to Israel later, Hezbollah fighters raided a military outpost in the occupied zone, and Israel resumed what it called "necessary" shelling of Lebanon.

"The cease-fire changed nothing," says Mohammed Fneich, a leading member of Hezbollah's Political Council. Israeli forces are occupying approximately one-tenth of Lebanon, tapping the region's rich water and agricultural resources and diverting them south. Israel is acting in defiance of the 1978 U.S.-sponsored UN resolution 425, which demanded Israel's immediate withdrawal from Lebanon. As long as the occupation continues, Hezbollah believes its fight is one of self-defense. Indeed, April's cease-fire reserves the right for each side to defend themselves, only outlawing the targeting of civilians. For both Lebanese and Israeli mothers, it is an absurd distinction that tries to separate the children who are armed from the kids in their arms. The point is, the war is still on.

In a ghostly white apartment building in the heart of south Beirut, Fneich, lounging in a pale green satin baseball jacket, has a right to sound so imperturbable. In 1982, the organization he helped to found was a marginalized guerrilla outfit, soon to gain world renown for its suicide bombings, hostage taking and Iranian-style fanaticism.

Today, Fneich is an elected member of the Lebanese parliament. He sits in the press office of Hezbollah, knowing his party garnered 200,000 votes in the Lebanese elections of 1992. Portraits of the Ayatollah Khomeini hang from lampposts outside, and a big part of Hezbollah's money still comes from Teheran. In 1983, April 18 was remembered for Hezbollah's suicide bombing of the U.S. embassy in Beirut. Now, this date will be remembered for Israeli terror—the day that, according to the UN official report, Israel probably intentionally fired its amputation weapons on Qana's refugees.

Asked how many U.S. dollars it will take to defeat his organization, Fneich flinches. "It has to do with belief and faith and the will to fight," he says, not finances.

"The last [Israeli] offensive…used hundreds of millions of dollars and ended up massacring 200 people, destroying more than 200 houses, damaging many economic installations. But they didn't accomplish anything. Maybe they'll have to destroy all of Lebanon and annihilate all of the Lebanese people; maybe they'll get somewhere then," he says.

Of course, there are various ways to destroy a country. Fneich is wrong when he says the conflict accomplished nothing. Among other things, it seems to have achieved even greater influence for Hezbollah.

"The occupation creates resistance," explains Lebanese Prime Minister Rafik al Hariri, "and under the word, or the cover of 'resistance,' everybody can join. [The Hezbollah] have a political ambition, I know that. They are using the fight against Israel and the occupation to exist politically…but you cannot expect the Lebanese government to go to war with those people who believe it is unfair that part of our country is occupied. Israel shows us that it doesn't deal with things by negotiation. It needs and it uses force."

The Lebanese authorities talk loudly against the evils of the occupation, but they leave the guerrillas to do the fighting. Like the Syrians, who shuttle Iranian support to the Hezbollah Shiite minority in southern Lebanon, Hariri knows better than to take on Israel himself. Entering into a war with Israel and the U.S. would be "suicide" says Hariri flatly. "They would crack us like this." He snaps his finger against his thumb.

So Hezbollah breeds martyrs, scampering across the border into the Israeli-occupied zones. In 1994, Hezbollah guerrillas killed 21 Israelis and 43 members of Israel's proxy, the South Lebanese Army, compared with 12 and 13 two years before. Another 23 Israeli soldiers died in 1995 and seven in the first quarter of '96. "Now it's scary," an 18-year-old Israeli enlistee on his way into Lebanon told the *Washington Post*. "The Hezbollah is getting better and better."

Members of Beirut's intellectual elite find the situation scary, too. Sitting in a sunlit living room, surrounded by Iraqi sculpture and abstract Egyptian oil paintings, Nidal Ashkar, a leading lady in the Lebanese theater, reflects. In the '80s, there were all sorts of resistance organizations: Christian, Communist, nonsectarian, irreligious, she says. "Now only Hezbollah is left."

A woman, a feminist, an artist, and a Christian, Ashkar sounds exasperated. "I can't believe we are combating Israel with their own weapons: a religious state against a religious resistance." If the Shiite fundamentalists ever won political control, Achkar knows she'd be in trouble.

Fneich leaves no doubt that women and men have different spheres of influence in the world of Hezbollah. But this April, when Israeli F-16s hit Beirut's brand-new, beautiful electricity plant in Bselim—no place that Hezbollah fighters had ever trod—the guerrillas found some unlikely allies.

"Right now, I don't have time to fight them. The most important thing right now is to resist Israel, and they are all we have," says Ashkar.

Over and over again, Lebanese civilians complain that Americans only want to talk about the end, not the beginning. The result, not the reason. At least one of the reasons is that, for years, the world's most powerful democracy has been fueling Israel's army even in occupations, and Iran has been propping up the feeble other side. At Qana, the two quite literally collided: M109A1 howitzers vs. Katyushas—then U.S. taxpayers coughed up $100 million for Israeli defense systems and then compatriots of dead mothers and children are asked to choose sides.

When women and men from MADRE, a 13-year old New York based women's organization arrived in Beirut, May 1, they were told they were the first and only U.S. organization to have made the trip to Lebanon to stand with the victims of the Israeli assault. A dark-eyed girl in an orphanage in Sidon smiled at the people who were bringing medicine and blankets and explained that she alone of all her family had survived the 16 days of shelling. "I am six years old. I am never afraid." she said.

"That fear has been replaced by rage, and it's incumbent on us to show that child humanity," said MADRE executive director Vivian Stromberg. "But a thousand delegations could come and show a thousand six-year-olds humanity. Until the U.S. stops funding the Israeli occupation and it ends, rage will prevail."

Reprinted by permission of the author and the Village Voice
May 28,1996

Bringing the War Home

Four years ago this fall, the cover of *People* magazine read "Mom Goes to War... American mothers are saying good-bye to their families to face unknown dangers in the Gulf." *Newsweek*'s cover celebrated women warriors. Inside, women were pictured in combat fatigues, swallowing tears, clutching children. On TV, pundits pondered the possible threat to the U.S. family posed by sending women to war.

Today many women who served in the Gulf are still in combat, only this time their fight is with the Department of Defense and the Veterans Administration. They have what some are calling the "Gulf War Syndrome," a web of debilitating symptoms denied an official diagnosis or treatment. Looking back, the most damaging "unknown danger" soldiers faced in the Gulf may have been the irresponsible actions of their own government. After months of struggle and increasing sickness, the tears are now of rage.

Sergeant Carol Picou served fifteen years in the Army before she was deployed to the Gulf. A nurse, mother, former model, commander of an intensive care unit, driver of a five-ton truck, today she sits at home, unable to work, struggling with memory and muscle loss. According to the unemployment office she's unemployable; according to Social Security, she's not disabled. When I interviewed her in her home this spring, Picou was like a fisherman pulling in a sodden line; she struggled to reel in her story and make sense of what had happened to her.

On November 3, 1990, Picou posed for the classic pre-dawn departure shot with her young son outside their house in San Antonio, Texas. Now she has such pain in her muscles and joints that she can't even pick him up. She's been known to go to get her son from school and come home without him, with no memory of why she left. To the right of her front door, a post-it sign reads "Don't forget the keys." Inside her car, her son attached a second sign:

"Don't forget the keys, or me."

"I'm not the same person that I was," said Picou, "Now I'm the one in trouble."

According to the Veterans Administration, approximately 3,500 veterans of the Gulf War have filed claims for disabilities they associate with their service in the Gulf. Unofficial estimates put the number afflicted with Gulf War Syndrome symptoms at closer to 20,000. Their illnesses range from muscle pains, memory loss and diarrhea to blurry vision, low blood pressure, nausea, night sweats, respiratory problems and bleeding gums.

As for causes, some cite environmental factors: pollutants from 600-plus oil-field petrochemical fires and pesticides sprayed from military planes over desert encampments. Others point to regional threats including a parasitic infection called leishmaniasis which is carried by sand flies indigenous to the Gulf. And others, like Picou, worry about depleted uranium used in shells, possible exposure to chemical and biological agents sold to the Iraqis in the years before the war, and several experimental drugs administered to Gulf War personnel without warning and without an option to refuse.

"It's not fair what's happening to our American families," says Picou, who now runs a support group with several dozen members. "We don't want money, we just want a treatment and an explanation."

When they arrived in Saudi Arabia, Picou and her unit, the 41st Combat Hospital, were stationed in an encampment that was sprayed regularly with pesticides. The flies were so numerous the soldiers joked that they'd been issued a hundred each. Latrines were overflowing, shower water collected in fetid pools on the ground and every so often the chemical alarms on base would go off. "When I alerted the officer," said Picou, "he told me to reset it, that there must have been a mistake." So she did.

When the ground war began, contrary to what the Pentagon was asserting publicly about keeping women out of combat zones, Picou was asked to recruit seven women to accompany troops into Iraq because so many men had begged to be excused from front-line duty. Driving a five-ton hospital truck, Picou led her unit into a devastated area unlike any she had ever seen. Charred and smoldering bodies of animals and humans lay beside the highway. Picou was familiar with burnt bodies, she'd body-bagged the victims of a 1988 air-show disaster, and she'd witnessed combat in Africa and Korea. "These bodies were different. They weren't normal," she said. A colleague, Linda Hughes, called the corpses "charred, crispy. Not right."

It wasn't until they returned home to the U.S. that Picou and her friends found out that shells made of depleted uranium (DU) had been used for the first time in combat in the areas they'd seen. The depleted uranium, extra hard and fast, makes great anti-tank artillery; its only drawback is that it generates tremendous heat on impact, igniting high-temperature fires and releasing a radioactive dust into the air. In February, 1994, an NBC *Dateline* producer dug up an Army Munitions Command memo which stated that any system struck by a DU penetrator should be assumed to be contaminated and that protective clothing and masks were to be worn in its vicinity. But the memo was written March 7, 1991, eight days after the ground war ended. Carol Picou and the 41st Combat Hospital knew nothing about it. They set up shop two miles from the contaminated battlefield and for two weeks lived there, treating injured soldiers from the front and Iraqi civilians from the nearby town of Basra.

Tending wounded soldiers and families hurt by grenades and shrapnel was difficult enough. Since the trek into Iraq began, Picou had been struggling with blurry vision, muscle twitching, bladder problems and sneezing. The symptoms hit her when she started taking pyridostigmine bromide, a nerve gas treatment the unit had been lined up in formation and forced to take before their departure for Iraq. Now it turns out that her symptoms were precisely those the Food and Drug Administration associates with pyridostigmine.

In hearings held by the Senate Veterans Affairs Committee on May 7, 1994, Robert J. Temple, MD, director of the office of drug evaluation at the FDA, testified that they were fully aware of the likely side-effects of the drug. "We knew all about the gastrointestinal problems, blurry vision, all that," said Temple. "What was not expected was that they would persist."

But no one told Picou or her colleagues. In the face of what was considered a "military combat exigency" the FDA waived its own requirement that the drug be used only with informed consent. Although the Pentagon contends that soldiers took the drug voluntarily, Carol Picou says she was ordered to continue taking pyridostigmine even after she had linked it to her physical problems.

A chemical believed to enhance the effectiveness of established drugs for the treatment of nerve gas poisoning, pyridostigmine is a nerve agent in itself. Since 1955 it has been approved for use in the treatment of myasthenia gravis, a neuromuscular disease. But its administration as a general-use prophylactic treatment against possible biological and chemical warfare agents was new. So was its distribution to over 695,000 troops and its use by approximately two-thirds of those regardless of their weight, age and medical histories.

According to the Department of Defense, studies on pyridostigmine prior to the war had concluded that the drug was safe for healthy men. Several groups, most of them including fewer than 35 people, were given the drug for three days and observed in a hospital setting. Those with a hypersensitivity to pyridostigmine were screened out of the tests; those with medical conditions, high blood pressure and asthma, as well as smokers and those on medication, were excluded. Even with such precautions the DOD reported severe adverse reactions, including memory loss, anemia and even respiratory arrest. But pyridostigmine was still considered the military's best available option. Without precautions or pre-screening of any kind, and without evaluating the synergistic effects that might occur in an already toxic environment, the drug was issued to all Gulf War service personnel in amounts sufficient not for three days, but for three weeks. No one at DOD had ever seen fit to test the drug on women.

"The attitude about the use of women in combat has changed dramatically in the last decade," explained Edward Martin, MD, of the Department of Defense. Old protocols excluding women from combat were still in effect, said Martin, when the drug was being tested in the late eighties. "If we did the study again today we would definitely include women."

Three and a half years after she returned from the Gulf, almost three years after she was declared medically unfit for service and discharged, Carol Picou sat in the second row of the lofty Senate hearing room and choked back tears. Her private doctor, Thomas Callander, has diagnosed neurological damage to the left side of her brain, affecting vision, memory and speech. Unable to control her vaginal, bowel or bladder muscles, she's been forced to catheterize herself to urinate and to wear diapers. Her period comes in two-week cycles, one black and tarry, the next clotted and profuse.

Frightened by all the drugs she's been given and all her health problems, a couple of years ago Carol had her tubes tied. Women who have borne babies since the war have confirmed her fears. In Mississippi, Aimee West, herself a National Guard member, started asking questions after her daughter was born with severe birth defects. It turned out that thirteen of sixteen babies born to members of her unit since its return had similar problems. The Veterans Administration has legal authority to treat only vets, not their children, so it has fallen to the Mississippi state health department to do a statewide survey of Gulf War children. So far their research has found that 36 of 56 babies born to members of four Mississippi units have birth defects, including missing eyes and ears, malformed lungs, and kidney and liver problems.

Without a diagnosis, the U.S. victims of the Gulf War are struggling to get treatment. Carol Picou's VA doctors will not accept Dr. Callander's assessment because, they say, his diagnosis was based on "nontraditional medical techniques." Like thousands of other Gulf War vets, her official medical records include no mention of pyridostigmine or uranium exposure, or any report of several other vaccines she was given (some also called "investigational" by the FDA).

And for all the talk of "Women Warriors," women are almost invisible in current discussions of Gulf War Syndrome. Long features in *GQ* and *Esquire* this spring interviewed only male victims. (No one yet has done a feature about Iraqis.) A magazine reporter who had worked with Picou on a photo documentary recently informed her that she'd been told to refocus the story on the babies. "We're not all service wives or mothers of babies," said Picou. "Where are all the women?" For this mom and thousands of others like her, the "Mom's War" has just begun.

Originally published in the Women's Review of Books

July 1994

The frequent media presentations of soldiers as moms reinforced a view of women as mothers first and foremost. The U.S. Armed Forces are 89 percent men, but have you ever seen a war presented as a fathers' war?

Marginalized Experts

Beyond Beijing
(Remarks to the NGO Forum
on Women, China 1995)

I'd like to start by thanking all the members of the NGO Forum who have made this program possible. And I'd also like to thank our hosts—the Chinese people.

I have the privilege of living in New York City—the media capital of the world—so of course, thanks to all the radio stations, television networks and newspapers I have access to, I am lucky enough to know absolutely nothing about your ideas and your way of life. And that's part of why I'm here.

I shouldn't have to travel halfway around the world to hear from the Chinese people—the words of your government leaders and your corporate lobbyists and tourist board officials seem to get through just fine.

Nor should any of us really have to make this expensive trip to hear from the women at this forum. It's kind of ironic that so much of the press coverage of this event has focussed on the difficulties that women are having getting heard and seen in Beijing: the problems here are nothing in comparison to what most women face every day trying to get access to the media in their home towns.

This NGO Forum isn't just the largest gathering of women in history, it's probably the largest gathering of marginalized experts the world has ever seen.

Unlike some women's media watch groups, at FAIR, we don't believe in women's issues. We're against the very idea that men and women have mutually exclusive areas of concern. What we call for is reporting that covers the world as it is—more than half populated by women, with ideas and experiences and bodies that matter—regardless of their race, their age, their sexual orientation, political power, physical abilities or class.

Consider any topic, whether it's the global economy, health care, education, human relations or how to avoid war. You are experts because you, as people who are focussed on women and the marginalized, are paying attention to the majority of people on the planet—the very people who are on the cutting edge of current policy. In many cases, it's an edge that doesn't just cut, it kills. And you'd think that would make your information good to share.

So here you are... 20,000 or more of the world's most rarely-heard-from experts—all gathered more or less conveniently in one place. Being discussed here are some of those key issues, some of them the very issues that the boring men in suits discuss on television every night. The press are here, a lot of them, and I'm glad—as a reporter myself—my sympathies are with you. I wish you well. But what do we get? Stories about justice, equality and how women are moving an international agenda from the bottom up? Hardly.

I turn on my TV in the hotel room and read a U.S. paper over lunch and what do I find? The same U.S. media that remained tight-lipped when Ronald Reagan approved sales of police equipment to China's internal security force, and praised Vice President Bush's visit here in 1985, are now suddenly concerned about security levels and whether or not Hillary Rodham Clinton is disrespecting human rights by coming to a rights conference. People think the media's soundbites are short: that's nothing in comparison to their memory. Has anyone seen *Time* magazine this week refer to the fact that in 1985, they selected Deng Xiao Ping as *Time* "Man of the Year?"

Sure, there are traces of the discussion that's happening here, but those traces are edged out by the same government and establishment faces and the same rhetoric that always dominate the news. We call what's happening here, "wildlife reporting." People like yourselves, who represent vast, popular movements may get captured in a shot or two: speaking at a demonstration or waving a fist in the air, but you're not allowed to set the agenda. You're not invited into the television studios, to sit on the comfortable chairs like the Generals and the Bankers. They get to explain themselves in a number of paragraphs. You get to shout a slogan in the street. And then, having been exiled to the margins, you're called "marginal" or "not representative." It's a cute trick. And it happens over and over again.

What has changed in 20 years? Well, women get into a few more pictures. This weekend's *Herald Tribune,* for example, put two women from this Forum on the cover (Sept. 2-3). But the women were gagged: in the picture, and in the paper. Look inside for the follow-up story having read the caption and there's not a word from the two protesting Tibetans. It was interesting over the past few days to watch how the big cameras came into this hall when celebrities were talking or when women were telling their personal stories, but left when women were giving analysis of things like the global economy or the rise of the right .

We want women seen but we also want them heard. And we want women's expertise as well as their experience. We are not just bodies, but minds—and some of you can argue the pants off some of those boring men in suits.

These days there are more women in the industry, but unfortunately, as we've seen here, without other changes, adding female reporters does not necessarily guarantee a sea change in the coverage. CNN for example, has a particularly high proportion of women correspondents on staff. But according to a study by one of the groups we work with, Women, Men and Media, the network uses particularly few women among the people they choose to interview.

A woman in front of the camera may be a good new role model, but gender parity without a broadening of the political spectrum will only help the individuals who scramble to the top, it doesn't guarantee a change in the reporting.

We also have to be more subtle in our call for more women opinion-givers. The same issue of the *Herald Tribune* this weekend published an opinion piece by a woman—but the author, Camille Paglia, who seems to believe that only Americans worry about reproductive rights or homophobia, is not a women's rights expert or an activist. She's an art critic who's made a name for herself echoing old familiar arguments against the women's rights movement. She once said that "feminism misses the bloodlust in rape, the joy of violation and destruction." The call for women pundits needs to be more sophisticated. We need to say which ones.

It is no academic question who gets to speak in mainstream media. In the U.S., the people who frame the media debate are often framing political policy and public opinion for years. Take crime for example: the number of victims of violent crime decreased by 9 percent from 1981 to 1990, but in the same time, the number of stories about street crime soared. The most common victims of violent crime are Black men, who are 50 percent more likely than white men and two and half times more likely than white women to be the victims of violent street crime—yet U.S. newspapers are full of racially-coded stories about "suburban victims" of "urban crime"— the suburbs being a code word for white—and the city, the symbol of people who are not. In opinion polls now, the public put "fear of crime" close to the top of their list of worries—and politicians get support to invest the public wealth into prisons—the criminal industrial complex Mab Segrest talked about last week.

Meanwhile, corporate crime is doing the big-dollar damage: banking scandals, fraud, and stock-cheating swindle people out of millions—but predominantly white, male corporate criminals don't feel the heat, because crime in the suites doesn't get the same coverage as crime in the streets, and as a result, there's little pressure to put the corporate crooks in jail. A greater diversity of viewpoints on the subject of crime could at least open up this debate, if not get it back on the rails. So at FAIR we look at who gets to talk.

We monitor the media: we record the national news off the television every night and watch as much of it as we can bear. We read the newspapers and newsmagazines and produce data on who is participating in the public-opinion shaping debate.

FAIR's first study was of a single, influential program, called *Nightline*—it's a nightly news discussion show broadcast nationally by ABC. We recorded 40 months of programs and compiled statistics on who got to speak in the studio discussion. What we thought was bad, we found out was even worse.

The most frequently featured guests on *Nightline* during that period from 1985 to 1988 were Henry Kissinger, Alexander Haig, Elliot Abrams and Jerry Falwell: one former war-monger now a corporate consultant, a laid-off member of Ronald Reagan's cabinet; a cabinet member who was found guilty of lying to Congress—and an evangelical minister who manipulates people's religious beliefs to promote a roll-back of feminism and civil rights. We also found that 89 percent of the guests were male, and 92 percent were white—not a big surprise.

Faced with that data, the host of the program responded "Ours is a news program... we go to people involved in making the news..." And that spoke volumes about how the media defines news and power. "Is it only what people in D.C. do?" we asked reporters— and the project got attention around the country. We've done several similar studies since, and the idea has also been taken up by other groups.

The goal of this sort of study is an expanded debate. FAIR isn't interested in preventing the airing of viewpoints we disagree with—we're working for the inclusion of more. A more pluralistic media would be nice—it would certainly be more entertaining, but that's not the point either. The slighting of public interest and minority viewpoints is dangerous. This spring, for example, we watched in horror while the mainstream media looked for Arab terrorists in their effort to explain the bombing of the federal building in Oklahoma City. The mainstream media were so convinced the terrorists were foreign, that when a white, christian man was arrested in the case, the *New York Times* ran headlines like "New Images of Terror... A suspect, a white drifter, evokes new fear."

The sort of coverage that followed the Oklahoma City bombing showed the price we pay for racism, homophobia and sexism in mainstream media. Right-wing terror is hardly surprising to those who've been on the receiving end of it over the years. Nor would the pale image of the suspect have been "new" to mainstream readers if the media had been doing their job.

In the U.S. today, there are right wing demagogues who provide easy solutions to real problems by pandering to popular ignorance and prejudice. In my home town, New York, the most popular host on the most listened-to station routinely refers to African Americans as "savages". He once urged NYC cops to show up to the gay pride parade with machine guns "and mow them down." A man who broadcasts weekly to over 20 million people calls advocates of human rights for women, "feminazis." And the mainstream media's alternative to that? Respectable "polite" debate about the the intellectual inferiority of Black Americans and the threat that gay men and lesbians may pose to the military and the family—as if we don't have families—and "softly, softly" coverage of anti-abortion violence that long before Oklahoma had already killed five health clinic workers and burnt or bombed 169 clinics in 33 states in the USA. When the *New York Times* published a graph to illustrate "other bombings in America" the chart spanned four decades but none of the documented bombings of women's health clinics made it onto the list. None of the attacks on civil rights offices or gay and lesbian homes. Not one.

As a lesbian, the fact of invisibility is painful, but to me and my friends at FAIR—invisibility is not the only problem. I know what's going on. It is the people who are in the dark that I worry about. The price of homophobia in the press is ignorance—and ignorance and hate can cost us all our lives.

Rather than damning reporters to hell as some right wing critics have done—we engage with journalists directly, and we begin, at least, by appealing to their higher natures. "We're not asking you to do us any favors," we say, "we're just asking you to do good reporting—better reporting." And we come to them with ideas.

After a short study of several weeks of the media's coverage of NAFTA, the North American Free Trade Agreement, we found that working women were not being heard from. Female business owners showed up a couple of times, and some U.S. women politicians, but women workers weren't cited even once, although women workers are the largest single group likely to feel the effects of the not-so-free free trade pact. The majority of workers in the multinational factories that were at that time likely to expand under NAFTA and the most vulnerable workers facing lay-offs in the states if the jobs relocated south were women. Covering them wasn't doing us any favors, we told journalists. It's just covering the news. We suggested that perhaps they might want to take a break from quoting representatives of the World Bank and the International Monetary Fund. "Just to relieve the boredom if nothing else, why don't you talk to the folks at a grassroots organization, like MADRE, a 12-year-old women's group that works with women in Central America, or the National Labor Committee, a labor group that works with unions in the South"—and we offered names and numbers of suggested guests—and a documented case that was hard to ignore.

Just recently, a number of stories have focussed on the impact of NAFTA on workers in Honduras. We don't know whether our work helped, but it certainly didn't hurt.

We try to correct the record by writing opinion-pieces and letters to the press: to editors, publishers, even members of the company's corporate board. And we help give people tools to do the same. But even while we're doing all that, we know that media institutions are not about to change. The industry is an industry and it is serving its corporate interest just fine, thank you. The *Wall Street Journal* is not about to see the light and say "ok—you're right—we're wrong."

In 1986, when we started FAIR, a few months after the Nairobi Conference, media institutions were owned by a small—and shrinking—number of powerful businesses. Now the number's even smaller. In 1986, 29 corporations dominated broadcasting, publishing and cable. By the end of 1993, the number was down to 20. Some have estimated that before the end of the century, an oligopoly of about half a dozen hugely profitable giant firms will have consolidated control of the mass media worldwide.

Today newspapers can be published simultaneously on five continents and a single satellite can beam information to half the globe. As one speaker put it this week, now CNN brings you the world—

and all of it in 22 minutes—whether you want it or not. The way that CNN covered the Gulf War affected not just Americans, but Europeans and Australians, even people in whose neighborhoods the U.S. bombs were being dropped.

Media companies are no longer businesses in your neighborhood, vying with one another for your support: they're major political players on the national and even international scene. For example, if current merger plans go ahead, soon two out of three of the world's richest television networks would be controlled by nuclear power companies, both of which have the U.S. military as their most important client. You can expect plenty of critical reporting on the issue of military spending on NBC and CBS—I don't think.

Media moguls have become even more explicit about the fact that they pursue corporate profits, not the public's interest. The head of Tele-Communications International—the man who's currently poised to have a virtual monopoly over the U.S. cable industry—recently scoffed at the notion of ever developing a media system that would serve the public interest. Private corporations are not set up to serve the public interest, he said. "One would be fired as the CEO (the Director) of a profit-making company if he did that." So that's settled.

And the corporate interest puts profits first. As the head of the Disney corporation put it recently, after announcing his plan to buy up ABC which also owns the sports network, ESPN. "There are many places in the world, like China, India and other places, that do not want to accept programming that has political content but they don't have a problem with sports and ...the Disney kind of programming. The leverage of those two together in what used to be Third World ... or closed countries is enormous," he said. In other words, you can make a lot of money down-playing reality.

The world as reported by multinational corporations like these is certainly not a world where women and marginalized people get many starring roles. So at the same time that we pursue what you might call a policy of "constructive engagement" (and it's about as effective as "constructive engagement" policies usually are) we also produce our own independent media: a syndicated column, a bi-monthly magazine called *EXTRA!*, an activists' newsletter and a weekly syndicated radio program called *CounterSpin*, which is now heard on about 100 college and community radio stations and from Radio for Peace International on short wave. We also have a web page and exchange information with reporters and others on line. And in all the work we do, we work hard to applaud hard-hitting independent journalism that cuts against the conventional grain. High-minded reporters who do that sort of work usually get pretty discouraged in the mainstream—so we think it's our job to high-light work that challenges the establishment. If anyone asks me what can they do about the problems we're facing, I say, "Step one support your local independent media: whether it's a radio station or a newsletter or a flyer or a story-teller." Unfortunately, the means of communication have become far too expensive for freedom of the press to belong only to those who can buy one. So we have more to do as well. We have to fight for our right to communicate.

In the 1930s, it was determined that under U.S. law, the airwaves, like the air and the water, belonged to the public. With the growth of cable and telecommunications that principle, long unenforced, is in danger of dying a quietly unreported death. Internationally, the first UN General Assembly declared freedom of information the "touchstone of all freedoms to which the UN is consecrated." The individual and collective right to communicate is "an evolving principle in the democratization process," UNESCO declared in a study in 1979.

But no enforcement mechanism has ever evolved to protect that evolving principle. At present the power to communicate is resting in the hands of a few corporations and states—not for conversation, but for control.

Looking to the future, I'll make a proposal. Since these International Women's Conferences began, we have seen an environmental movement grow up to protect and share the scarce resource that is the planet; we have seen a women's and a human rights movement be built to protect the invaluable resource of human potential—all our people. What we need now is a global movement to assert the public's right to the resource of information and communication. We are entitled to exist in each other's lives and not just once in every ten years. And we're entitled to feel that we're not alone—because obviously we are not.

What's holding us back is access. But so what else is new? You and your friends are used to long, seemingly impossible uphill fights. The right to communicate is like any right. And like any right, it will not be given. It must be won.

September 1, 1995

Resources

Astraea National Lesbian
Action Foundation
116 E. 16th St. 7th Fl.
NYC 10003
212-529-8021

Center for Third World
Organizing
1218 E. 21st St.
Oakland, CA 94606
510-533-7583

Center on Budget and Policy
Priorities
777 N Capitol St. NE
Washington, DC
202-408-1080

Center for a New
Democracy
410 7th St. SE
Washington, DC 20003
202-543-0773

Center for Women's Global
Leadership
Douglass College
New Brunswick, NJ 08903
908-932-8782

CounterPunch
PO Box 18675
Washington, DC 20036
202-986-3665

Covert Action Quarterly
1500 Mass Ave. NW
Washington, DC 20005
202-331-9763

Democracy Now
Pacifica Radio
702 H St. NW
Washington, DC 20001
202-588-0988

Dollars & Sense
One Summer St.
Somerville, MA 02143
617-628-8411

Freedom Writer
PO Box 589
Great Barrington, MA
01230

Gay and Lesbian Alliance
Against Defamation
(GLAAD New York)
159 W. 26th St.
New York, NY 10001
212-0807-1700

Hampshire College
Population & Devt. Pgm
Amherst, MA 01002
413-582-5506

In These Times
2040 N. Milwaukee Ave.
Chicago, IL 60647
312-772-0100

Institute for Women's Policy
Research
1400 20th St. NW
Washington, DC
202-785-5100

MADRE
121 W. 27th St.
New York, NY 10001
212-627-0444

Media Network
39 W. 14th St.
New York, NY 10011
212-929-2663

MOUTH: *The Voice of
Disability Rights*
61 Brighton St.
Rochester, NY 14607
716-473-6764

Ms. Magazine
230 Park Ave.
New York, NY 10169
212-551-9595

The Nation
72 Fifth Ave.
New York, NY 10011
212 242 8400

National Gay and Lesbian
Task Force
2320 17th. St. NW
Washington, DC 20009
202-332-6483

National Labor Committee
275 7th Ave
New York, NY 10001
212-242-3003

On The Issues
97-77 Queens Blvd
Forest Hills, NY 11374
718-275-6020

Paper Tiger TV
339 Lafayette St.
NYC 10012
212-473-8933

Political Research Assocs.
120 Beacon St. Suite 202
Somerville, MA 02143
617-661-9313

Sojourners
2401 15th St. NW
Washington, DC 20009
202-328-8842

Sterling Research Assocs
1192 Park Ave.
New York, NY 10128
212-423-9237

Washington Feminist Faxnet
1735 S St. NW
Washington, DC 20009
202-797-0606

Welfare News
Center on Social Welfare
Policy and Law
1029 Vermont Ave. NW
Washington, DC
202-347-5615

Women's Economic Agenda
Project
518 17th St. Suite 200
Oakland, CA 94612
510-451-7379

Women's Review of Books
Wellesley Center
for Research on Women
Wellesley, MA 02181
617-283-2087

The Women's Project
2224 Main St.
Little Rock, AR 72206
501-372-5113

Z Magazine
18 Millfield St.
Woods Hole, MA 02543
508-548-9063

Available From FAIR

EXTRA! Special Issues:

(Single copies: $4. For 25 or more: $2.50 each.)

1992: "Missing Voices: Women and the Media"

July/August 1992: "Focus on Racism in the Media"

June 1993: "Confronting Homophobia:
Gays and Lesbians in the Media"

March/April 1994: "Media Take Aim at Youth"

July/August 1994: "Rush Limbaugh's Reign of Error"

March/April 1995: "The Right Wing Media Machine"

Audio Tapes:

"Marginalized Experts: A Report from Beijing"
Selected speeches: UN Global Conference on Women,
Sept.1995. Including speech by Laura Flanders
(Double cassette set: $15)

"Women and the Media"
Panelists from *Newsweek*, *Dyke TV*, MS
discuss women's gains in the industry.
Hosted by Laura Flanders ($9).

"Media and the Contract with America"
Speech by Laura Flanders,
presented by Alternative Radio's David Barsamian.
March 1995 ($9).

"Best of *CounterSpin* I & II"
Two hours of highlights from
FAIR's syndicated radio program ($9).

"Backlash to Backlash"
Susan Faludi discusses the press response to *Backlash* ($9).

All prices include shipping and handling.
Allow 6 - 8 weeks for delivery.

INDEX

About the Author

Photo by June Jordan

Laura Flanders is executive producer and host of *CounterSpin*, the nationally-syndicated radio program heard on 100 stations in the U.S. and Canada, and director of the Women's Desk at FAIR (Fairness & Accuracy In Reporting), the ten-year-old media watch group. She's a long-time writer and journalist and currently writes a column on women and media for the magazine *EXTRA!* and contributes regularly to such publications as the *Nation*, the *Progressive*, *On the Issues* and *The Village Voice*. She's been an international correspondent for the TV series *Rights and Wrongs* (aired on PBS) and a national anchor for Pacifica Radio. The Institute for Alternative Journalism named her one of ten "Media Heroes of 1994." As well as being an experienced broadcast host and interviewer, Flanders is a popular public speaker and interviewee. She lives in New York City with her partner, Elizabeth Streb.